OXFORD WORLD'S CLASSICS

===

ANDREW SANDERS

Charles Dickens

===

OXFORD
UNIVERSITY PRESS

OXFORD
UNIVERSITY PRESS

Great Clarendon Street, Oxford OX2 6DP

Oxford University Press is a department of the University of Oxford.
It furthers the University's objective of excellence in research, scholarship,
and education by publishing worldwide in

Oxford New York

Auckland Bangkok Buenos Aires Cape Town Chennai
Dar es Salaam Delhi Hong Kong Istanbul Karachi Kolkata
Kuala Lumpur Madrid Melbourne Mexico City Mumbai Nairobi
São Paulo Shanghai Taipei Tokyo Toronto

Oxford is a registered trade mark of Oxford University Press
in the UK and in certain other countries

Published in the United States
by Oxford University Press Inc., New York

First published as an Oxford World's Classics paperback 2003
Reissued 2009

British Library Cataloguing in Publication Data

Data available

Library of Congress Cataloging in Publication Data

Sanders, Andrew.
Charles Dickens/Andrew Sanders.
p. cm.—(Oxford world's classics. Authors in context)
Includes bibliographical references and index.
1. Dickens, Charles, 1812–1970—Criticism and interpretation.
2. Literature and society—Great Britain—History—19th century.
3. Literature and history—Great Britain—History—19th century.
4. Dickens, Charles, 1812–1870—Knowledge—London (England).
5. London (England)—History—1800–1950. 6. London (England)—In literature.
7. City and town life in literature. I. Title. II. Oxford world's classics
(Oxford University Press). Authors in context.
PR4588.S28 2003
823′.8—dc21
2002034591

ISBN 978-0-19-955609-0

2

Typeset in Ehrhardt
by RefineCatch Limited, Bungay, Suffolk
Printed in Great Britain by
Clays Ltd, St Ives plc

General Editor: PATRICIA INGHAM, University of Oxford
Historical Adviser: BOYD HILTON, University of Cambridge

CHARLES DICKENS

AUTHORS IN CONTEXT examines the work of major writers in relation to their own time and to the present day. The series provides detailed coverage of the values and debates that colour the writing of particular authors and considers their novels, plays, and poetry against this background. Set in their social, cultural, and political contexts, classic books take on a new meaning for modern readers. And since readers, like writers, have their own contexts, the series considers how critical interpretations have altered over time, and how films, sequels, and other popular adaptations relate to the new age in which they are produced.

ANDREW SANDERS is Professor of English at the University of Durham. He is the author of *The Victorian Historical Novel* (1978), *Charles Dickens: Resurrectionist* (1982), *The Companion to A Tale of Two Cities* (1988), *Anthony Trollope* (1998), *Dickens and the Spirit of the Age* (1999), and *The Short Oxford History of English Literature* (1994, 2000). He has edited several nineteenth-century novels and was formerly Editor of *The Dickensian*.

OXFORD WORLD'S CLASSICS

*For over 100 years Oxford World's Classics have brought
readers closer to the world's great literature. Now with over 700
titles—from the 4,000-year-old myths of Mesopotamia to the
twentieth century's greatest novels—the series makes available
lesser-known as well as celebrated writing.*

*The pocket-sized hardbacks of the early years contained
introductions by Virginia Woolf, T. S. Eliot, Graham Greene,
and other literary figures which enriched the experience of reading.
Today the series is recognized for its fine scholarship and
reliability in texts that span world literature, drama and poetry,
religion, philosophy and politics. Each edition includes perceptive
commentary and essential background information to meet the
changing needs of readers.*

For James

Walther: *Doch, wem der Lenz schon lang' entronnen,*
wie wird er dem im Bild gewonnen?
Sachs: *Er frischt es an, so gut er kann:*

Die Meistersinger

CONTENTS

LIST OF ILLUSTRATIONS

A CHRONOLOGY OF CHARLES DICKENS

Dickens's major fictions are indicated by bold type.

	Life	*Historical and Cultural Background*
1809	(13 June) John Dickens, a clerk in the Navy Pay Office, marries Elizabeth Barrow.	
1810	(28 Oct.) Frances Dickens ('Fanny') born.	
1811		Prince of Wales becomes Prince Regent. W. M. Thackeray born. Jane Austen, *Sense and Sensibility*
1812	(7 Feb.) Charles Dickens born at Mile End Terrace, Landport, Portsea (now 393 Old Commercial Road, Portsmouth).	Luddite riots. War between Britain and the United States. Napoleon's retreat from Moscow. Robert Browning and Edward Lear born. Lord Byron, *Childe Harold's Pilgrimage*, i and ii (completed 1818)
1813		Robert Southey becomes Poet Laureate. Napoleon defeated at Leipzig. Austen, *Pride and Prejudice*; Byron, *The Bride of Abydos*, *The Giaour*; P. B. Shelley, *Queen Mab*
1814	Birth (Mar.) and death (Sept.) of Alfred Allen Dickens.	Napoleon exiled to Elba. Austen, *Mansfield Park*; Sir Walter Scott, *Waverley*; William Wordsworth, *The Excursion*
1815	(1 Jan.) Dickens family moves to London.	Escape of Napoleon; Battle of Waterloo. Anthony Trollope born. Thomas Robert Malthus, *An Inquiry into Rent*; Scott, *Guy Mannering*
1816	(Apr.) Letitia Dickens born.	Charlotte Brontë born. Austen, *Emma*; S. T. Coleridge, *Christabel and Other Poems*; Thomas Love Peacock, *Headlong Hall*; Scott, *The Antiquary*, *Old Mortality*
1817	(Apr.) Dickens family settles in Chatham.	Jane Austen dies. Byron, *Manfred*; Coleridge, *Biographia Literaria*; John Keats, *Poems*; Robert Owen, *Report to the Committee on the Poor Law*; Scott, *Rob Roy*
1818		Emily Brontë born.

	Austen, *Northanger Abbey*, *Persuasion* (posth.); Keats, *Endymion*; Peacock, *Nightmare Abbey*; Scott, *The Heart of Midlothian*; Mary Shelley, *Frankenstein*
1819 (Sept.) Harriet Dickens born.	Princess Victoria born. Peterloo 'Massacre' (11 deaths). A. H. Clough, Mary Anne Evans (George Eliot), Charles Kingsley, John Ruskin born. Byron, *Don Juan*, i–ii (continued till 1824); Scott, *The Bride of Lammermoor*; Wordsworth, *Peter Bell*, *The Waggoner*
1820 Frederick Dickens ('Fred') born.	Death of George III; accession of Prince Regent as George IV. Trial of Queen Caroline. Anne Brontë born. John Clare, *Poems*, *Descriptive of Rural Life*; Keats, *Lamia*, *Isabella*, *The Eve of St Agnes and Other Poems*; Malthus, *Principles of Political Economy*; Charles Robert Maturin, *Melmoth the Wanderer*; P. B. Shelley, *The Cenci*, *Prometheus Unbound*; Scott, *Ivanhoe*
1821 CD goes to school run by William Giles.	Greek War of Independence starts. Napoleon dies. Keats dies. Clare, *The Village Minstrel and Other Poems*; Thomas De Quincey, *Confessions of an English Opium Eater*; Pierce Egan, *Life in London*; Thomas Moore, *Irish Melodies*; Scott, *Kenilworth*; P. B. Shelley, *Adonais*; Southey, *A Vision of Judgement*
1822 (Mar.) Alfred Lamert Dickens born; Harriet Dickens dies. CD stays in Chatham when family moves to Camden Town, London; rejoins them later, but his education is discontinued.	Shelley dies. Matthew Arnold born. Byron, *The Vision of Judgement*
1823 (Dec.) Family moves to 4 Gower Street North, where Mrs Dickens fails in her attempt to run a school.	Building of present British Museum begins. Coventry Patmore born. Charles Lamb, *Essays of Elia*; Scott, *Quentin Durward*
1824 (late Jan. or early Feb.) CD sent to work at Jonathan Warren's blacking-warehouse, Hungerford Stairs; (20 Feb.) John Dickens arrested and imprisoned for debt in the Marshalsea till 28 May; CD in lodgings; family moves to Somers Town.	National Gallery founded in London. Repeal of acts forbidding formation of trades unions. Byron dies. Wilkie Collins born. James Hogg, *The Private Memoirs and Confessions of a Justified Sinner*; Walter Savage Landor, *Imaginary Conversations* (completed 1829); Scott, *Redgauntlet*

1825 (9 Mar.) John Dickens retires from Navy Pay Office with a pension; (Mar./Apr.) CD leaves Warren's and recommences his schooling at Wellington House Academy.

Stockton–Darlington railway opens. Hazlitt, *Table-Talk*, *The Spirit of the Age*; Alessandro Manzoni, *I promessi sposi*

1826 John Dickens works as Parliamentary correspondent for *The British Press*.

University College London and Royal Zoological Society founded. J. Fenimore Cooper, *The Last of the Mohicans*; Benjamin Disraeli, *Vivian Grey* (completed 1827); Mary Shelley, *The Last Man*

1827 (Mar.) Family evicted for non-payment of rates; CD becomes a solicitor's clerk; (Nov.) Augustus Dickens born.

Battle of Navarino. William Blake dies. Clare, *The Shepherd's Calendar*; De Quincey, 'On Murder Considered as One of the Fine Arts'

1828 John Dickens works as reporter for *The Morning Herald*.

Duke of Wellington PM. George Meredith, D. G. Rossetti, Leo Tolstoy born. Pierce Egan, *Finish to the Adventures of Tom, Jerry and Logic*

1829 CD works at Doctors' Commons as a shorthand reporter.

Catholic Emancipation Act; Robert Peel establishes Metropolitan Police.

1830 (8 Feb.) Admitted as reader to British Museum; (May) falls in love with Maria Beadnell.

George IV dies; William IV succeeds. Opening of Manchester–Liverpool Railway. July revolution in France; accession of Louis-Philippe as emperor. Greece independent. Hazlitt dies. Christina Rossetti born. William Cobbett, *Rural Rides*; Sir Charles Lyell, *Principles of Geology* (completed 1832); Alfred Tennyson, *Poems, Chiefly Lyrical*

1831 Composes poem 'The Bill of Fare'; starts work as reporter for *The Mirror of Parliament*.

Reform Bill. Major cholera epidemic. Michael Faraday's electro-magnetic current. Peacock, *Crotchet Castle*; Edgar Allan Poe, *Poems*; Stendhal, *Le Rouge et le noir*

1832 Becomes Parliamentary reporter on the *True Sun*.

Lord Grey PM. First Reform Act. Jeremy Bentham, Crabbe, Goethe, and Scott die. Charles Lutwidge Dodgson (Lewis Carroll) born. Goethe, *Faust*, ii; Mary Russell Mitford, *Our Village*; Tennyson, *Poems*; Frances Trollope, *Domestic Manners of the Americans*

1833 Concludes relationship with Maria Beadnell; first story, 'A Dinner at Poplar Walk' (later called 'Mr Minns and his Cousin') published in *Monthly Magazine*.

First steamship crosses the Atlantic. Abolition of slavery in all British colonies (from Aug. 1834). Factory Act forbids employment of children under 9. First government grant for schools. Oxford Movement starts.
Robert Browning, *Pauline*; John Henry Newman, 'Lead, Kindly Light' and (with others) the first *Tracts for the Times*

1834 (Jan.–Feb.) Six more stories appear in *Monthly Magazine*; (Aug.) meets Catherine Hogarth; becomes reporter on *The Morning Chronicle*, which publishes (Sept.–Dec.) first five 'Street Sketches'; (Dec.) moves to Furnival's Inn, Holborn.

Robert Owen's Grand National Trades Union. 'Tolpuddle Martyrs' transported to Australia. Lord Melbourne PM; then Peel. Workhouses set up under Poor Law Amendment Act. Coleridge, Lamb, and Malthus die. William Morris born.
Balzac, *Eugénie Grandet*; Thomas Carlyle, *Sartor Resartus*; Harriet Martineau, *Illustrations of Political Economy*

1835 (?May) Engaged to Catherine Hogarth ('Kate'); publishes stories, sketches, and scenes in *Monthly Magazine*, *Evening Chronicle*, and *Bell's Life in London*.

Lord Melbourne PM. Municipal Corporations Act reforms local government. Cobbett and James Hogg die.
Browning, *Paracelsus*; Alexis de Tocqueville, *La Démocratie en Amérique*

1836 (Feb.) Takes larger chambers in Furnival's Inn; (8 Feb.) *Sketches by Boz, First Series* published; (31 Mar.) first monthly number of *Pickwick Papers* issued; (2 Apr.) marries Catherine Hogarth; (June) publishes *Sunday Under Three Heads*; (Oct.) leaves the *Morning Chronicle*; (17 Dec.) *Sketches by Boz, Second Series*; (?Dec.) meets John Forster.

Beginning of Chartism. First London train (to Greenwich). Forms of telegraph used in England and America. Augustus Pugin's *Contrasts* advocates Gothic style of architecture. Browning, 'Porphyria's Lover'; Nicolai Gogol, *The Government Inspector*; Frederick Marryat, *Mr Midshipman Easy*

1837 (1 Jan.) First monthly number of *Bentley's Miscellany*, edited by CD, published; (6 Jan.) birth of first child, Charles ('Charley'); (31 Jan.) serialization of *Oliver Twist* begins in *Bentley's*; (3 Mar.) *Is She His Wife?* produced at the St James's; (Apr.) family moves to 48 Doughty Street; (7 May) sudden death of his sister-in-law,

William IV dies; Queen Victoria succeeds.
Carlyle, *The French Revolution*; Isaac Pitman, *Stenographic Short-Hand*; J. G. Lockhart, *Memoirs of the Life of Sir Walter Scott*

Mary Hogarth, at 17; CD suspends publication of *Pickwick Papers* and *Oliver Twist* for a month; (Aug.–Sept.) first family holiday in Broadstairs; (17 Nov.) *Pickwick Papers* published in one volume.

1838   (Jan.–Feb.) Visits Yorkshire schools with Hablot Browne ('Phiz'); (6 Mar.) second child, Mary ('Mamie'), born; (31 Mar.) monthly serialization of *Nicholas Nickleby* begins; (9 Nov.) *Oliver Twist* published in three volumes.

Isambard Kingdom Brunel's *Great Western* inaugurates regular steamship service between England and USA. London–Birmingham railway completed. Irish Poor Law. Anti-Corn Law League founded by Richard Cobden. People's Charter advocates universal suffrage.
Carlyle, *Sartor Resartus*; John Ruskin, *The Poetry of Architecture*; R. S. Surtees, *Jorrocks's Jaunts and Jollities*; Wordsworth, *Sonnets*

1839   (31 Jan.) Resigns editorship of *Bentley's*; (23 Oct.) *Nicholas Nickleby* published in one volume; (29 Oct.) third child, Kate ('Katey'), born; (Dec.) family moves to 1 Devonshire Terrace, Regent's Park.

Opium War between Britain and China. Chartist riots. Louis Daguerre and W. H. Fox Talbot independently develop photography.
Carlyle, *Chartism*; Darwin, *Journal of Researches into the Geology and Natural History of . . . Countries Visited by HMS Beagle*; Harriet Martineau, *Deerbrook*

1840   (4 Apr.) First weekly issue of *Master Humphrey's Clock* (also published monthly) in which *The Old Curiosity Shop* is serialized from 25 Apr.; (1 June) moves family to Broadstairs; (11 Oct.) returns to London; (15 Oct.) *Master Humphrey's Clock*, Vol. I published.

Queen Victoria marries Prince Albert. Maoris yield sovereignty of New Zealand to Queen Victoria by Treaty of Waitangi. Rowland Hill introduces penny postage. Fanny Burney dies.

1841   (8 Feb.) Fourth child, Walter, born; *The Old Curiosity Shop* concluded and *Barnaby Rudge* commenced in *Master Humphrey's Clock* (6 and 13 Feb.); operated on for fistula (without anaesthetic). *Master Humphrey's Clock*, Vols. II and III published (Apr. and Dec.); one-volume editions of *The Old Curiosity Shop* and *Barnaby Rudge* published (15 Dec.).

Peel PM. Hong Kong and New Zealand proclaimed British. *Punch* founded.
W. H. Ainsworth, *Old St Paul's*; Browning, *Pippa Passes*; Carlyle, *On Heroes, Hero-Worship, and the Heroic in History*; R. W. Emerson, *Essays*. Dion Boucicault's *London Assurance* acted

1842 (Jan.–June) CD and Catherine visit North America; (Aug.–Sept.) with family in Broadstairs; (Oct.–Nov.) visits Cornwall with Forster and others; (19 Oct.) *American Notes* published; (31 Dec.) first monthly number of *Martin Chuzzlewit* published.

End of wars with China and Afghanistan. Mines Act: no underground work by women or by children under 10. Chadwick report on sanitary condition of the working classes. Chartist riots. Copyright Act. Stendhal dies.
Browning, *Dramatic Lyrics*; Gogol, *Dead Souls*; Thomas Babington Macaulay, *Lays of Ancient Rome*; Tennyson, *Poems*

1843 (19 Dec.) *A Christmas Carol* published.

British annexation of Sind and Natal. I. K. Brunel's *Great Britain*, the first ocean screw-steamer, launched. Southey dies; Wordsworth becomes Poet Laureate.
Carlyle, *Past and Present*; Thomas Hood, 'Song of the Shirt'; Macaulay, *Essays*; J. S. Mill, *System of Logic*; Ruskin, *Modern Painters*, i (completed 1860)

1844 (15 Jan.) Fifth child, Francis, born; (16 July) takes family to Genoa; one-volume edition of *Martin Chuzzlewit* published; (30 Nov.–8 Dec.) returns to London to read *The Chimes* (published 16 Dec.) to his friends.

Factory Act restricts working hours of women and children. 'Rochdale Pioneers' found first co-operative society. Ragged School Union.
William Barnes, *Poems of Rural Life in the Dorset Dialect*; E. B. Barrett, *Poems*; Disraeli, *Coningsby*; Dumas, *Les Trois Mousquetaires*; A. W. Kinglake, *Eōthen*

1845 Travels in Italy with Catherine before returning to London from Genoa; (20 Sept.) directs and acts in first performance of the Amateur Players, Ben Jonson's *Every Man In His Humour*; (28 Oct.) sixth child, Alfred, born; (20 Dec.) *The Cricket on the Hearth* published.

Disappearance of Sir John Franklin's expedition to find a North-West Passage from the Atlantic to the Pacific. War with Sikhs. 1845–9: potato famine in Ireland: 1 million die; 8 million emigrate. Thomas Hood and Sydney Smith die.
Browning, *Dramatic Romances and Lyrics*; Disraeli, *Sybil*; Engels, *Condition of the Working Class in England*; Poe, *The Raven and other Poems, Tales of Mystery and Imagination*

1846 (21 Jan.–9 Feb.) Edits *The Daily News*; (May) *Pictures from Italy* published; (31 May) leaves with family for Switzerland via the Rhine; (11 June) settles in Lausanne; (30 Sept.) monthly serialization of *Dombey and Son* commences; (Oct.) family moves to Paris; (Dec.) *The Battle of Life* published.

Corn Laws repealed; Peel resigns; Lord John Russell PM. Ether first used as a general anaesthetic. Robert Browning and Elizabeth Barrett marry secretly and leave for Italy.
Balzac, *La Cousine Bette*; *Poems by Currer, Ellis and Acton Bell* (i.e. Charlotte, Emily, and Anne Brontë); Edward Lear, *Book of Nonsense*

1847 (28 Feb.) Returns from Paris; (18 Apr.) seventh child, Sydney, is born; (June–Sept.) with family at Broadstairs; (27–8 July) performs in Manchester and Liverpool with the Amateurs; (Nov.) Urania Cottage, Miss Coutts's 'Home for Homeless Women', in whose administration CD is involved, opened in Shepherd's Bush.

Factory Act limits working day for women and young persons to 10 hours. James Simpson discovers anaesthetic properties of chloroform. Louis Napoleon escapes to England from prison.
A. Brontë, *Agnes Grey*; C. Brontë, *Jane Eyre*; E. Brontë, *Wuthering Heights*; Tennyson, *The Princess*. J. M. Morton's *Box and Cox* acted

1848 (12 Apr.) One-volume edition of *Dombey and Son* published; (May–July) the Amateurs perform in London, Manchester, Liverpool, Birmingham, Edinburgh, and Glasgow; (2 Sept.) sister Fanny dies; (19 Dec.) *The Haunted Man* published.

Outbreak of cholera in London. Public Health Act. End of Chartist Movement. Pre-Raphaelite Brotherhood founded. 'The Year of Revolutions' in Europe. Louis Napoleon becomes President of France. Emily Brontë, Branwell Brontë die.
A. Brontë, *The Tenant of Wildfell Hall*; Elizabeth Gaskell, *Mary Barton*; Marx and Engels, *Communist Manifesto*; J. S. Mill, *Principles of Political Economy*; Thackeray, *Vanity Fair*

1849 (16 Jan.) Eighth child, Henry ('Harry'), born; (1 May) monthly serialization of *David Copperfield* begins; (July–Oct.) with family at Bonchurch, Isle of Wight.

Revolt against the British in Montreal. Punjab annexed. Rome proclaimed a republic; later taken by the French. Suppression of Communist riots in Paris. Californian gold rush. Anne Brontë, E. A. Poe die.
C. Brontë, *Shirley*; Sir John Herschel, *Outlines of Astronomy*; Macaulay, *History of England*, i–ii (unfinished at his death, in 1859); Ruskin, *The Seven Lamps of Architecture*

1850 (30 Mar.) First issue of *Household Words*, a weekly journal edited and contributed to by CD; (16 Aug.) ninth child, Dora, born; (Aug.–Oct.) at Broadstairs; (15 Nov.) one-volume edition of *David Copperfield* published.

Restoration of Roman Catholic hierarchy in England. Factory Act: 60-hour week for women and young persons. Public Libraries Act. Dover–Calais telegraph cable laid. Balzac and Wordsworth die. Tennyson becomes Poet Laureate.
E. B. Browning, 'Sonnets from the Portuguese', in *Poems*; Nathaniel Hawthorne, *The Scarlet Letter*; Tennyson, *In Memoriam A.H.H.*; Thackeray, *The History of Pendennis*; Wordsworth, *The Prelude* (posth.)

1851 (25 Jan.) *A Child's History of England* starts serialization in *Household Words*; (31 Mar.) John Dickens dies; (14 Apr.) Dora dies suddenly, aged 8 months; (May) directs and acts in Bulwer-Lytton's *Not So Bad As We Seem* before the Queen, in aid of the Guild of Literature and Art; (May–Oct.) last family holiday at Broadstairs; (Nov.) moves to Tavistock House.

Great Exhibition in the Crystal Palace, Hyde Park. Fall of French Second Republic. Gold found in Australia. George Borrow, *Lavengro*; Henry Mayhew, *London Labour and the London Poor*; Herman Melville, *Moby Dick*; George Meredith, *Poems*; Ruskin, *The King of the Golden River*, *The Stones of Venice*, i (completed 1853)

1852 (28 Feb.) Monthly serialization of *Bleak House* begins; (14 Apr.) birth of tenth child, Edward ('Plorn'); (Feb.–Sept.) provincial performances of *Not So Bad As We Seem*; (July–Oct.) family stays in Dover.

Lord Derby becomes PM; then Lord Aberdeen. Louis Napoleon proclaimed Emperor Napoleon III. 1852–6: David Livingstone crosses Africa. Tom Moore and the Duke of Wellington die. M. P. Roget, *Roget's Thesaurus of English Words and Phrases*; Harriet Beecher Stowe, *Uncle Tom's Cabin*; Thackeray, *Henry Esmond*

1853 (June–Oct.) Family stays in Boulogne; (12 Sept.) one-volume edition of *Bleak House* published; (Oct.–Dec.) in Switzerland and Italy with Wilkie Collins and Augustus Egg; (10 Dec.) *A Child's History of England* concluded in *Household Words*; (27–30 Dec.) gives public readings of *A Christmas Carol* and *The Cricket on the Hearth* in Birmingham.

Arnold, *Poems*; C. Brontë, *Villette*; Gaskell, *Ruth*, *Cranford*; Surtees, *Mr Sponge's Sporting Career*

1854 (28–30 Jan.) Visits Preston; (1 Apr.–12 Aug.) weekly serialization of *Hard Times* in *Household Words*; (June–Oct.) family stays in Boulogne; (7 Aug.) *Hard Times* published in one volume; (Dec.) reads *A Christmas Carol* in Reading, Sherborne, and Bradford.

Reform of the Civil Service. France and Britain join Turkey against Russia in the Crimean War; battles of Alma, Balaclava, Inkerman and siege of Sebastopol; Florence Nightingale goes to Scutari. Patmore, *The Angel in the House*, i (completed 1862); Tennyson, 'The Charge of the Light Brigade'; H. D. Thoreau, *Walden*

1855 (Feb.) Meets Maria Winter (née Beadnell) again; (27 Mar.) reads *A Christmas Carol* in Ashford, Kent; (June) directs and acts in Collins's *The Lighthouse* at

Lord Palmerston PM. Newspaper tax abolished. *Daily Telegraph*, first London penny newspaper, founded. Fall of Sebastopol. 1855–6: G. J. Mendel discovers laws of heredity.

Tavistock House; family stays in Folkestone, where CD reads *A Christmas Carol* on 5 Oct.; (15 Oct.) settles family in Paris; (1 Dec.) monthly serialization of *Little Dorrit* begins; (Dec.) reads *A Christmas Carol* at Peterborough and Sheffield.

Charlotte Brontë and Mary Russell Mitford die.
R. Browning, *Men and Women*; Gaskell, *North and South*; Longfellow, *Hiawatha*; Tennyson, *Maud and other Poems*; Thackeray, *The Newcomes*, *The Rose and the Ring*; A. Trollope, *The Warden*; Walt Whitman, *Leaves of Grass*

1856 (Mar.) Buys Gad's Hill Place, Kent; (29 Apr.) family returns from Paris; (June–Sept.) family stays in Boulogne.

End of Crimean War. Britain annexes Oudh; Sir Henry Bessemer patents his steel-making process. Synthetic colours invented. Henry Irving's first stage appearance. National Gallery founded in London.
Mrs Craik (Dinah Maria Mulock), *John Halifax, Gentleman*; Flaubert, *Madame Bovary*

1857 (Jan.) Directs and acts in Collins's *The Frozen Deep* at Tavistock House; (13 Feb.) moves to Gad's Hill Place; (30 May) *Little Dorrit* published in one volume; Walter leaves for service with the East India Company; (June–July) visited by Hans Andersen; gives three public readings of *A Christmas Carol*; (July–Aug.) performances of *The Frozen Deep* in London and, with Ellen Ternan, her sister and mother in the cast, in Manchester.

Divorce courts established in England. Arnold becomes Professor of Poetry at Oxford. Museum—later, the Victoria and Albert Museum—opened in South Kensington. Beginning of Indian mutiny; siege and relief of Lucknow.
Baudelaire, *Les Fleurs du mal*; C. Brontë, *The Professor* (posth.); E. B. Browning, *Aurora Leigh*; Gaskell, *The Life of Charlotte Brontë*; Hughes, *Tom Brown's Schooldays*; Livingstone, *Missionary Travels and Researches in South Africa*; A. Trollope, *Barchester Towers*

1858 (19 Jan.; 26 Mar; 15 Apr.) Reads *A Christmas Carol* for charity; (29 Apr.–22 July) series of 17 public readings; (May) separation from Catherine; (7 and 12 June) publishes 'personal' statement about it in *The Times* and *Household Words*; (Aug.) *Reprinted Pieces* published; (Aug.–Nov.) first provincial reading tour, extending to Ireland and Scotland (85 readings); (24 Dec.) first series of London Christmas readings begins.

Derby PM. Indian Mutiny suppressed; powers of East India Company transferred to the Crown. Queen Victoria proclaimed Empress of India. Launch of I. K. Brunel's *Great Eastern*. Darwin and A. R. Wallace give joint paper on evolution.
R. M. Ballantyne, *The Coral Island*; Clough, *Amours de Voyage*; Eliot, *Scenes of Clerical Life*; A. Trollope, *Doctor Thorne*

1859 (30 Apr.) Begins to edit *All the Year Round* in which *A Tale of Two Cities* appears weekly till 26 November; (28 May) final number of *Household Words*; (Oct.) gives 14 readings on second provincial tour; (21 Nov.) *A Tale of Two Cities* published in one volume; (24 Dec.) begins series of three London Christmas readings.

Palmerston PM. Franco–Austrian War: Austrians defeated at Solferino. War of Italian Liberation. The abolitionist John Brown hanged for treason at Charlestown, Virginia. Thomas De Quincey, Leigh Hunt, and Lord Macaulay die. Darwin, *On the Origin of Species by Means of Natural Selection*; Eliot, *Adam Bede*; Edward FitzGerald, *The Rubáiyát of Omar Khayyám*; J. S. Mill, *On Liberty*; Samuel Smiles, *Self-Help*; Tennyson, *Idylls of the King*

1860 (17 July) Katey marries Charles Collins; (27 July) CD's brother Alfred dies, at 38; (21 Aug.) sells Tavistock House; settles permanently at Gad's Hill; (1 Dec.) weekly serialization of *Great Expectations* begins in *All the Year Round*, continuing till 3 Aug. 1861.

Abraham Lincoln elected US president; Carolina secedes from the Union. Collins, *The Woman in White*; Eliot, *The Mill on the Floss*; Faraday, *Various Forces of Matter*. Boucicault's *The Colleen Bawn* acted

1861 (Mar.–Apr.) Series of 6 London readings; (6 July) *Great Expectations* published in three volumes; (Oct.–Jan. 1862) gives 46 readings on third provincial tour; (19 Nov.) Charley marries Elizabeth ('Bessie') Evans: CD refuses to be present.

Abolition of Paper Tax. Prince Albert dies. Victor Emmanuel becomes King of Italy. Serfdom abolished in Russia. Outbreak of American Civil War. E. B. Browning and A. H. Clough die. Mrs Isabella Mary Beeton, *Book of Household Management*; Eliot, *Silas Marner*; J. S. Mill, *Utilitarianism*; F. T. Palgrave, *The Golden Treasury*; Reade, *The Cloister and the Hearth*; A. Trollope, *Framley Parsonage*; Mrs Henry Wood, *East Lynne*

1862 (Feb.–May) Exchanges Gad's Hill Place for a house in London but also uses rooms at the office of *All the Year Round*; (Mar.–June) London readings; (June–Oct.) makes several visits to France; (Oct.) settles Mamie and her aunt, Georgina Hogarth, in Paris; (Dec.) returns to Gad's Hill for Christmas.

Famine among Lancashire cotton workers. Bismarck becomes Chancellor of Prussia. Thoreau dies. Mary Elizabeth Braddon, *Lady Audley's Secret*; Hugo, *Les Misérables*; Meredith, *Modern Love*; Christina Rossetti, *Goblin Market and Other Poems*; Herbert Spencer, *First Principles*; Turgenev, *Fathers and Sons*

1863 (Jan.) Gives 3 readings for charity at British Embassy in Paris; (Feb. and Aug.) makes further visits to France; (Mar.–May) London readings; (13 Sept.) Elizabeth Dickens dies; (31 Dec.) Walter dies in Calcutta, India, aged 22.

Beginning of work on London underground railway. Lincoln's Gettysburg Address; emancipation of US slaves. Thackeray and Frances Trollope die.
Eliot, *Romola*; Margaret Oliphant, *Salem Chapel*

1864 (1 May) Monthly serialization of *Our Mutual Friend* begins; (27 June–6 July) probably in France; (Nov.) in France.

Karl Marx organizes first Socialist International in London. Louis Pasteur publishes his theory of germs as the cause of disease. International Red Cross founded. John Clare, W. S. Landor, R. S. Surtees, and Hawthorne die.
Sheridan Le Fanu, *Uncle Silas*; Newman, *Apologia pro Vita Sua*; Tennyson, *Enoch Arden and Other Poems*; Trollope, *The Small House at Allington, Can You Forgive Her?*

1865 (Feb.–June) Three trips to France; (Feb.–Apr.) first attack of lameness from swollen left foot; (29 May) sees Alfred off to Australia; (9 June) returning from France with Ellen Ternan and her mother, is in fatal railway accident at Staplehurst, Kent; (Sept.) visit to France; (20 Oct.) *Our Mutual Friend* published in two volumes.

Russell PM. William Booth founds Christian Mission in Whitechapel, known from 1878 as the Salvation Army. Completion of transatlantic cable. End of American Civil War. Abraham Lincoln assassinated. Elizabeth Gaskell dies.
Arnold, *Essays in Criticism, First Series*; Lewis Carroll, *Alice's Adventures in Wonderland*

1866 (Apr.–June) Readings in London and the provinces; (June) CD's brother Augustus Dickens dies in Chicago, aged 38.

Derby PM. Second Reform Bill. Fenians active in Ireland: Habeas Corpus suspended. Elizabeth Garrett opens dispensary for women. Dr T. J. Barnardo opens home for destitute children in London's East End. Peacock and John Keble die.
Fyodor Dostoevsky, *Crime and Punishment*; Eliot, *Felix Holt, the Radical*; Gaskell, *Wives and Daughters* (posth., unfinished); Swinburne, *Poems and Ballads*, First Series

1867 (Jan.–May) Readings in England and Ireland; (Nov.) begins American reading tour in Boston; (Dec.) *No Thoroughfare*, written jointly with Collins, published in *All the Year Round*.

Fenian outrages in England. Second Reform Act. Factory Act. Joseph Lister practises antiseptic surgery. Building of Royal Albert Hall commenced.
Arnold, 'Dover Beach', 'Thyrsis', in *New Poems*; Walter Bagehot, *The English Constitution*; Henrik Ibsen, *Peer Gynt*; Karl Marx, *Das Kapital*, i; A. Trollope, *The Last Chronicle of Barset*; Emile Zola, *Thérèse Raquin*

1868 (22 Apr.) Sails home from New York, having cancelled planned readings in the USA and Canada; (26 Sept.) Plorn sails to Australia to join Alfred; (Oct.) Harry enters Trinity College, Cambridge; CD begins Farewell Reading Tour; CD's brother Fred dies, aged 48.

Disraeli PM; Gladstone PM. Trades Union Congress founded. Basutoland annexed.
Louisa May Alcott, *Little Women*; Collins, *The Moonstone*; Queen Victoria, *Leaves from a Journal of Our Life in the Highlands*

1869 (5 Jan.) Introduces 'Sikes and Nancy' into his repertoire; (22 Apr.) serious illness forces CD to break off reading tour after 74 readings.

Girton College for Women founded. Suez Canal opened.
Arnold, *Culture and Anarchy*; R. D. Blackmore, *Lorna Doone*; R. Browning, *The Ring and the Book*; J. S. Mill, *On the Subjection of Women*; Leo Tolstoy, *War and Peace*; A. Trollope, *Phineas Finn, He Knew He Was Right*; Paul Verlaine, *Fêtes galantes*

1870 (Jan.– Mar.) Farewell readings in London; (9 Mar.) received by Queen Victoria; (1 Apr.) first of six completed numbers of *The Mystery of Edwin Drood* issued; (9 June) dies, aged 58, following a cerebral haemorrhage, at Gad's Hill; (14 June) buried in Westminster Abbey.

Gladstone's Irish Land Act. Married Women's Property Act gives wives the right to their own earnings. Elementary Education Act for England and Wales. Outbreak of Franco–Prussian War: Napoleon III defeated and exiled; siege of Paris (till 1871).
E. C. Brewer, *Dictionary of Phrase and Fable*; D. G. Rossetti, *Poems*

ABBREVIATIONS

Life   John Forster, *The Life of Charles Dickens* (1872–4), ed. J. W. T. Ley (1928)

Letters Madeline House, Graham Storey, Kathleen Tillotson, *et al.* (eds.), *The Letters of Charles Dickens*, 12 vols. (The Pilgrim Edition, Oxford: Clarendon Press, 1965–2002)

CHAPTER I

DICKENS'S LIFE

ON 10 February 1812 Charles Dickens's father, John Dickens, proudly, and more than a little pompously, announced the birth of his son three days earlier:

BIRTHS—On Friday, at Mile-end Terrace, the Lady of John Dickens, Esq. a son.[1]

John Dickens was not only celebrating the arrival of his second child, and his first son, he was also proclaiming to his friends and acquaintance in the port and garrison town of Portsmouth that he laid claim to a social dignity that was not necessarily his by right, status, or inheritance. John Dickens, and his 'lady', Elizabeth, and their 18-month-old daughter, Fanny, made up a relatively obscure lower middle-class provincial family, but they evidently had pretensions to gentility. That claim to gentility was precarious. John, the second son of the butler and the housekeeper to the aristocratic Crewe family, had married the sister of a seemingly respectable friend in 1809, but in February 1810 Elizabeth's father had been obliged to take refuge on the Isle of Man on the discovery of his having embezzled the then huge sum of £5,689. 13s. 3d., thus provoking the wrath and legal action on the part of his employers, the Navy Pay Office and the Lords of the Admiralty.

Money, the misuse of money, and the lack of money were to continue to haunt Charles Dickens's childhood and early adolescence. His father worked for the Navy Pay Office as an 'extra clerk'. John Dickens had been sent to Portsmouth, then, as now, Britain's chief naval port, in 1808 and, once married, had established himself in a modest seven-roomed, terraced house in the parish of Portsea on the main Portsmouth to London road. The novelist was later to describe his birthplace disparagingly as 'an English seaport town principally remarkable for mud, Jews, and Sailors' (*Letters*, i. 423: ?July 1838). In 1812, with the long-drawn-out war against Napoleonic France still being waged both at sea and on land,

Portsmouth was a busy, various, but generally unlovely town. It sprawled around its dockyard and its economy depended on the trade generated by its shifting population of sailors, soldiers, and marines (the Jews Dickens recalled were likely to have been both moneylenders and tradesmen engaged in various forms of ships' chandlery). The Dickenses were to move house twice during the first two years of Charles's life and the novelist later recalled Portsmouth with considerable vagueness. His factotum, George Dolby, was to describe an incident during a visit to Portsmouth in 1866:

On the morning after our arrival we set out for a walk, and turning the corner of a street suddenly, found ourselves in Landport Terrace. The name of the street catching Mr. Dickens's eye, he suddenly exclaimed, 'By Jove! Here is the place where I was born'; and, acting on his suggestion, we walked up and down the terrace for some time, speculating as to which of the houses had the right to call itself his cradle. Beyond a recollection that there was a small front garden to the house he had no idea of the place for he was only two years old when his father was removed to London from Portsmouth.[2]

Perhaps because the Dickens family were always on the move, as a consequence of John Dickens's employment as much as of economic necessity, the novelist seems to have felt little attachment to his birthplace. Unlike Chatham, Rochester, and London where he spent later periods of his childhood, Portsmouth seems to have stimulated few vivid memories and even less of a sense of belonging. Nor, apart from the fact that it figures briefly in *Nicholas Nickleby* as the setting for the Crummles company's theatrical enterprise, was it to directly stimulate his literary imagination.

In 1815 the Dickenses moved briefly to London, but between 1817 and 1822 they passed their most ostensibly prosperous, secure, and happy time as a growing family in Chatham. London was to become the central phenomenon in Charles Dickens's work, but the port and garrison town of Chatham and its neighbouring cathedral city of Rochester were to foster his imagination in another sense. These two contiguous towns on the River Medway were to be whimsically described by Mr Pickwick in Dickens's first full-length work of fiction as having as their principal production 'soldiers, sailors, Jews, chalk, shrimps, officers, and dockyard men'. Chatham was later to be revisited and pictured, not particularly flatteringly, as 'Dullborough Town' in one of the *Uncommercial Traveller* essays, while Rochester was to figure anonymously in *Great Expectations* and as the dusty Cloisterham in *The Mystery of Edwin Drood*. All three later accounts convey the distinct impression that both towns were, and had remained, slightly eccentric backwaters. Nevertheless, despite the adult Dickens's evocations of a mood of small-town small-mindedness, he had been conspicuously happy as a boy in Chatham. By the time his family moved to the dockyard town the Dickenses numbered five (a second daughter, Letitia, had been born in 1816). The household also included Charles's maternal aunt, Mary Allen, and two servants. One of these servants, Mary Weller, it has sometimes been suggested, was instrumental in fostering Dickens's imagination by telling him the gorily sensational bedtime stories which he recalled in the *Uncommercial* essay 'Nurse's Stories'.[3] Whether or not Mary was the nurse concerned, Dickens's distinctive turn of mind was certainly shaped by much of his experience of the Medway towns and their surrounding countryside. Here, by his own account, he staged mock battles and sieges in hay-ricks, invented games in fields, and wonderingly speculated amongst the marshes and creeks in the estuary of the River Thames ('running water is favourable to day-dreams, and a strong tidal river is the best for mine', Dickens later insisted in his essay 'Chatham Dockyard'). Here, despite the limited resources of the Theatre Royal, Rochester, he was introduced to the professional stage for the first time, seeing, amongst other plays, Shakespeare's *Richard III* and *Macbeth*, and two high-flown and once highly esteemed eighteenth-century dramas, Nicholas Rowe's *The Tragedy of Jane Shore* and George Lillo's *The London Merchant, or the History of George Barnwell*. Here in Chatham, Dickens received his first formal education, initially at a preparatory day-school, which he vaguely remembered in the essay 'Our School' as having been over a dyer's shop, with its entry guarded by 'a puffy pug-dog, with a personal animosity towards us', and, secondly, at an institution run by the Revd William Giles, a local Baptist minister. Dickens remembered Giles's encouragement with much affection. John Forster records that when, half-way through the spectacularly successful serialization of *Pickwick Papers*, Giles sent Dickens a silver snuff-box 'with the admiring inscription to "the inimitable Boz," it reminded him of praise far more precious obtained by him at his first year's examination' (*Life*, p. 7). At Giles's school Dickens was also stimulated to develop his natural talent for

elocution, recitation, and acting (he recalled with pleasure the
double encore demanded after his performance of a piece from an
anthology entitled the *Humourist's Miscellany*). This relish for acting
out texts and for imagining himself in other roles, and the love of the
well-rounded sentence and of the resonance of words and rolling
phrases, were to remain central aspects of Dickens's character and of
his art. His boyhood passion for words and books was also fostered
by his early discovery of the established literary classics of European
comic fiction: Smollett's *Roderick Random*, *Peregrine Pickle*, and
Humphry Clinker; Fielding's *Tom Jones*; Goldsmith's *The Vicar of
Wakefield*; Defoe's *Robinson Crusoe*; Cervantes's *Don Quixote*; and Le
Sage's *Gil Blas*. He also fell in love with *The Arabian Nights*. When,
as an established writer himself, he allotted to David Copperfield this
same reading list and a similar desire to escape imaginatively into the
lives of fictional characters, Dickens was stressing the importance of
the kind of literature that 'kept alive my fancy and my hope of
something beyond that time and place' (*David Copperfield*, ch. 4).
Dickens, like David, craved that vital imaginative resource as
much as, in an earlier generation, Wordsworth and Coleridge sought
the spiritual restoration given to them by the recall of natural
landscape.

The Dickenses in London 1822–1825

In June 1822 John Dickens was transferred from Chatham Dockyard
to a post at Somerset House in London. He took a small suburban
house in Bayham Street, Camden Town, and at some point in the
autumn of 1822, his family moved up to town to join him. By this
time the family numbered six (although two of her children had died
in infancy, Elizabeth Dickens had given birth to another boy, Frederick, in 1820 and two more boys, Alfred and Augustus, were to follow
in 1822 and 1827 respectively). The house in Bayham Street was
almost certainly the model for the Cratchits' modest home in *A
Christmas Carol* and the fact that the winter of 1822 was especially
cold may well have contributed to the influential pictures of snowy
Christmases in that story and in *Pickwick Papers*. Camden Town was
a slightly dowdy, lower middle-class district. In chapter 27 of *David
Copperfield* David goes in search of his friend Traddles who has
taken a house close to Bayham Street and finds the address 'not as

desirable a one as I could have wished it to be . . . the inhabitants appeared to have a propensity to throw any little trifles they were not in want of, into the road: which not only made it rank, and sloppy, but untidy too, on account of the cabbage leaves'. It was, however, from Bayham Street that Dickens first began to explore the vast and varied metropolitan spaces which stretched southwards from Camden Town. This was not simply a matter of being drawn towards the centre of a teeming city symbolized by 'the cupola of St. Paul's looming through the smoke'. John Forster describes the excitement and mixed emotions stimulated by excursions from the northern suburbs:

To be taken out for a walk into the real town, especially if it were anywhere about Covent-garden or the Strand, perfectly entranced him with pleasure. But, most of all, he had a profound attraction of repulsion to St. Giles's. If he could only induce whomsoever took him out to take him through Seven-dials, he was supremely happy. 'Good Heaven!' he would exclaim, 'what wild visions of prodigies of wickedness, want and beggary, arose in my mind of that place!' (*Life*, p. 11)

Dickens's vision of London remained consistent with this childhood response to the city's inherent anomalies and ambiguities. The 'profound attraction of repulsion', stimulated by the seamier side of London, was to prove a key to Dickens's creativity.

During these first months in London a distinct economic shadow was beginning to eclipse the Dickenses' tenuous claim to lower middle-class respectability. John Dickens was running steadily into financial trouble. Although he was earning a healthy-enough salary of £350, his income had dropped by £90 since his transfer and, probably as a result of personal financial mismanagement and an inability to honour outstanding debts, he seems to have found it hard to make ends meet. In September 1823 Elizabeth Dickens attempted to provide a second income by setting up a private school for girls in a somewhat more capacious house in Gower Street North and the family moved accordingly. The school and the second income remained a dream. As Dickens later recalled, with a real note of bitterness: 'I left at a great many doors, a great many circulars calling attention to the merits of the establishment. Yet nobody ever came to school, nor do I recollect that anybody ever proposed to come, or that the least preparation was made to receive anybody' (*Life*, p. 13). The family increasingly slipped further and further into debt. The

atmosphere at 4 Gower Street North probably resembled that at
the Micawbers' house described in chapter 11 of *David Copperfield*.
Mrs Micawber has placed a brass plate on her front door proclaiming it to be 'Mrs. Micawber's Boarding Establishment for Young
Ladies', but no young lady pupil has ever materialized. Moreover,
as David recalls, there were regular callers of a distinctly ungenteel
kind:

The only visitors I ever saw or heard of, were creditors. *They* used to come
at all hours, and some of them were quite ferocious. One dirty-faced man,
I think he was a boot-maker, used to edge himself into the passage as early
as seven o'clock in the morning, and call up the stairs to Mr. Micawber—
'Come! You ain't out yet, you know. Pay us, will you? Don't hide, you
know; that's mean. I wouldn't be mean if I was you. Pay us, will you? You
just pay us, d'ye hear ? Come!' Receiving no answer to these taunts, he
would mount in his wrath to the words 'swindlers' and 'robbers;'
and these being ineffectual too, would sometimes go to the extremity of
crossing the street, and roaring up at the windows of the second floor.

This embarrassment, an embarrassment which was as much social as
it was economic, was to usher in the darkest period of Charles
Dickens's life.

At some point early in 1824, shortly before Charles's twelfth
birthday, James Lamert, a friend of Dickens's father, suggested that
the boy might be found employment in the shoeblacking factory
which he was managing, Warren's of 30 Hungerford Stairs, between
the Strand and the River Thames. In the 1820s it was by no means
extraordinary that a working-class boy of Dickens's age should be
out at work. What humiliated Dickens, however, was the fact that
he, a middle-class boy, with social aspirations and expectations of
a professional career, should suffer such an acute loss of status.
He had probably not been sent to school since the move to London,
but now he was reduced, by his own estimate, to a singularly miserable and demeaning working existence. Recalling it painful detail
by painful detail, he described his situation in the unfinished
autobiography which was first published in Forster's posthumous
biography:

The blacking warehouse was the last house on the left-hand side of the
way, at old Hungerford-stairs. It was a crazy, tumble-down old house,
abutting of course on the river, and literally overrun by rats. Its wainscot-

ted rooms, and its rotten floors and staircase, and the old grey rats swarming down in the cellars, and the sound of their squeaking and scuffling coming up the stairs at all times, and the dirt and decay of the place, rise up visibly before me, as if I were there again. The counting-house was on the first floor, looking over the coal barges and the river. There was a recess in it, in which I was to sit and work. My work was to cover the pots of paste-blacking; first with a piece of oil-paper, and then with a piece of blue paper; to tie them round with a string; and then to clip the paper close and neat, all round, until it looked as smart as a pot of ointment from an apothecary's shop. When a certain number of grosses of pots had attained this pitch of perfection, I was to paste on each a printed label; and then go on again with more pots.

This mechanical and repetitive work was certainly uncongenial, but so in a different way was the company that Dickens was obliged to keep. His comments on one of these fellow labourers is especially revealing:

Two or three other boys were kept at similar duty down stairs on similar wages. One of them came up, in a ragged apron and a paper cap, on the first Monday morning, to show me the trick of using the string and tying the knot. His name was Bob Fagin; and I took the liberty of using his name, long afterwards, in *Oliver Twist*.   (*Life*, p. 25)

This comment is more than a little disingenuous on Dickens's part. Bob Fagin not only taught him how to perform his menial tasks more efficiently, he was also to prove a singularly good-natured workmate during this period in the blacking-warehouse. He once physically defended the boy against the onslaughts of another boy who resented Dickens's special status as 'the young-gentleman'. On another occasion he filled an empty blacking-bottle with hot water in order to relieve excruciating pains in Dickens's side, after which he attempted to accompany him home to be sure that he had sufficiently recovered (though Dickens deliberately deceived him when it came to revealing where he lived). To give this good-hearted boy's surname to the arch-villain of *Oliver Twist* suggests the degree to which Dickens had come to associate his kindness with entrapment in the world of Warren's, and by extension in the culture and non-aspirant ethos of the working class. Bob seems to have been cast in the role of a devil, one who had tried to make Dickens's private hell more habitable and therefore more acceptable. The transfer of Bob's surname to that of the diabolic Fagin, the 'merry old gentleman' who is hospitable and murderous by turns, seems to have been an expression of Dickens's fear of never being able to escape from the world that Bob Fagin took for granted. In a passage from the autobiographical fragment, sentiments which he later gave, virtually word for word, to David Copperfield, Dickens described the 'secret agony' of his soul as he had 'sunk' into the companionship of Bob and the other working boys and had compared these 'everyday associates' with those of his happier childhood:

[I] felt my early hopes of growing up a learned and distinguished man, crushed in my breast. The deep remembrance of the sense I had of being utterly neglected and hopeless; of the shame I felt in my position; of the misery it was to my young heart to believe that, day by day, what I had learned, and thought, and delighted in, and raised my fancy and my emulation up by, was passing away from me, never to be brought back any more. (*Life*, p. 26)

To add to what Dickens felt to be the neglect and hopelessness of this dire period of his life on 20 February 1824 his father was arrested for debt. John Dickens was detained briefly in a 'sponging house' (similar to 'Coavinses' described in chapter 6 of *Bleak House*) and his son was required to run errands and carry urgent messages for him. As nothing further to satisfy John Dickens's creditors could be extracted from him, he was carried off to the Marshalsea Prison in Southwark, remarking to his son as he left him that 'the sun was set on him for ever'. This Micawberesque turn of phrase left Charles convinced that 'they' (perhaps the Marshalsea officers, perhaps his parents themselves) had broken his heart (*Life*, p. 13). The Marshalsea Prison, which was chiefly given over to debtors, had moved in the late eighteenth century to premises situated just to the north of St George's church in Borough High Street. It is described in *Little Dorrit* as 'an oblong pile of barrack building, partitioned into squalid houses standing back to back, so that there were no back rooms; environed by a narrow paved yard, hemmed in by high walls duly spiked at the top'. When he visited his desolate father for the first time Dickens received not only the famous advice about personal finances later placed in the mouth of Mr Micawber, but also instructions to go upstairs to request the loan of a knife and fork from another inmate in order to partake in a 'gipsy-like' dinner. Some weeks later Elizabeth and her three younger children moved into the Marshalsea while Charles lodged with a family friend in Camden

Town (a woman who became the original for Mrs Pipchin in *Dombey and Son*). After some weeks of this lonely existence, and after pleading with his father, he moved into a back attic in Lant Street, close to the prison. When he took possession of his humble room he thought it paradise. The period of John Dickens's incarceration (February–May 1824) was for the most part, however, a dismal and miserable one in his son's experience. Nevertheless, it obliged him to discover an enforced maturity, an unwonted independence, and, perhaps most influentially, a real familiarity with the streets, alleys, byways, and short cuts of London. He had regularly criss-crossed the metropolis on his walks to and from Hungerford Stairs and to and from the Marshalsea (which he visited with his sister on Sundays). Moreover, prisons were to loom large, gloomily, and always oppressively throughout his later work. Mr Pickwick and Mr Micawber are both incarcerated for debt (respectively in the Fleet and the King's Bench prisons), while William Dorrit shares much of John Dickens's experience in the Marshalsea. Newgate Prison figures prominently in *Sketches by Boz*, *Oliver Twist*, *Barnaby Rudge*, *A Tale of Two Cities*, and *Great Expectations*; the notorious Bastille in Paris both entombs the silent Dr Manette and is stormed by the noisy mob in *A Tale of Two Cities*, a novel which also describes the confinement of Charles Darnay in the Abbaye and the Conciergerie during the Reign of Terror; Heep and Littimer emerge as 'model' prisoners in a new 'model' prison at the end of *David Copperfield*, while Dickens expresses his concerns about the horror of the abuse of solitary confinement in its eighteenth-century form in *A Tale of Two Cities* and in its experimental modern American ramification in *American Notes*. Even as a tourist in *Pictures from Italy* he dwells fascinatedly, even luridly, on the subterranean dungeons of the Papal Palace at Avignon, on the ancient Mamertine prison in Rome, and on the 'dismal, awful, horrible, stone cells' in the prison adjacent to the Doge's Palace in Venice. As with the dark side of London, Dickens's 'profound attraction of repulsion' to prison life served to fire both his indignation and his imagination.

John Dickens was released from the Marshalsea on 28 May 1824 under the provisions of an Act of Parliament which required him to declare himself an insolvent debtor, to detail all of his debts, and to hold goods valued at no more than £20 (even Charles's clothes had to be inspected by an official appraiser to make sure that this amount was not exceeded). During his time in prison John Dickens had continued to receive his salary from the Admiralty. This was probably on medical grounds, for, within a fortnight of his imprisonment, he had applied for retirement due to 'a chronic infection of the Urinary Organs'. This illness was to cause him considerable discomfort in the years to come, and to finally lead to his death. In addition to his salary John inherited the sum of £450 on the death of his mother in April. Thus the immediate financial embarrassment passed and the social stigma of imprisonment for debt was, as far as it was possible, blotted out. Yet while the family as a whole seemed set for respectable new beginnings, for Charles there was no immediate prospect of a release from Warren's Blacking. The business had moved to Chandos Street in Covent Garden where he worked by a window looking out on the street and where his humiliating drudgery was exposed to public view. Things only came to a head when, after a quarrel between his father and his employer, Lamert, it became clear that his services were no longer required. His mother attempted to mend fences, but his father insisted instead that he should go to school. 'I can never forget', Dickens bitterly wrote, 'that my mother was warm for my being sent back.' He never seems to have quite forgiven her. It appears that he only left Warren's in March or April 1825. His formal education had been replaced by manual grind for just over a year.[4]

Dickens, like his parents, was to remain almost completely silent about this dark but formative period in his life. Only in the 1840s was he privately prepared to record the painful details and to show them to his wife and to his friend, John Forster. It was Forster who published most of this self-pitying autobiographical fragment after the novelist's death. For the most part, Dickens's boyhood misery was translated into fiction. The memory of his months in the blacking-factory became part of a habit of secrecy. It may also be integral to Dickens's awareness of the significance of leading a double life, a doubleness so frequently practised by his later characters.

School and First Employment

The Dickens family spent the months following the Marshalsea episode in various lodgings in the new, marginally respectable, suburbs of north London. Late in December 1824 they had moved into a

house in Johnson Street, Somers Town (close to where Harold
Skimpole lives in *Bleak House*). From here Dickens walked the short
distance to his new school, the Wellington House Classical and
Commercial Academy in Hampstead Road. As Dickens himself
noted, the schoolroom was later to be 'sliced away' by the works on
the London–Birmingham Railway which are so dramatically
described in chapter 15 of *Dombey and Son*. At Wellington House
Dickens seems to have responded to his resumed education with
much of the alacrity of David Copperfield at Dr Strong's school,
working 'very hard, both in play and in earnest'. Although an older
Dickens generally felt inclined to flatter both the quality of his educational experience and the social cachet of the Wellington House
Academy, as the essay 'Our School' (published in *Household Words* in
October 1851) suggests, his schoolmaster, William Jones, had in fact
more of the brutish Mr Creakle than of the gentlemanly Dr Strong
about him:

We were old enough to be put into Virgil when we went there, and to get
Prizes for a variety of polishing on which the rust has long accumulated. It
was a School of some celebrity in its neighbourhood—nobody could have
said why—and we had the honour to attain and hold the eminent position
of first boy. The master was supposed among us to know nothing, and one
of the ushers was supposed to know everything. We are inclined to think
the first-named supposition perfectly correct.[5]

Dickens was to remain at Wellington House until March 1827 when,
at the age of 15, he was abruptly withdrawn. His father, stumbling
economically yet again, had found it difficult to pay the school fees.[6]

In this same March Dickens went to work at the offices of Charles
Molloy, a solicitor with chambers in the now defunct Symond's Inn.
In May he transferred as a junior clerk to the firm of Ellis and
Blackmore in a 'poor old set of chambers of three rooms' in Holborn
Court (now South Square) in Gray's Inn at a starting salary of 10s.
6d. a week, rising to 15s. At the end of the year the firm moved to
Raymond Buildings. Dickens was not articled, but worked as a hum-
ble 'writing clerk', a position which did not necessarily promise a
radiant future in the legal profession.[7] Dickens was bored by his job.
'A lawyer's office', he later told a German correspondent, 'is a very
little world, and very dull one' (*Letters*, i. 423: July 1838). This
period in his working life introduced him to the geographical area

now often known as 'legal London', an area which encompassed both the larger Inns of Court (Lincoln's Inn, Gray's Inn, and the Inner and Middle Temple), and the smaller Inns of Chancery (Staple Inn, Clifford's Inn, Clements Inn, and Lyon's Inn). All of these 'nests of lawyers' were to figure regularly in Dickens's novels, offering both chambers for those who actually practise the law (such as Eugene Wrayburn and Mortimer Lightwood in *Our Mutual Friend*) and convenient bachelor apartments for aspiring young male professionals (such as Pip and Herbert Pocket in *Great Expectations*). As a newly married man Dickens was himself to take a set of rooms at Furnival's Inn in Holborn, a former Inn of Chancery. His experience as a legal clerk was to give him a consistent antipathy to the servants, functionaries, officials, and practitioners of the English Law. This antipathy was to reach its apogee in *Bleak House* (a novel physically centred on the area around Lincoln's Inn), but it was also to determine the unfavourable picture of lawyers from the attorneys Dodson and Fogg ('mean, rascally, pettifogging robbers') of *Pickwick Papers*; through that 'sort of monkish attorney', Francis Spenlow, a proctor in Doctors' Commons in *David Copperfield*; to the punctilious and elusive solicitor Mr Jaggers in *Great Expectations*. The Law, as we generally observe its functions in Dickens's novels, generally serves to justify Mr Bumble's ungrammatical assertion that it is 'a ass—a idiot'.

After a mere eighteen months at Ellis and Blackmore's, Dickens was sufficiently bored by his job to actively seek a change of professional direction. Since his release from the Marshalsea and his retirement from the Admiralty John Dickens appears to have taken sporadic employment as a journalist reporting for *The British Press* on parliamentary affairs. His son was resolved to follow him, having for some years contributed 'penny-a-line' reports on minor incidents, accidents, and crimes to newspapers willing to take copy from impecunious amateurs. Dickens accordingly taught himself the Gurney method of shorthand, or 'brachygraphy', and practised for a prospective career as a freelance parliamentary reporter by taking down court proceedings (at Doctors' Commons), thus probably compounding his low view of the legal profession and of the slick tongues of advocates. He was rapidly to discover that Members of Parliament were no less serpentine in their cant and hypocrisy. At some point in early 1831 Dickens joined the staff of *The Mirror of*

Parliament (a journal owned and edited by an uncle for whom his father also worked as a reporter). *The Mirror of Parliament* was a serious rival to *Hansard* as a recorder of the often fraught debates in the House of Commons in the crucial period in British constitutional history that led up to the passage of the Great Reform Bill of 1832. Dickens, who steadily acquired a reputation as an accurate shorthand writer, was to be taken on as a regular reporter for *The True Sun* in March 1832 and transferred his services to *The Morning Chronicle*, at a salary of five guineas a week, in 1834. Again, like David Copperfield, he came to find that he was 'sufficiently behind the scenes to know the worth of political life' and to be 'quite an infidel about it'. In the essay 'A Parliamentary Sketch' (published in revised form in December 1836) Dickens was to remark of the Commons that he had 'made some few calls at the aforesaid house in our time' and that he had 'visited it quite enough for our purpose, and a great deal too often for our personal peace and comfort'. The House itself is unflatteringly described as full of members 'all talking, laughing, lounging, coughing, oh-ing, questioning, or groaning' and as 'presenting a conglomeration of noise and confusion, to be met with in no other place in existence, not even excepting Smithfield on a market day, or a cockpit in its glory'. 'Sentiment', a tale of 1834, later republished in the *Sketches by Boz*, contains the first in a line of Dickens's pompous fictional MPs, Cornelius Brook Dingwall: 'very haughty, solemn, and portentous . . . he was wonderfully proud of the MP attached to his name, and never lost an opportunity of reminding people of his dignity. He had a great idea of his own abilities, which must have been a great comfort to him, as no one else had.' This line continues through the self-important Mr Gregsbury, 'a tough, burly, thick-headed gentleman, with a loud voice [and] a pompous manner', who offers Nicholas Nickleby the position of his secretary. It culminates in the interchangeably self-seeking Buffys, Cuffys, and Duffys, the parliamentary associates of Sir Leicester Dedlock MP in *Bleak House*. Dickens was never to be an enemy of representative government but his early experience of the noisy workings and the creaky misworkings of parliament was to condition his view of the British constitution, a view which was to become more jaded as he grew older.

The Beginning of Dickens's Literary Career: 1833–1839

In the summer of 1833, when a parliamentary recess left him with relatively little to do as a reporter, Dickens began work on the first of a proposed series of articles to be entitled 'Our Parish'. In a preface to a new edition of *Pickwick Papers* in 1847, he left an account of his trepidation as he submitted this first stab at fiction to the editor of a contemporary journal. He described how 'stealthily one evening at twilight' he dropped his manuscript 'with fear and trembling into a dark letter box, in a dark office, up a dark court in Fleet Street'. This was the office of the *Monthly Magazine*. Dickens proved to be fortunate in his choice of journal. Its editor admired his piece, published it in the December issue under the title 'A Dinner at Poplar Walk', and asked for further contributions (though no remuneration was forthcoming). He supplied six more tales to the *Monthly Magazine* during 1834, and for the publication of the second instalment of the fifth story he signed himself by his new pen-name: 'Boz'.[8] Over the next two years a steady stream of further 'sketches' of London life were to appear in a variety of magazines and newspapers. Although some twelve such sketches appeared under the pseudonym 'Tibbs', it was as 'Boz' that Dickens first really established his reputation as a new writer to be reckoned with. After his initial unpaid experience with the *Monthly Magazine* he was also to develop into a canny and demanding negotiator of contracts and financial terms with his future publishers.

Thus Dickens's dazzling literary career opened. He had begun his rise to fame with the kind of social disadvantage not shared by most of his male literary contemporaries. His birth had been relatively humble, he had never attended a public school, and he had not proceeded to a university. He was not, therefore, by the conventional nineteenth-century definitions of the term, a gentleman by birth, breeding, or education, and neither his father's history of debt nor his own experience of poverty as a 12-year-old added any glamour or romance to his status. What he learned and experienced during his adolescence and early manhood could scarcely be described by Goethe's terms *Lehrjahre* or *Wanderjahre*. Compared to Thackeray or Trollope, to Tennyson or Arnold, to Ruskin or Browning, Dickens had experienced little in the way of social and educational privilege; he lacked both inherited status and financial resource, and he had established no network of influential school and university friends to assist his advance. As he was to remark to his friend Wilkie Collins on 6 June 1856, he had begun to write 'without any interest or introduction of any kind' (*Letters*, viii. 130–1). Dickens knew that he had to make his own way in the world of letters, and once doors were opened to him, he took a deep pride in his achievement as a professional writer. As the surviving contracts for his books also suggest, he was determined that his success should also be generously rewarded.

The opening years of the 1830s were a vital transitional period in Dickens's life. They were years in which uncertainties were ironed out and ambitions realized. For a time he contemplated a career on the professional stage, having put on amateur productions at his parents' home and, as he told John Forster, privately practised acting techniques for up to 'four, five, or six hours a day' (*Life*, pp. 59–60). Having missed a crucial audition at Covent Garden, thanks to an untimely head cold, this histrionic ambition was to be deflected into his continuing involvement with private theatricals and into the public readings from his own work which were such a feature of the latter part of his career. He was also reading widely and avidly. He obtained a reader's ticket for the British Museum Library as early as 1830 and surviving call slips suggest that he was devouring the plays of Shakespeare, history, and a good deal of eighteenth-century prose literature (*Life*, p. 47).[9] By the latter half of 1831 he was also courting the first great love of his life, Maria Beadnell, the daughter of a City banker. Despite Dickens's infatuation, and a flood of bad poetry addressed to her, the coquettish Maria proved to be non-committal about the relationship. It is possible that her father had caught wind of John Dickens's earlier embarrassments, or that he considered Charles's economic and professional prospects unsatisfactory, but the affair appears to have fizzled out by the middle of 1833. As the once-besotted Dickens told Maria some twenty years later, this courtship had been faithfully reflected in that of David and Dora in *David Copperfield* (*Letters*, vii. 538–9: 15 Feb. 1855). Far less flatteringly, the 'extremely fat' Maria whom Dickens met again in 1855 was to be the model for the garrulously sentimental Flora Finching, Arthur Clennam's old flame in *Little Dorrit*.

From 1834 Dickens's career as a journalist, and then as an author, advanced by rapid strides. In that year he became a regular contributor to the influential liberal newspaper the *Morning Chron-icle*, a journal with a circulation second only to that of *The Times*. He was to remain with the *Morning Chronicle* until October 1836, when he resigned to assume the editorship of the humorous monthly magazine *Bentley's Miscellany* (the owner of which, Richard Bentley, a keen recruiter of young talent, had already signed a contract with Dickens for two novels). It was, however, through George Hogarth, an Edinburgh lawyer by training and now a senior colleague on the *Morning Chronicle*, that in the spring of 1835 Dickens met his future wife, Catherine. Catherine, Hogarth's eldest daughter, was four years Dickens's junior. Her family had been influentially linked to the literary culture of Edinburgh (her mother was the daughter of an associate of Robert Burns's, while her father had been an intimate friend of, and legal adviser to, Sir Walter Scott). Dickens's affection for her, and his feeling of real mutual warmth, is evident enough in the letters that survive their courtship but the surviving correspond-ence suggests little of the adolescent passion that he seems to have felt for Maria Beadnell. The couple were married in London on 2 April 1836 and moved into Dickens's chambers in Furnival's Inn in Holborn. Nine months later she bore him a son, christened Charles Culliford Boz, the first of their ten children. Soon after the marriage the three rooms at Furnival's Inn also accommodated Catherine's younger sister, Mary, who came on a month-long visit and fre-quently returned, keeping house for Dickens during her sister's confinement. In the spring of 1837 the Dickenses escaped these cramped conditions and moved to a larger, middle-class terraced house at 48 Doughty Street.

In October 1837 a critic writing in the *Quarterly Review* noted that the popularity of 'Boz' was 'one of the most remarkable literary phenomena of recent times'. Although the critic acknowledged that 'Boz' had made 'the whole reading public' talk about his characters and that he was without doubt the first among the comic writers of his day, the critic went on to warn that if his literary fecundity were not curtailed he might exhaust himself too early: 'he has risen like a rocket, and he will come down like the stick'.[10] It was a warning that Dickens took to heart. In October 1837 he was writing with a truly phenomenal energy and with an exacting dedication which had been tested both by experience and by circumstances. He had begun the monthly serialization of *Pickwick Papers* in March of the previous year and there still remained one further monthly number to publish in November. Since January 1837 he had been engaged on the parallel serial publication in *Bentley's Miscellany* of *Oliver Twist* (which was not to finish its run until April 1839). Once *Pickwick Papers* was complete he gave himself a month's break before beginning work on his third novel, *Nicholas Nickleby*, in January 1838 (it was serialized in monthly parts between March 1838 and October 1839). Dickens was more than simply an *efficient* writer. He had a natural comic talent, a fine ear for words and phrases, and, thanks to his journalistic experience, a facility in writing to time, but these qualities had now, of necessity, been combined with a flair for the art of serialization. Dickens's innate creativity was also enhanced by his naturally tidy mind and by a scrupulous self-discipline.

As he had also painfully discovered in May 1837, however well he had disciplined himself as a writer, circumstances beyond his control could effectively wreck his working regime. On 6 May his 17-year-old sister-in-law, and regular house guest, Mary Hogarth, had accompanied the Dickenses to the theatre. During the night Mary was taken suddenly and dangerously ill. She died, in Dickens's arms, the following afternoon, probably of some kind of heart disease. He was emotionally devastated and found himself quite incapable of writing the next month's instalments of both *Pickwick Papers* and *Oliver Twist*. Public announcements to his prospective readers explained that he had lost 'a very dear young relative to whom he was most affectionately attached, and whose society [had] been, for a long time, the chief solace of his labours'. Many biographers and critics have dwelt at length on this profound 'affectionate' attachment to Mary, some even seeing it as exaggeratedly perverse and as somehow eclipsing his love for his wife. His letters of the period certainly reiterate his acute sense of loss and his intensely emotional recall of Mary's youthful perfection ('I have lost the dearest friend I ever had'; 'I solemnly believe that so perfect a creature never breathed . . . She had not a fault' (*Letters*, i. 259, 263: 17 and 31 May 1841)). He had taken a ring from her dead finger and wore it until his own dying day. He dreamed of her nightly for months and for many years he insisted that he was to be buried by her side, though a brother of hers was to take precedence over Dickens in assuming that privilege in 1841. In that same 1841 he was to reanimate his grief for Mary when he came to describe the death of the equally 'angelic' Little Nell in *The Old Curiosity Shop* ('Dear Mary died yesterday, when I think of this sad story' (*Letters*, ii. 182: 8 Jan. 1841)). Mary Hogarth seems to have been the model on which Dickens based the line of his passive, loving, generous-minded, young heroines, a line that stretches from Rose Maylie in *Oliver Twist*, through Agnes Wickfield in *David Copperfield*, to Amy Dorrit. These young women, who sometimes seem caught between adolescence and young womanhood, have frequently been condemned by critics as more sisterly than sexual, more idealized than real. They nonetheless sprang from something deep both in Dickens's consciousness and in early Victorian culture, albeit a consciousness and a culture which happily acknowledged and celebrated the power of the ideal.

What remains more extraordinary about Dickens's first three novels is not the quality of their heroines (or the lack of it), but the originality and variety of their male protagonists. *Pickwick Papers* has as its central character a confirmed bachelor, the rotund, middle-aged Samuel Pickwick, possessed of a 'bald head and circular spectacles' and dressed in slightly old-fashioned and (for the 1830s) somewhat preposterous 'tights and gaiters'. Mr Pickwick, the founder and chairman of an amateurish antiquarian club, is a good-natured innocent, more at home in male than in female company. He is a long way from the kind of dashing, susceptibly young, occasionally moody, romantic hero whom readers of 1836 might have expected to have been shaped by culture associated with the recently deceased Byron and Scott. The genesis of the novel, in a commission to write a text to accompany a series of cockney sporting prints, explains the decision to issue *Pickwick Papers* in twenty monthly parts, but it does not help us to grasp the essential originality of Dickens's hero and the nature of that hero's adventures and misadventures. The idea of a serial predominantly concerned with hunting, shooting, and fishing was rapidly dropped, for, as Dickens was to insist, 'I objected, on consideration that although born and partly bred in the country I was no great sportsman.' As he went on to explain to his readers in a preface to the novel added in 1847, he was determined to 'take my own way, with a freer range of English scenes and people, and I was afraid I should ultimately do so in any case . . . My views being deferred to, I thought of Mr. Pickwick, and wrote the first number.' This last, seemingly casual, statement can be taken as exemplary of Dickens's confident bravura. *The Posthumous Papers of the Pickwick Club* ('posthumous' because the club is defunct at the end of the retrospective story) was serialized between March 1836 and November 1837 (with a break in June following Mary Hogarth's death). Each of these green paper-covered parts was priced at one shilling, thus potentially making the story available to a wide, socially diverse readership (much shorter contemporary novels, generally published in three volumes, would cost a guinea and a half, or thirty-one shillings). After a relatively slow start, *Pickwick Papers* became a runaway success, selling some 14,000 of the February 1837 number and some 40,000 of the numbers published towards the end of the same year. As the story develops, so does the character and status of its unlikely hero. Not only does Mr Pickwick establish his vital relationship with his sharp, even cynical, cockney servant Sam Weller, but he also becomes less open to ridicule and less patently innocent. His essentially benign nature remains constant, but it is threatened by misfortune, by calumny, and by imprisonment. He nevertheless ends in happy retirement in a London suburb having been subtly and steadily advanced morally, and indeed socially, by his creator.

Samuel Pickwick is, like the 'divers unmarried ladies' he observes at Bath, 'past his climacteric', past, that is, the most sparkling period of his life and unlikely to find future stimulating experience. By contrast, Dickens's second protagonist, Oliver Twist, experiences what seems set to be *his* climacteric in an intensely fraught boyhood. Oliver is, of necessity, condemned to an eternal, fictional childhood, for the novel in which he appears centres on the conflict between his vulnerability and the encroachments of an essentially exploitative adult world. Oliver is obliged to oscillate between two states: at times the unhappy victim of adult self-interest, at others the blessed recipient of adult benevolence. In either case, he remains passive. *Oliver Twist: or the Parish Boy's Progress* is essentially a two-pronged satire, attacking the malfunctioning of the 1834 Poor Law in its first part, and then savagely undermining the 'romance' of London criminal life, a 'romance' cultivated by the so-called 'Newgate Novelists' popular at the time. Unlike *Pickwick Papers*, *Oliver Twist* was recognized by its first readers as a social document, a thesis novel of the first order, one which successfully intermixed propaganda and wit, comedy and tragedy, narrative archness and the ultimate comic triumph of good over evil. Having thus built his first two full-length fictions respectively around the experiences of a middle-aged bachelor and a pre-adolescent boy, it was only with *Nicholas Nickleby* (serialized 1838–9) that Dickens gave his readers a more conventional central male character. When it was published in volume form, the novel's full title—*The Life and Adventures of Nicholas Nickleby*—stressed Nicholas's central role, but the title used for the monthly parts suggested more uncertainty as to his role. This original title saw him as part of a larger canvas, as integral to a family unit which passes through a series of 'Fortunes, Misfortunes, Uprisings [and] Downfallings'. *Nicholas Nickleby* too is an overtly propagandist novel, variously exposing the scandalous conditions of the Yorkshire schools typified by Dotheboys Hall, criticizing the speculative capitalism which had brought about a commercial crisis in the 1820s, and satirizing the snobbery and abuse of privilege by the upper classes. Thanks to his innate moral strength, the young, energetically upright, enterprising adaptable Nicholas triumphs in the end despite the multiple set-backs he experiences on his wanderings through England and despite the corruption which he finds manifest in the world in which he forges his own destiny.

To some degree Nicholas Nickleby's struggle for independence and self-realization mirrors Dickens's own, but Nicholas was by no means a self-portrait, nor did his adventures resemble his creator's. What is remarkable about Dickens's first three novels is the extent to which they eschew any direct reflection of their author's own experience and any attempt to write a closet autobiography. The account of Oliver Twist's painful childhood may be coloured by Dickens's feelings about his own blighted boyhood and Nicholas Nickleby's triumph over adversity may have Dickens's wholehearted endorsement, but their histories remain detached from direct autobiographical reference. These three first novels are therefore unlike the early self-reflective fiction of writers such as Thackeray, Charlotte Brontë, George Eliot, James Joyce, or D. H. Lawrence. Not until *David Copperfield*, his eighth novel, did Dickens feel the need to quarry his own experience. Significantly too, the fragmentary diaries that survive for the years 1838–41 contain little except a succinct catalogue of social engagements, domestic details, and particulars of his journeys through England.[11] Dickens did not yet seem to feel the need to leave a record of his emotional, intellectual, or spiritual life whether in fiction or in any other written form. This does not imply that he was without an acute sense of selfhood, personal vanity, or justified pride in his achievement. When the three-volume edition of *Oliver Twist* was reissued in November 1838 the name 'Boz' was omitted from its title-page and replaced by the proud declaration 'by Charles Dickens. Author of "The Pickwick Papers"'. When *Nicholas Nickleby* was published in volume form in October 1839 Dickens was again named as its author. Moreover, the identification of the now celebrated and no longer pseudonymous writer with his text was emphasized by an engraved frontispiece which reproduced the head and shoulders of Daniel Maclise's recent portrait of him The portrait was complemented by an engraving of the equally flamboyant flourish of Dickens's signature.

The Novels of the 1840s

On 11 December 1839 the Dickens family, now including three children, moved from the house in Doughty Street to far larger premises at 1 Devonshire Terrace, just south of Regent's Park. The house was, he told John Forster, 'of great promise (and great premium) "undeniable" situation and excessive splendour' (*Letters*, i. 598: 7 Nov. 1839). The move set the seal on Dickens's new status and bore testimony to his literary success and prosperity. Here, in a house with thirteen rooms, there was not only proper accommodation for his growing family, but also ample space for his books and for his entertaining. The lease was only relinquished in 1851. At Devonshire Terrace Catherine was to bear Dickens five further children, and here too the family was to be joined by Catherine's younger sister, Georgina Hogarth. Georgina initially seems to have helped with the running of the household. She was gradually to become invaluable to Dickens as an essential domestic mainstay, companion, and confidante, remaining with him, and defensively loyal to him, despite the strains on, and eventual breakdown of, his marriage.

In March 1840 Dickens signed a contract for a new work of fiction, or rather for a popular weekly journal to be written entirely by him under the title *Master Humphrey's Clock*. The journal, which ran from April 1840 until December 1841, was to be a miscellany, and, as Dickens had told Forster some months previously, its roots were to be bedded in eighteenth-century precedents (*The Tatler, The*

Spectator, and Goldsmith's *The Bee*), while also reflecting back on his own work;

I should propose to start, as *The Spectator* does, with some pleasant fiction relative to the origin of the publication; to introduce a little club or knot of characters and to carry their personal histories and proceedings through the work; to introduce fresh characters constantly; to reintroduce Mr. Pickwick and Sam Weller, the latter of whom might furnish an occasional communication with great effect; to write amusing essays on the foibles of the day as they arise; to take advantage of all passing events; and to vary the form of the papers by throwing them into sketches, essays, tales, adventures, letters from imaginary correspondents and so forth, so as to diversify the contents as much as possible.   (*Letters*, i. 563–4: 14 July 1839)

Master Humphrey's Clock was to prove to be one of Dickens's rare commercial and literary miscalculations. After an initial enthusiasm on the part of his readers, sales began to fall off, then to plummet, obliging Dickens to expand and extend the story he had begun in the fourth number. This was to become *The Old Curiosity Shop*. By the eighth issue it took up the entire number. The central figure of the miscellany, the dowdy, reclusive Master Humphrey, was only to reappear to briefly introduce a second long story, *Barnaby Rudge*. Although this experimental journal ceased publication with the completion of *Barnaby Rudge*, it was the vehicle for two of Dickens's most extraordinary (if now most critically neglected) early fictions. *The Old Curiosity Shop*, which eventually attracted some 100,000 readers, was centred on the story of the escape of an old man and his granddaughter, Nell, from the encroachments both of London and of the predatory dwarf Daniel Quilp. What seems to have held original readers spellbound was the account of Little Nell's frailty, vulnerability, and, ultimately, mortality. Dickens, in his turn, cleverly exploited the serial form of his narrative in order to build up, and then to demolish hopes, and to play with suspense. *Barnaby Rudge* is, by contrast, an ambitious historical novel, set at the time of the Gordon Riots of 1780. With it Dickens laid serious claim to be the heir of the most popular novelist of the generation before his own: Sir Walter Scott. Despite the slow beginning, which establishes character, the historical situation, and the idea of mental and moral dysfunction, Dickens's narrative first flickers and then blazes with something akin to the fire with which the rioters devastate London.

Dickens completed *Barnaby Rudge* in November 1841. Early in the following January, after a period of preparatory reading of guide-books and other appropriate travel literature, he and his somewhat reluctant wife let Devonshire House, left their children in the care of his brother, and set sail from Liverpool for the United States. After an extremely stormy crossing, they touched land at Halifax, Nova Scotia, on 19 January and reached Boston three days later. Enthused by his reception Dickens journeyed southwards to New York, Philadelphia (where he met Edgar Allan Poe), Washington (where he was introduced to President Tyler), and Richmond, Virginia (where he found the reality of slavery repulsive). He turned northwards again, and then westwards to Pittsburgh, Cincinnati, and St Louis, which they reached on 12 April. They visited the Niagara Falls at the end of April, then headed north to Canada, seeing Toronto and Montreal, before returning to New York in early June, leaving the city by steamer on 7 June, en route for Liverpool and home. It was an extraordinarily enterprising and demanding trip for its date, though American transportation systems (railroads, stage-coaches, and steam-boats) were already generally of a high order. Dickens, who had been lionized by his American readers in virtually every city he visited, responded to the physical and social demands of his journey with characteristic energy. Although he managed to offend his hosts with constant reference to the fact that the United States had not signed any international copyright agreements (and had therefore deprived him of income from his books), he seems to have been fascinated by most of what he saw of America and delighted by his celebrity amongst Americans. Nevertheless, he had crossed the Atlantic convinced that the Republic represented an ideal of an aristocrat-free, radical, breezily new, self-fashioning society. He left it jaded and disillusioned. In March 1842 he wrote to his friend W. C. Macready expressing his disappointment with America, American institutions, and American society in virulent terms:

This is not the Republic I came to see. This is not the Republic of my imagination. I infinitely prefer a liberal Monarchy . . . to such a Government as this. In every respect but that of National Education, the country disappoints me. The more I think of its youth and strength, the poorer and more trifling in a thousand respects, it appears in my eyes. (*Letters*, iii. 156: 12 and 21 Mar. 1842)

Although he did not allow this disillusion to exclusively determine the account of his travels recorded in *American Notes for General Circulation* (1842), it certainly did help to shape his criticisms of American manners (or lack of them), American pushiness, American rowdiness, and American anomalies (and notably the institution of slavery). His travel book has continued to vex certain American readers, as has the largely satirical account of the American misadventures of the equally disillusioned (but fictional) hero of *Martin Chuzzlewit*.

Dickens's jaundiced view of the United States was not shaped by a naïvely patriotic presupposition of the moral and social superiority of Great Britain. Throughout his life Dickens continued to be vexed not only by desuetude in the political life of his homeland, but also by the divisions between economic groups and social classes which had been accentuated by the advances of urbanism and industrialism. When he visited Manchester in October 1843 in order to speak at the newly opened Athenaeum (which provided reading rooms and educational facilities for working men), his acute awareness of the inequalities and innate conflicts of industrial England helped provoke the composition of *A Christmas Carol*. Dickens was not blind to the economic potential of a short book tailored for the growing Christmas market, but he was also determined to write a punchy tract for the times. When in stave 3 of that story the Ghost of Christmas Present shows Ebenezer Scrooge two horribly degraded waif children—identified as Ignorance and Want—the accompanying illustration shows the smoking factory chimneys of Manchester behind them. *A Christmas Carol* reiterates and reinforces the moral that healthy societies, like sound family relationships, are based on mutual responsibility and mutual responsiveness. In the case of *A Christmas Carol* Dickens proved shrewd both as a popular moralist and as a writer attuned to his public. The book, published in an edition of 6,000 copies on 19 December, sold out in a few days. By the May of the following year, this ostensibly seasonal tale had exhausted its seventh printing. Despite the healthy sales of the four subsequent Christmas Books (*The Chimes* of 1844, *The Cricket on the Hearth* of 1845, *The Battle of Life* of 1846, and *The Haunted Man* of 1848), none ever attained the enduring popularity, or the singularly mythic quality, of *A Christmas Carol*. Its immediacy and its moral resonance for Dickens's contemporaries were to be reinforced when he read it in public in Birmingham on 27 and 30 December 1853. These were to prove the first of his highly successful public readings from his works. The reading text, gradually curtailed from its original three-hour performance length, was to remain a standard part of his repertoire and figured as the main item in his farewell reading two months before his death in 1870.[12]

In November 1845 Dickens was appointed editor of a new liberal morning newspaper, the *Daily News*, the first issue of which appeared on 21 January of the following year. He was not to remain long in the post. A combination of falling sales and the uncongenial demands of the editorship drove him to resign on 9 February but not before he had begun the publication of eight 'Travelling Letters' descriptive of his year-long sojourn in Italy from July 1844 to July 1845. These letters, revised and extended, were to be the basis for his second travel book, *Pictures from Italy* (1846). In composing his narrative Dickens had drawn extensively on the correspondence he had sent home to friends and relatives. Since its publication it has proved a rather less contentious book than *American Notes*, despite its irreverent tone, its frequent expressions of hostility to Roman Catholicism and its occasionally downright philistine responses to the complex artistic heritage of Italy. Dickens emerges from the narrative as an alert, often amused, observer, but also as one determined not to be awed by Italy and its history. The distant prospect of Rome, for example, occasions the remark, 'it was so like London, at that distance, that if you could have shown it me, in a glass, I should have taken it for nothing else'. Cities generally excite him more than landscapes, living communities more than ruins, and, despite the thoroughness of his Italian sightseeing, only the exoticism of Venice seems to utterly enchant him.

Dickens had taken a break from novel writing after the completion of *Barnaby Rudge*. His two novels of the middle 1840s, *Martin Chuzzlewit* and *Dombey and Son*, mark the transition between his early, expansive, predominantly comic fiction and his later, tighter, darker work. Although the mood of both novels remains confidently optimistic and broadly comic, both also suggest a new concern with thematic consistency and with character. *Martin Chuzzlewit*, serialized between January 1843 and July 1844, was advertised as being concerned with 'English life and manners' but its setting shifts to America in the fifth number when its central character announces his intention of emigrating in order to make his fortune. Hypocrisy, the leading trait of Mr Pecksniff in the early phases of the plot, takes on a national and political dimension once Martin and his servant Mark Tapley cross the Atlantic. Dickens seems to have been delighted by the effect of the American chapters on American readers, remarking on 15 August 1843 that his book had 'made them all stark staring raving mad across the water' (*Letters*, iii. 541–2). *Dombey and Son* was 'to do with Pride what its predecessor had done with Selfishness', Dickens insisted to John Forster. It was, therefore, to take a leading trait of character, in this instance the uncompromising, unbending business ethic of a London merchant, and to trace its damaging development and its ultimate, purgative downfall. The leading ideas of the novel were established early on in Dickens's mind and the pacing of the novel, with its balance of life and death, love and the denial of love, was, as the surviving complete set of numbers demonstrates, carefully established. *Dombey and Son*, serialized between October 1846 and April 1848, has long been recognized as a key work in the development of Dickens's craft as a novelist, notable especially for its almost symphonic pattern of reiterated imagery. It is also one of his profoundest explorations of family life, relating the unhappiness of the dysfunctional Dombeys to the condition of a wider dysfunctional society.

Much of the early part of *Dombey and Son* had been written in Switzerland during the Dickens family's extended sojourn in Lausanne (June–November 1846). In Lausanne Dickens conspicuously missed the stimulus that London gave to his imagination. In August he confessed to John Forster that the street life of the metropolis 'supplied something to my brain, which it cannot bear, when busy, to lose . . . the toil and labour of writing, day after day, without that magic lantern, is IMMENSE!!' (*Letters*, iv. 612: 30 Aug. 1846.) This yearning for the 'magic lantern' of London may also be related to the fact that in writing *Dombey* Dickens stirred certain dark memories of his urban childhood. His schoolroom had been demolished for the mighty railway cutting which figures so prominently in the novel, while the siting of the Toodles' house at 'Camberling [Camden] Town' and the modelling of Mrs Pipchin on his boyhood landlady, Mrs Roylance ('Mrs. Pipchin's establishment . . . is from the life, and I was there' he told Forster), indicate that he was, in part, revisiting uncomfortable locations. He was extraordinarily vexed when his illustrator, H. K. Browne, sketched a Mrs Pipchin who did not resemble the original that he alone would have recognized in the flesh.[13] These imaginative, if still indirect, revisitings of his unhappy London boyhood may also have prompted Dickens to consider the prospect of an autobiography.

The autobiographical fragment which John Forster published in his *Life of Charles Dickens* cannot be precisely dated, but Dickens seems to have returned to work on an already existing manuscript in the winter of 1848–9. This manuscript he showed to Forster and to his wife early in 1849, and then, he later told a correspondent, he burnt it.[14] The process of writing, and then destroying what he had written, may have been doubly purgative. What is now certain is that the genesis of Dickens's new novel, *David Copperfield*, coincided with an attempt to confront his secret and traumatic past. This is not to suggest that *David Copperfield* is a particularly moody or self-obsessed novel, but to imply that this highly proficient novelist, one who was also decidedly a public figure, was now prepared to quarry his own experience in a first-person narrative. *David Copperfield*, serialized between May 1849 and November 1850, is one of Dickens's most ebullient and confidently optimistic novels. It is also perhaps the last of his novels in which a central character is seen not only overcoming adverse circumstances but also ending his narrative in a state of emotional, spiritual, and financial serenity. If David's boyhood agonies, the death of Dora, and the betrayal of his friendship by Steerforth, threaten to push the novel into the tragic realm, this tragedy is balanced at each stage of the hero's life by the timely appearance of assertively positive characters (Micawber, Betsey Trotwood, Agnes Wickfield). Above all, *David Copperfield* celebrates the triumph of a determined spirit thanks to what David describes in chapter 42 as 'thorough-going, ardent, and sincere earnestness'.

Household Words and the Novels of the Mid-1850s

A month before he completed the serialization of *David Copperfield* Dickens published the first number of his new, miscellaneous, cheaply priced weekly journal, *Household Words*. Unlike *Bentley's Miscellany* and *Master Humphrey's Clock*, the new magazine was to contain articles on the issues of the day, instructive and whimsical essays, short fiction, and poetry and it was to be aimed at a middle-brow readership. On 31 January 1850 he wrote to a prospective contributor, the novelist Elizabeth Gaskell, describing 'the general mind and purpose' of his journal as 'the raising up of those that are down, and general improvement of our social condition (*Letters*, vi. 21–2). *Household Words* was to run for nine years and was to contain within its pages Gaskell's *Cranford* and *North and South*, and fiction by Dickens's literary friends Wilkie Collins and Edward Bulwer-Lytton. It was also to be a vehicle for Dickens as an essayist, both as a fanciful observer and as an earnestly satiric social critic. In his 'A Preliminary Word' he insisted that 'no mere utilitarian spirit, no iron binding of the mind to grim realities' would give a 'harsh tone' to *Household Words*, and he ended in a breezily optimistic spirit: 'Go on, is all we hear, Go on! In a glow already, with the air from yonder height upon us, and the inspiriting voices joining in this acclamation, we echo back the cry, and go on cheerily.' As the journal progressed, however, its cheer steadily diminished as a stream of 'grim realities' were brought to the attention of readers.[15] In Dickens's short essay 'A December Vision', for example, the end of the magazine's first year of publication was marked with a darkly prophetic denunciation of a society that allowed acres of slum-land to fester in its midst:

I saw a poisoned air, in which Life drooped. I saw Disease, arrayed in all its store of hideous aspects and appalling shapes, triumphant in every alley, bye-way, court, back-street, and poor abode, in every place where human beings congregated—in the proudest and most boastful places most of all. I saw innumerable hosts fore-doomed to darkness, dirt, pestilence, obscenity, misery and early death.

This is no longer the earnestly upbeat, essentially private world of *David Copperfield*. It is essentially the dark social vision that was to mould *Bleak House* and its successors.

The year 1851 was to prove a singularly melancholy and disruptive one for Dickens and his family. In the months following the birth of her ninth child, Dora Annie, in August 1850, Catherine Dickens began to show symptoms of an incapacitating, nervous complaint, possibly related to postnatal depression. On medical advice, Dickens took Catherine to the spa at Great Malvern early in March so that the 'water cure' on offer there might alleviate her condition. Dickens remained with her as much as his professional commitments in London permitted, taking the train backwards and forwards. On 25 March, however, his father, John, was taken critically and painfully ill when a long-standing urinary infection became critical. Dickens described the onset of this crisis to Catherine. His father had been

in that state from active disease (of the bladder) which he had mentioned to nobody, that mortification and delirium, terminating in speedy death, seemed unavoidable. Mr. Wade was called in, who, instantly performed (without chloroform) the most terrible operation known in surgery . . . he bore it with astonishing fortitude . . . his room, a slaughter house of blood . . . (*Letters*, vi. 333: 25 Mar. 1851)

John Dickens died on 31 March and was buried five days later at Highgate Cemetery. His tombstone was to bear a tribute, composed by his son, to his 'zealous, useful, cheerful spirit'. Nine days later, as Dickens rose from the chair at a charitable dinner, news was brought to him that his ailing daughter, the 8-month-old Dora Annie, had died. He was obliged to hint delicately at the dire news to his invalid and still absent wife. Even after telling Catherine to read his letter 'very slowly and carefully', he felt obliged to skirt around the horrid truth, merely informing her that Dora was 'very ill' and that he did 'not think her recovery at all likely' (*Letters*, vi. 353: 15 Apr. 1851). The baby was interred close to John Dickens at Highgate.

By May Catherine was in good-enough spirits to take a small part in Dickens's amateur production of Bulwer-Lytton's play *Not So Bad As We Seem*. In the summer months the Dickenses' house in Marylebone was let and the family moved to the seaside at Broadstairs. This was partly a distraction from his active house-hunting in London, a search which ended when negotiations to lease a yet more substantial home, Tavistock House in Tavistock Square in Bloomsbury, were finally concluded in late autumn. The flurry of frenetic activity over the furnishing and redecoration of Tavistock House seems to have been almost exclusively Dickens's. A letter of 31 October describes his own 'convulsions of repairing and moving', but, with a note of irritation, disparages Catherine's contribution as appearing 'all over paint' and seeming to think 'it is somehow being immensely useful to get into that condition' (*Letters*, vi. 532–3).

The weather of that summer and autumn was rainy and non-conducive to an easy domestic removal, while the autumn of the following year was to prove the wettest on record. The mention of such climatic, domestic, and biographical details is, however, not merely incidental to the conception and composition of *Bleak House*. Dickens finally began work on his new novel in November 1851, having found the move to Tavistock House extremely disruptive to his established patterns of planning and composition (he mentioned to a correspondent on 7 October 'the distraction of the new book— the whirling of the story through one's mind, escorted by workmen—the Pantechnicon's imbecility, the wild necessity of beginning to write, the not being able to do so' (*Letters*, vi. 510)). His search for a title for his novel is also indicative of domestic restlessness and domestic discontinuity. The trial titles include 'Tom-All-Alones: The Ruined House', 'Tom-All-Alones: The Solitary House That was always shut up', and 'Tom-All-Alones: The Solitary House where The Wind howled'.[16] Even when he settled on the title under which the novel was serialized between March 1852 and September 1853, first readers might have remained confused as to which of the many bleak houses of the story was *the* Bleak House (it is not fully identified until chapter 6, half-way through the second number). When published in volume form the frontispiece represents Chesney Wold, while a vignette on the title-page shows the notably house-*less* Jo, standing with his broom on a corner in the slum to which the name 'Tom-all-Alone's' was ultimately transferred. The novel is haunted by death and by the diseases generated by the slum. Its characters die variously of the effects of neglect, drugs, fever, murder, suicide, and despair. Its established gloominess of tone, and its determining theme of frailty and human mortality, may well have been accentuated during the process of composition by the deaths of two further close friends of Dickens: Richard Watson (the dedicatee of *David Copperfield*) in July 1852 and Alfred D'Orsay in August of the same year. Nevertheless, *Bleak House* is not a conspicuously negative novel. Its trenchant satire is directed at the creaking institutions of Victorian Britain, the Law above all, but also at a do-nothing government and a self-perpetuating governing class. Its truest claim to singularity amongst Dickens's novels lies, however, in its narrative daring, equally divided as it is between two distinctive narrators and two distinctive points of view. Although *Bleak House* sold exceptionally well, the demands it made on its readers (both in terms of its social criticism and its structure) meant that it was not uniformly well received by contemporary critics. Its stature was not universally recognized until the late twentieth century.

Bleak House's successor, *Hard Times*, was far less daring in terms of its narrative innovation but equally provocative of readers' social and political sensitivities. The novel, serialized in *Household Words* between April and August 1854, was intended to raise the flagging sales of the journal. It was to be generally condemned by Victorian reviewers as 'dreary' and, to use Macaulay's description, 'sullen' (though John Ruskin later praised it for being 'grossly and sharply told').[17] *Hard Times* is Dickens's most schematic novel, a consistent, if occasionally abrupt, attack on the Utilitarian philosophy of 'fact' as opposed to the free play of fancy. It is also the one novel that is set exclusively beyond that energizing force for Dickens's imagination, London. Its provincial substitute, grimy, red-brick Coketown, was partly based on the strike-bound manufacturing town of Preston which Dickens had visited professionally in January 1854 and the town's industrial relations were the subject of the long essay 'On Strike', published in *Household Words* on 11 February.

'Preston has not the strong relish for personal altercation that Westminster hath', Dickens noted in his essay, comparing the nature of a northern working-class debate with that of a parliamentary one. 'The deliberate collected manner' of the Preston strikers had impressed him, but the main message of his article was that the poisoned relationship between masters and men in one strike-ridden town might come to infect all class relationships in Victorian Britain ('And from the ever-widening circle of their decay, what drop in the ocean shall be free!').[18] These concerns about a potentially revolutionary Britain and a do-nothing parliament were to haunt most of his writings in the 1850s. They were to be accentuated by the evidence of gross government mismanagement during the Crimean War of 1854–6. On 10 April 1855, for example, Dickens wrote to his friend, the reforming MP A. H. Layard, expressing his dismay at 'the alienation of the people from their own public affairs'. Parliament and the institutions of state, he insisted, conducted themselves in a manner which seemed little more than a 'game' in which the people had laid down their cards and had 'taken to looking on'. The players who were left were refusing to see beyond that 'game' and therefore could not 'conceive that the gain and loss and all the interest of the play are in their hands—and will never be wiser until they and the table and the lights and the money are all overturned together' (*Letters*, vii. 586–7). This dismay at such a moribund, buck-passing mentality is reflected in the working title of *Little Dorrit*: 'Nobody's Fault'. *Little Dorrit*, which Dickens began in the summer of 1855, was serialized in monthly parts between December 1855 and June 1857. It is perhaps the most sombre of all of his novels and it dwells almost obsessively on prisons as physical institutions and as states of mind. Despite the fact that a substantial part of the action takes place abroad (in France, Switzerland, and Italy) the sense of confinement seems to travel with those who want to believe that they are free, both mentally and physically.

The Acquisition of Gad's Hill Place and the Breakup of Dickens's Marriage

Little Dorrit sold conspicuously well despite its supposedly despondent tone. Dickens appears to have relieved much of his private frustration with public affairs by realizing a particular domestic ambition in 1856. In March he completed the purchase of Gad's Hill Place, a detached late Georgian house in the country near Rochester. He took particular pleasure in the fact that his father had pointed the house out to him as a boy as a place he might own one day 'if he would only work hard enough'. He also liked its tenuous Shakespearian associations, for here on Gad's Hill Falstaff's bungled attempts at highway robbery take place in *Henry IV Part One*. This association was marked by a framed page of calligraphy which was displayed in the entrance hall. Dickens relished his new property and made 'improvements' both to its structure and to its gardens for the rest of his life. He was not, however, to relinquish the lease on his London house until 1860. Tavistock Place had proved a particularly agreeable residence for his family and it had also offered a reasonably commodious location for his ambitions as the producer of, and spirited actor in, amateur theatricals. Here, in June 1855, in a temporary set constructed in the children's schoolroom, he played the part of Aaron Gurnock, the old lighthouse-keeper in Wilkie Collins's melodrama *The Lighthouse* (the scenery for which was painted by his friend, the marine painter Clarkson Stanfield). In January 1857 a second play by Collins, *The Frozen Deep*, received its première in the converted schoolroom. Collins and Dickens took the leading roles as rival lovers while the other parts were played by friends and by members of the Dickens family. As the temporary theatre held a maximum audience of twenty-five, four performances were given. A private command performance, with the same cast, was also given for Queen Victoria and her family on 4 July and three public benefit performances were given in London in order to raise money for the widow of Dickens's friend, Douglas Jerrold.

When *The Frozen Deep* was again publicly staged at the Free Trade Hall in Manchester in August, professional actresses replaced the female members of the Dickens family whose sense of propriety forbade public exposure on the stage. These Manchester perform-ances were to have a doubly influential impact on the next phase of Dickens's life. The actresses concerned were all members of the Ternan family, the youngest of whom, Ellen, took the minor part of Lucy Crayford. Dickens played the role of Richard Wardour, a rejected lover who sacrifices his life in order to save his rival in love. It was perhaps symptomatic of his restlessness in this period that he had thrown himself so wholeheartedly into the play's production which was, he told a correspondent, like 'writing a book in company' (*Letters*, viii. 255–6: 9 Jan. 1857). He also seems to have played Wardour with an extraordinarily intense passion, a passion which was gradually but inexorably to be redirected towards the young Ellen Ternan with whom he rapidly became infatuated. Dickens had for some time shown manifest signs of irritation with his wife. He blamed Catherine with clumsiness and domestic incompetence, and by 1857 his friends were noticing a pronounced strain in the rela-tionship. The meeting with Ellen brought things to an emotional head, at least as far as Dickens was concerned. In October he moved out of the marital bedroom into a neighbouring dressing room, ordering the communicating door to be sealed with shelves. By the following March he told John Forster that his married life was 'des-pairingly over' and that 'a dismal failure has to be borne' (*Letters*, viii. 539: 30 Mar. 1858). A separation was agreed in the summer of 1858 and Catherine was obliged to move out (with an annual income of £600). Dickens's domestic situation was made more complex, as far as his friends, and then his gossiping wider public, were con-cerned, due to the fact that Catherine's sister, Georgina, remained both loyal to him and resident in his household. On 7 June he issued a public, self-justifying statement about his personal affairs which was printed in *The Times* and other newspapers, reproducing it on the front page of *Household Words* five days later. It was somewhat intemperately expressed ('all the lately whispered rumours ... are abominably false ... whoever repeats one of them ... will lie as wilfully and as foully as it is possible for any false witness to lie, before Heaven and earth'). With more than a degree of touchy self-righteousness he also expected his publishers, Bradbury and Evans, to reprint this long statement in *Punch*, which they also owned. They refused, and thereby provoked Dickens into terminating his partnership with them. Despite having been his printers since 1836 and his publishers since 1845, Bradbury and Evans were never to print anything else that Dickens wrote. By mid-1859 it was not only his marriage that was at an end. So was his long-standing relationship with his publishers, certain of his friendships (notably that with Thackeray), and, somewhat ironically, his domestically titled journal.[19]

Typically undaunted, and full of restless energy, Dickens began a new weekly magazine in April 1859. Having been strongly, and sagely, advised by Forster not to call it *Household Harmony*, he settled on the title *All the Year Round*. He was already at work on a new novel which was to appear both as a weekly serial to launch *All the Year Round* and as a separately published monthly serial. This novel, *A Tale of Two Cities*, was also rooted in the production of *The Frozen Deep* and in Dickens's still tense and uncertain relationship with Ellen Ternan. Despite its charged setting in the period of the French Revolution, the germ of the plot, the rivalry of two lovers for the hand of Lucie Manette and the final redemptive sacrifice of Sydney Carton, was a clear reflection of the theme of Collins's melodrama. Dickens was to weave a good deal of his private life into the developing destinies of its characters. Lucie bore many of the physical characteristics of Ellen (who had played a character called Lucy in *The Frozen Deep*), while the connection between the two central male figures was originally to have been emphasized by the interchangeable initials of characters originally to be called *Charles* Darnay and *Dick* Carton (Dickens had played the role of *Richard* Wardour). This patent self-identification was to prove too much even for Dickens and he changed Carton's first name to Sydney early on in the manuscript. Nevertheless, the sense of a split personality, or of an alter ego, acting out Dickens's still uncertain and perhaps unrequited love for Lucie/Ellen suggests something of his intensely private involvement with his developing narrative. This should not, however, distract us from the wider political and moral implications of *A Tale of Two Cities*. It is a novel which re-explores in a historical context Dickens's anxieties about the state of a rancorous, class-divided society and its potential descent into revolutionary violence. It is, at the same time, a profound meditation on strangeness, on the principle of reconciliation, and on the meaning of resurrection.

The Public Readings, the *Uncommercial Traveller*, and Dickens's Last Years

The role-playing, the divided selves, and the interchangeability of identity which so mark the plot of *A Tale of Two Cities* can also be related to Dickens's new-found interest in reading his works in public. After the success of his charity performances of *A Christmas Carol* in Birmingham in 1853, the restlessness associated with the breakdown of his relationship with Catherine found some real release in the earnestness with which Dickens took up a new series of London readings in April 1858. Such was the success of these performances that they were to become a major element in his life. These stage-managed, carefully gaslit, highly emotional readings gave him an immediate rapport with his audiences. He could both act out *and* revisit his own texts; he could lose himself by playing parts *and* vividly remind his public of why he was the most popular writer alive. He was to move beyond the Christmas Books to a repertoire which would eventually include retailored extracts from *Pickwick Papers*, *Oliver Twist*, *Nicholas Nickleby*, *Martin Chuzzlewit*, *Dombey and Son*, *David Copperfield*, and some of his minor works. He did not confine himself to London audiences, but, in those periods when he was not engaged on the composition of a novel, undertook exhausting tours of England, Scotland, and Ireland, sometimes managing seven performances in a week. He was also to read with triumphant success in the United States, and even, to a somewhat more recherché audience, at the British Embassy in Paris. Although he made a good deal of money from this enterprise, the readings seem also to have answered Dickens's insecure craving for applause and for palpable evidence of his readers' affection for him.

Dickens at his reading desk, as if posed for a Reading, 1858.

The acute restlessness and the emotional insecurity which Dickens felt in the period after his separation from Catherine were to manifest themselves in a different form in *Great Expectations*. Although, like *David Copperfield*, this is a first-person narrative, telling the story of a boy's growth to manhood, it is a far less personal one. Dickens was well aware of the possible pitfalls of what he was doing. To be quite sure that he had fallen into 'no unconscious repetitions' he reread *David Copperfield* and told John Forster that he was 'affected by it to a degree you would hardly believe' (*Letters*, ix. 325: early Oct. 1860). Pip comes from a far lower social class than David and is promoted to the status of a 'gentleman' by mysteriously coming into a fortune rather than earnestly labouring to overcome his disadvantages. Unlike David he ends his narrative with an air of disappointment about him: sad but probably, if not certainly, wiser. The novel was serialized weekly in *All the Year Round* between December 1860 and August 1861, and then, unusually for Dickens, published in three unillustrated volumes. It was not especially well received by contemporary critics.

All the Year Round was to place a far greater emphasis on publishing new fiction than had its predecessor. In addition to the two Dickens novels, Wilkie Collins's *The Woman in White* (1860) and *The Moonstone* (1868) and works by Elizabeth Gaskell, Charles Reade, and Edward Bulwer-Lytton were to appear in its pages. Apart from the fiction, the most memorable, and still underrated, aspect of Dickens's achievement in his second journal is the series of thirty-six essays published between 1860 and 1869, later collected as *The Uncommercial Traveller*. Dickens's persona of an *un*-commercial traveller reflected the increasing importance of commercial travellers in mid-Victorian England. These representatives of companies travelled round the country displaying samples to prospective customers and taking orders. Dickens's narrator wryly defines himself against them in the first essay. His 'General Line of Business' consists of travelling in both town and country as a representative 'for the great house of Human Interest Brothers' with 'rather a large connexion in the fancy goods way . . . seeing many little things, and some great things, which, because they interest me, I think may interest others'.[20] Through these extraordinarily inventive essays Dickens variously explored aspects of his childhood ('Dullborough Town', 'Nurse's Stories'), contemporary issues such as emigration ('Bound for the Great Salt Lake'), poverty ('Wapping Workhouse') and slumland ('On an Amateur Beat'), popular entertainment ('Two Views of a Cheap Theatre'), and, perhaps most revealingly, his now obsessive habit of lonely nocturnal wandering ('Night Walks') and his fascination with the dead bodies exposed in the Paris Morgue ('Some Recollections of Mortality'). With the *Uncommercial Traveller* his well-honed journalistic skills found their ideal medium.

Dickens was not to begin the serialization of his last completed novel, *Our Mutual Friend*, until May 1864. There had been plenty to distract him from the customarily heavy demands made on him by the composition of a novel. Domestically, the early 1860s had been marked by upheaval. He moved his household permanently to Gad's Hill Place in August 1860 soon after the marriage of his daughter, Katey. In November of the following year his eldest son, Charley, was also to marry. But there were also events which did not call for celebration. In July 1860 Dickens's younger brother, Alfred, died leaving him with the responsibility of caring for the widow and the five surviving children. His mother's health, both mental and physical, had been steadily deteriorating, evidently to her son's irritation. On 19 August 1860 he wrote somewhat tetchily from Gad's Hill describing the funereal gloom that surrounded him:

My mother, who was also left to me when my father died (I never had anything left to me but relations), is in the strangest state of mind from senile decay: and the impossibility of getting her to understand what is the matter, combined with her desire to be got up in sables like a female Hamlet, illumines the dreary scene with a ghastly absurdity that is the chief relief I can find in it.   (*Letters*, ix. 287)

Elizabeth Dickens died in September 1863 at the age of 74. In a terse footnote to a business letter to W. H. Wills, his assistant editor at *All the Year Round*, he commented, seemingly with little regret: 'My poor mother died quite suddenly at last. Her condition was frightful' (*Letters*, x. 289: 14 Sept. 1863). It was a private comment, but it was the only epitaph he provided. His letters suggest that he was much more profoundly moved by the melancholy news of the sudden deaths of Thackeray (to whom he had been recently reconciled) at Christmas 1863 and of his son, Walter, who died in India on the last day of 1863 (see especially *Letters*, x. 355–6: 12 Feb. 1864). Both deaths seem to have haunted him in a season of the year that he had always readily associated with ghosts.

Our Mutual Friend was serialized in monthly parts between May 1864 and November 1865. Dickens had never really liked the constrictions imposed upon him by weekly publication in *All the Year Round* (indeed, he had disparaged such brief episodes as 'teaspoons' (*Letters*, ix. 113: 28 Aug. 1859)). He seems, nevertheless, to have experienced some real difficulty with both the gestation and the planning of the novel. On 25 January 1864, however, he was able to write to Wilkie Collins announcing that he had already completed two numbers and was at work on a third: 'It is a combination of drollery with romance which requires a deal of pains and a perfect throwing away of points that might be amplified; but I hope it is *very good*. I confess, in short, that I think it is' (*Letters*, x. 346). His confidence was not unjustified. *Our Mutual Friend* is one of his very finest achievements: complex, expansive, specific, and sharply characterized, while at the same time playing with mystery and with the strangeness attendant upon explorations of identity. It is also one of the greatest of urban novels, using London's detritus and London's river to suggest complementary impulses to death and to life. Initially at least, the novel sold sensationally well (sales of the opening numbers reached some forty thousand). As Dickens announced to readers of the completed novel, however, the serialization had not run smoothly. In his Preface (published in November 1865) he revealed that on 'Friday the Ninth of June in the present year, Mr. and Mrs. Boffin . . . were on the South-Eastern Railway with me, in a terribly destructive railway accident'. This was a somewhat whimsical way of putting it. When Dickens was returning from an expedition to France with Ellen Ternan and her mother, the train in which he was travelling was derailed at Staplehurst in Kent. Dickens and his companions were seriously shaken but unhurt. Ten people died in the accident and Dickens, who had been obliged to climb through a window of his compartment, was assiduous in tending to his wounded and dying fellow passengers. Only after his ministrations were no longer required did he realize that he had left a portion of the manuscript of *Our Mutual Friend* in the wrecked train. In the following month he was also to fall behind with the serialization, finding that he had underwritten the sixteenth number by two and a half pages ('a thing I have not done since *Pickwick*', he confessed to John Forster (*Letters*, xi. 67: July 1865)). Dickens never fully recovered from the effects of the accident.

He was, understandably, very wary of train travel in his last remaining years. This worry was not allowed to disrupt the hectically demanding pace of his reading tours, however, for his progress up and down the country was dependent on the relative efficiency of the railway. His factotum, George Dolby, records that Dickens would nerve himself one hour into each journey with a draught of brandy.[21] In April and May 1866 he read in London, Liverpool, Manchester, Edinburgh, Glasgow, Bristol, Birmingham, Aberdeen, and Portsmouth. Between January and May of the following year, after launching his tour in London, he revisited Liverpool and went on to performances in Chester, Wolverhampton, Leicester, Leeds, Manchester, Bath, Glasgow, Edinburgh, York, Bradford, Newcastle-upon-Tyne, Wakefield, Dublin, Belfast, Cambridge, Norwich, Gloucester, Swansea, Cheltenham, Worcester, Hereford, Bristol, Preston, Blackburn, Stoke-on-Trent, Hanley, Warrington, and Croydon. Since 1858 he had contemplated a second visit to the United States but his plans had been, of necessity, postponed due to the outbreak of the Civil War. In early November 1867, however, he set sail from Liverpool en route for Boston and what he anticipated would be an exceptionally lucrative North American reading tour (he in fact made a clear profit from the seventy-six readings he gave of some £19,000). This time there seems to have been no prospect of a new *American Notes* and a far less edgy and fastidious Dickens seems to have found the citizens and institutions of the post-bellum United States more to his taste (though some of those citizens had neither forgotten nor forgiven his earlier abuse of them). He began his performances in Boston in December, and concluded them, after an exceptionally full schedule, in New York in the following April.

Dickens returned to England in a state of exhaustion and general debilitation which was not to be relieved either by rest or medication. John Forster noted:

There was a manifest abatement of his natural force, the elasticity of bearing was impaired, and the wonderful brightness of eye was dimmed at times. One day, too, as he walked from his office . . . he could read only the halves of the letters over the shop doors that were on his right as he looked . . . It was an additional unfavourable symptom that his right foot had become affected as well as the left . . . but all disappeared upon any special cause for exertion. (*Life*, pp. 798–9)

Dickens seems to have suffered a series of minor strokes, and to have been troubled with gout in his left foot ('a mere bag of pain') and a persistent head cold which he had christened his 'American catarrh'. All of these symptoms left him as soon as he ascended the rostrum to read, though, latterly, he took the precaution of having a doctor in attendance in the wings. For the so-called 'Farewell Season' of 1868–9 Dickens added a new reading to his repertoire, one that he performed with particular, even obsessive passion. This was the celebrated 'Sikes and Nancy', an adaptation of the scenes surrounding the murder of Nancy from *Oliver Twist* which was apt to set his pulse racing with particular ferocity. A witness to the very last performance of this reading saw the sudden upsurge in Dickens's extraordinary energy as he went on stage:

As he stepped upon the platform, resolved, apparently, upon out-doing himself, he remarked, in a half-whisper to the present writer, just before advancing from the cover of the screen to the familiar reading-desk, 'I shall tear myself to pieces.' He certainly never acted with more impassioned earnestness—though never once, for a single instant, however, overstepping the boundaries of nature. His pulse just before had been tested, as usual keenly and carefully, by his most sedulous and sympathetic medical attendant. It was counted by him just as keenly and carefully afterwards—the rise then apparent being something startling, almost alarming, as it seemed to us under the circumstances.[22]

The nationwide 'Farewell' series had had to be abandoned prematurely in April 1869 due to a further breakdown in Dickens's health. Perhaps ill-advisedly, his doctors allowed him to give a further twelve readings between 11 January and 15 March 1870, though they insisted that no railway journeys should be involved. Nevertheless, these readings, given exclusively to London audiences featured the extraordinarily draining 'Sikes and Nancy' more than any other item from his regular repertoire. Wilkie Collins was later to record the opinion that this reading 'did more to kill Dickens than all his work put together'.[23]

At the very last reading, on 15 March, Dickens announced to his audience that he was going to vanish 'from these garish lights . . . for evermore with a heartfelt, grateful, respectful and affectionate farewell'. He had, however, promised them that 'in but two short weeks from this time' he hoped that they might enter, in their own homes, 'on a new series of readings' at which his assistance would be

Mourners at the grave of Charles Dickens, from the *Illustrated London News*, 1870.

indispensable. He meant that a new serially published novel, *The Mystery of Edwin Drood*, was about to begin publication. It was intended that *Drood* should appear in twelve monthly parts beginning in April 1870. The novel, set both in London and in the dusty cathedral city Cloisterham (based on Rochester), was evidently to be centred on the mysterious disappearance (and probably the murder) of its title character. It was also to have been a further study of the criminal mind, a psychology dramatically explored in the cases of Bill Sikes (in *Oliver Twist* and in its adapted form as 'Sikes and Nancy') and Bradley Headstone (in *Our Mutual Friend*). The new novel was, however, to be left tantalizingly unfinished and, as the many floundering followers of Dickens have proved, effectively unfinishable. On 8 June he worked all day on the story in the chalet in his garden at Gad's Hill. At dinner that evening he announced that he was feeling 'very ill' and collapsed as the result of a cerebral haemorrhage. He died in his fifty-eighth year in the course of the following evening without having regained consciousness. Despite having expressed a wish to be buried 'in the small graveyard under Rochester castle wall', he was interred in Poets' Corner in Westminster Abbey on 14 June. His estranged wife survived him by nine years, leaving her collection of his letters to her to the library of the British Museum in order 'that the world may know he loved me once'. Ellen Ternan, who was bequeathed £1,000 in Dickens's will, married a clergyman in 1876, and spent the rest of her life in respectable obscurity in Margate and Southsea. She died in 1914, and is buried in the same cemetery in Portsmouth as Maria Beadnell. For the first and last loves of Dickens's life to be buried in the town of his birth is perhaps a coincidence worthy of one of his novels.

CHAPTER 2

'THESE TIMES OF OURS': DICKENS, POLITICS, AND SOCIETY

In terms of his reaction to two of the greatest spectacles of his time, the Great Exhibition of 1851 and the state funeral of the Duke of Wellington in 1852, Dickens was decidedly out of sympathy with his time. The first was a celebration of the energy and creativity of nineteenth-century British life; the other was an elaborate and very public celebration of death. The Victorians were particularly good at celebrating both.

Dickens visited the 'Great Exhibition of the Works of Industry of all Nations' twice, both times without much evident relish. The Exhibition and the Crystal Palace that housed it were generally regarded as phenomenal and were lauded as such. It was the first of a succession of international exhibitions and world fairs which have run into our own day. The term 'Crystal Palace' had been coined by the satirical magazine *Punch*, once a determined opponent of the whole scheme but readily converted by the sensational effect of the building and its contents. The highly innovative structure, designed by Dickens's friend Joseph Paxton, had been erected in Hyde Park and was regarded by Queen Victoria herself as a 'wonderful creation'.[1] It had been opened by the Queen, with great ceremony, on 1 May 1851, a ceremony described by *The Times* in terms of religious awe and apocalyptic prevision:

It was felt to be more than what was seen, or what had been intended. Some saw in it the second inauguration of their Sovereign; some a solemn dedication of art and its stores; some were most reminded of that day when all ages and climes shall be gathered around the Throne of their Maker; there was so much that seemed accidental, and yet had a meaning, that no one could be content with simply what he saw.[2]

By 15 October, when the Exhibition was formally closed to the public to the strains of the national anthem, it had been seen by over six million visitors drawn from all social classes.

During the planning stages of the Exhibition in March 1850
Dickens, who had established a reputation as a campaigner for
improved educational and entertainment facilities for the poor, had
been officially asked to serve on what was styled the 'Central Working Class Committee of the Great Exhibition'. This committee,
which also included Thackeray, John Stuart Mill, and John Forster,
had been established to disseminate information about the forthcoming Exhibition and to arrange visits and cheap accommodation in
London for prospective working-class visitors. It found its activities
hampered by an uncooperative government commission, and, on
Dickens's suggestion the committee dissolved itself on 6 June.[3]
Although, as it proved, well-behaved members of the working classes
visited the Exhibition in great numbers, Dickens was probably vexed
enough by the official obstruction he had encountered never to be
reconciled to the grand scheme. Although, as a recent commentator
has noted, it took time for the Exhibition to be 'redefined by the
public in a symbiotic relationship', Dickens seems to have been determined not to be part of that process of redefinition.[4] He decamped
from London with his family for an extended summer holiday in
Broadstairs in order to avoid the crowds drawn to the Crystal Palace,
wryly referring to the period as his 'expositional absence' (*Letters*, vi.
349: 7 Apr. 1851). As to the Exhibition itself, he jadedly complained
to a friend on 11 July that he felt 'used up': 'I don't say "there's
nothing in it"—there's too much . . . So many things bewildered me.
I have a natural horror of sights, and the fusion of so many sights in
one has not decreased it' (*Letters*, vi. 428). Nevertheless, though he
recognized the dead hand of the British Establishment in both the
preliminary planning and in what we might now call the ideology of
the Exhibition, he was also prepared to see that what was on show in
London in the summer of 1851 provided evidence of the benefits of
the cultural and political progress of the nation. In a co-written
article published in *Household Words* in July 1851 Dickens contrasted
the conservatism of Imperial China with the dynamism of industrialized Britain. Chinese artefacts had been on display in a separate
gallery in Hyde Park Place, a 'Little' exhibition detached from the
'Great' one:

We consider that our present period recognises the progress of humanity,
step by step, towards a social condition in which nobler feelings, thoughts

and actions, in concert for the good of all, instead of in general antagonism, producing a more refined and fixed condition of happiness, may be
the common inheritance of great and small communities, and of all those
nations of the earth who recognise and aspire to fulfil this law of human
progression. . . . Reader, in the comparison between the Great and Little
Exhibition, you have the comparison between Stoppage and Progress,
between the exclusive principle and all other principles, between the good
old times and the bad new times, between perfect Toryism and imperfect
advancement. Who can doubt that you will be led to conclusions, unhappily a little at a discount in this degenerate age, and that you will mentally
take suit and service in the favored Chinese Empire, with Reason's
Glory![5]

The irony of the last sentence is palpable. However repugnant the
smug, materialistic ethos of the Great Exhibition appeared to
Dickens, it nevertheless served to define something of the advantages of progress and to stress the superiority of European
civilization.

It is in Dickens's hearty espousal of the benefits of political, social,
and economic evolution that we can also root his antipathy to the
pomp of the Duke of Wellington's funeral. When the Iron Duke
died in September 1852, Dickens seems to have been happier
remembering 'the great old man' as the victor of Waterloo rather
than as the reactionary Tory prime minister of his youth (*Letters*,
vi. 762: 14 Sept. 1852). Once expressions of public grief became
overt and plans for an elaborate state funeral were announced,
his letters begin to express a fundamental distaste for what was
happening:

The whole Public seems to me to have gone mad about the funeral of the
Duke of Wellington. I think it a grievous thing——a relapse into semi-
barbarous practices . . . a pernicious corruption of the popular mind, just
beginning to awaken from the long dream of inconsistencies, mon-
strosities, horrors and ruinous expences, that has beset all classes of society in connexion with Death—and a folly sure to miss its object and to be
soon attended by a strong reaction on the memory of the illustrious man
so *mis*represented. (*Letters*, vi. 764–5: 23 Sept. 1852)

He was later to complain that the idea of a *State* funeral was 'wrong
in the Court estimate it implies of the People' for so public an occasion would merely prove to be 'a vulgar holiday, with a good deal of
business for the thieves and the public houses' (*Letters*, vi. 794–5:

3 Nov. 1852). When he was offered the rare honour of a ticket to the funeral service at St Paul's Cathedral by the Dean, he claimed to have 'made engagements' which did not leave him at liberty to accept the invitation. He told the Duke of Devonshire that he could not have contemplated 'the waiting in St Pauls, with any sort of philosophy' but he accepted the Duke's offer to watch the great procession as part of a private party at Devonshire House in Piccadilly and was later prepared to concede that 'the military part of the show was very fine'.[6]

What seems most to have offended Dickens was the fact that the State was wasting its resources so unnecessarily on a vain show of public grief. Moreover, it was also indirectly encouraging private indulgence in the kind of elaborate funeral ceremonial that he detested. He had a deep-seated loathing of the panoply of the Victorian funeral: mummers, mutes, plumes, palls, and all. He had conspicuously mocked undertakers and their stock-in-trade in *Oliver Twist*, *Martin Chuzzlewit*, and *David Copperfield*. His rage at the Wellington funeral 'show' reached its climax in the article he published in *Household Words* on 27 November under the title 'Trading in Death'.[7] The article expresses a horror at the 'barbarity' of the 'unmeaning mummeries, dishonest debt, profuse waste, and bad example in an utter oblivion of responsibility'. The Duke's state funeral had merely provided a means by which the unscrupulous had exploited the susceptibilities of a gullible public. To prove his case Dickens reprinted a succession of 'To Let' notices posted in windows along the processional route and added a selection of advertisements for personal mementoes and relics of the Duke. What he seems to have had no time for was the fact that this very public celebration of the Duke's fame might well have had some kind of therapeutic or cathartic effect on the British nation. He stated his emphatic sense of grievance at the climax of the essay:

We believe that a State Funeral at this time of day—apart from the mischievously confusing effect it has on the general mind, as to the necessary union of funeral expense and pomp with funeral respect, and the consequent injury it may do to the cause of a great reform most necessary for the benefit of all classes of society—is, in itself, so plainly a pretence of being what it is not: is so unreal, such a substitution of the form for the substance: is so cut and dried, and stale: is such a palpably got up theatrical trick: that it puts the dread solemnity of death to flight, and encourages these shameless traders in their dealings on the very coffin-lid of departed greatness.[8]

Dickens viewed Wellington as a figure who represented a past age, both as a general and as a politician but, once dead, the Duke's memory was being effectively dishonoured by a new generation which seemed to be improperly attuned to the progressive 'spirit of the age'.

Dickens's antipathetic responses to the Great Exhibition and to the Duke of Wellington's state funeral serve to suggest how uncomfortable he was with what latter-day historians might point to as leading aspects of his time. His antipathy also indicates the extent to which he detached himself from the way in which many self-congratulatory mid-Victorians looked at themselves. The Duke's funeral seemed to him to be an unhappy revival of the empty pomps of the past which the modern world would do better to forget. The Exhibition, by contrast, was largely an exercise in self-congratulation, a vulgar celebration of national commercialism which ignored the very modern social problems attendant upon industrialization. Although Dickens was consistently intolerant of the unreformed Victorian social, legal, and constitutional inheritance from the past, he was equally restless with those of his contemporaries who looked uncritically at the state of modern society. That 'eminently respectable man', Mr Podsnap, who figures so prominently in *Our Mutual Friend*, is typical of the kind of blinkered advocate of the moral and commercial superiority of all things British that Dickens profoundly mistrusted:

Mr Podsnap's world was not a very large world, morally; no, nor even geographically: seeing that although his business was sustained upon commerce with other countries, he considered other countries . . . a mistake, and of their manners and customs would conclusively observe, 'Not English!' when, PRESTO! with a flourish of the arm, and a flush of the face, they were swept away. (bk. 1, ch. 11)

Dickens characterizes Podsnap as a 'representative man', 'representative' that is of the pervasive smugness of much of middle-class Victorian Britain. Podsnap is convinced that Britain's moral, political, and cultural superiority over other nations has been decreed by Providence, but he is equally persuaded that 'what Providence meant, was invariably what Mr. Podsnap meant'. Dickens's accounts of the state of contemporary society ought, therefore, to be seen in the light of his own prejudices against two different kinds of conservative thinking. He is, on the one hand, a determined and often noisy advocate of reform in the face of Tory resistance to change. On the other, he emerges as a man who seeks to set himself apart from the self-satisfaction which marked those amongst his contemporaries who held that Britain was uniquely blessed in its system of government, in its liberties, and in its capitalist and imperial enterprise. In 1934, when new debates about the nature of society and its governance were rife, the historian G. M. Young shrewdly remarked on the nature of Dickens's radicalism in the novels of the 1830s and early 1840s:

They have the Radical faith in progress, the Radical dislike of obstruction and privilege, the Radical indifference to the historic appeal. But they part from the Radicalism of the Benthamites in their equal indifference to scientific appeal. Dickens's ideal England was not very far from Robert Owen's. But it was to be built by some magic of goodwill overriding the egoism of progress; not by law, and most emphatically not by logic.[9]

We should not expect consistency in Dickens's broad comments on the ills and abuses of his time. Despite the commonly held view of many of G. M. Young's contemporaries, Dickens was not primarily a social reformer or even a particularly sharp analyst of how and why reform was necessary (Young himself described the novelist's political satire as 'tedious and ignorant').[10] What generally renders Dickens a significant commentator on his times, is, however, his *imaginative* presentation of what latter-day readers can readily identify as 'representative' figures, types, scenes, incidents, and situations. This was precisely what another political satirist, George Bernard Shaw, recognized when he described Mr Podsnap as the direct ancestor of his character Britannus in *Caesar and Cleopatra*.[11] This was also what Shaw implied when he somewhat rashly claimed in 1937 that *Little Dorrit* was a more seditious book than *Das Kapital*.[12]

To readers in the twenty-first century it is just as important to recognize that Dickens can seem to be blinkered both by his own predilections, and, equally significantly, by certain of the cultural prejudices of his time, prejudices that we may not readily share. The social and political concerns of his fiction, his essays, and his letters do not, therefore, necessarily reflect those that modern historians and socio-literary critics might seek to identify as leading character-istics of his age. As we have already seen, Dickens's disillusion with the workings of the post-Reform parliament, which he acquired as a young reporter, was to influence him throughout his working life. He had an active distaste for parliament and the motives of most of his political contemporaries. Despite his adeptness at making his way professionally, he was never particularly skilled at grasping and describing the nature of Victorian Britain's creation and acquisition of wealth through imperial trade. This may help explain his antipathy to the Great Exhibition, but as the general marginalization of such matters in his novels suggests, he was substantially indiffer-ent to the contemporary expansion of the British Empire. His only real interest in British colonialism lay in its opening up of new terri-tories for emigration from an overpopulated homeland. Lastly, he was either intolerant of, or troubled by, the changing status of women. Each of these issues does, however, deserve to be addressed.

Dickens and the 'Age of Reform'

Dickens seems to have struck certain of his contemporaries as a quintessential representative of what was once commonly referred to as the 'Age of Reform'. In January 1857, for example, Sir James Fitzjames Stephen, who was by no means an enthusiast for the novel-ist's work, noted in the *Saturday Review*:

As every system is said to culminate, and every idea to be embodied, it might have been expected *a priori* that an era of reform would find, sooner or later, its representative man. We do not know whether the restless, discontented, self-sufficient spirit which characterizes so large a portion of modern speculation—especially on political and social subjects—could have had a more characteristic Avatar than it has found in Mr. Dickens.[13]

Stephen confessed that he viewed Dickens's 'curious commentary on a vast mass of phenomena' with 'profound disquiet'. Neverthe-less, this identification of the man and the political moment was to be repeated a year later by the distinguished economist and constitutional theorist Walter Bagehot:

Mr. Dickens's . . . has shown, on many occasions . . . the desire to start as a political reformer. The most instructive political characteristic of the years from 1825 to 1845 is the growth and influence of the scheme of opinion which we call radicalism . . . Mr. Dickens['s] . . . is what we may call the 'sentimental radicalism;' and if we recur to the history of the time, we shall find that there would not originally have been any opprobrium attaching to such a name. The whole course of the legislation, and still more of the administration, of the first twenty years of the nineteenth century were marked by a harsh unfeelingness which is of all faults the most contrary to any with which we are chargeable now . . . All the social speculation, and much of the social action of the few years succeeding the Reform Bill bear the most marked traces of the reaction. The spirit which animates Mr. Dickens's political reasonings and observations expresses it exactly.[14]

Dickens may have appeared to be an inept and impractical political reasoner to his intellectual contemporaries, but he was, nonetheless, a representative figure of forthright, no-nonsense, middle-class, middle-brow radicalism. He was, as John Ruskin later styled it, the quintessential 'modernist' who was 'the leader of the steam-whistle party *par excellence*', one who was intolerant both of the past and of modern complacency.[15] He believed in the virtues of the present only in so far as they were an expression of progress. In Dickens's eyes to stand still in a mood of self-congratulation was as grievous a sin against the 'spirit of the age' as an indulgent nostalgia for an improbable lost age.

In his article 'Old Lamps for New Ones', published in *Household Words* in June 1850, Dickens launched a bitter attack on John Everett Millais's painting *Christ in the House of his Parents*. The painting had been hung at the Royal Academy's exhibition that summer and had caused a small sensation. Dickens claimed to be offended not just by Millais's stiffly and formally posed treatment of a sacred subject but also by his representation of the child Jesus as 'a hideous, wry-necked, blubbering, red-headed boy, in a bed-gown' and of his mother as a woman 'so horrible in her ugliness that . . . she would stand out from the rest of the company as Monster, in the vilest cabaret in France, or the lowest gin-shop in England'.[16] What was really wrong with the painting in Dickens's eyes was neither its subject nor the details of its design, but that it represented a public display of the Pre-Raphaelite principles that he loathed. For him Pre-Raphaelitism appeared to be an integral part of a concerted cultural conspiracy to put the clock back. His article went on to dismiss the Pre-Raphaelite Brotherhood (PRB) as the 'Pre-Perspective Brotherhood', one that was prepared to discard the advances made in art since the High Renaissance. Dickens then attempted to draw absurdly satirical parallels between the PRB and a possible new spirit of revisionism in science and the sister arts:

A Society to be called the Pre-Newtonian Brotherhood, was lately projected by a young gentleman, under articles to a Civil Engineer, who objected to being considered bound to conduct himself according to the laws of gravitation . . . Several promising students connected with the Royal College of Surgeons have held a meeting, to protest against the circulation of the blood . . . A Pre-Harvey Brotherhood is the result, from which a great deal may be expected—by the undertakers . . . In literature, a very spirited effort has been made, which is no less than the formation of a P. G. A. P. C. B., or Pre-Gower and Pre-Chaucer-Brotherhood for the restoration of the ancient English style of spelling, and the weeding out from all libraries, public and private, of those and all later pretenders, particularly a person of loose character named SHAKESPEARE.[17]

Here is the progressivist, liberal Dickens protesting against what he considers to be the *wrong* sort of radicalism and the *wrong* sort of innovation. He knows what perspectives and what barriers he wants shifted and he insists that both must be consistently shifted forwards.

In this same *Household Words* essay Dickens also referred scathingly to the 'Young England hallucination . . . the notion of ignoring all that has been done for the happiness and elevation of mankind during three or four centuries of slow and dearly-bought amelioration'.[18] The 'Young England' to which Dickens refers here was what would now be known both as a 'splinter group' and a 'ginger group' within the Tory party led by Sir Robert Peel. Its influence was strongest in the years 1839–45 when it sought to forge a convergence of interest between a paternalist aristocracy and a deferential working class, both urban and rural. This prospective alliance was aimed at undermining the increasing political influence of middle-class industrialists, both in the Tory party and in the country as a whole. This was an influence that Peel had deliberately cultivated in the hope of gaining new ground for his party in the years following the passing of the Reform Act. Many of the ideas emanating from, and associated with, 'Young England' had a distinct, if ill-based, nostalgia about them. For Dickens they represented a naïve attachment to an elusive and unspecified vision of 'the Good Old Days'. In a parodic version of the traditional song 'A Fine Old English Gentleman' written in 1841, he hit out at what he believed were the abuses of aristocratic privilege in the past (this would be a subject to which he returned much later in *A Tale of Two Cities*). In one verse he introduced a sideswipe at the repressive legal system of the seventeenth and eighteenth centuries (again something he criticized in his earlier historical novel, *Barnaby Rudge*) :

> The good old laws were garnished well with gibbets, whips and chains,
>> With fine old English penalties and fine old English pains,
> With rebel heads and seas of blood once hot in rebel veins,
>> For all these things were requisite to guard the rich old gains
>>> Of the fine old English Tory times,
>>> Soon may they come again.

In *The Chimes*, Dickens's Christmas Book for 1844, a rubicund, self-satisfied associate of the contemptible Alderman Cute considers the demeanour of the City ticket porter Trotty Veck in a similarly 'fine old English Tory' light:

'What *is* to be said? Who can take an interest in a fellow like this,' meaning Trotty; 'in such degenerate times as these? Look at him! What an object! The good old times, the grand old times, the great old times! *Those* were the times for a bold peasantry, and all that sort of thing. Those were the times for every sort of thing, in fact. There's nothing now-a-days. Ah!' sighed the red-faced gentleman. 'The good old times, the good old times!'
   The gentleman didn't specify what particular times he alluded to; nor did he say whether he objected to the present times, from a disinterested consciousness that they had done nothing very remarkable in producing himself.   (First Quarter)

As the distinctly time-haunted narrative of *The Chimes* consistently implies, however, it is the evolving future, and not the past, which should be allowed to shape the political and social concerns of the present. In the third section of the story Trotty Veck is harangued in no uncertain terms by a Phantom with a decidedly Dickensian inflection in his voice:

'The voice of Time,' said the Phantom, 'cries to man, Advance! Time is for his advancement and improvement; for his greater worth, his greater happiness, his better life; his progress onward to that goal within its knowledge and its view, and set there, in the period when Time and He began. Ages of darkness, wickedness and violence, have come and gone: millions unaccountable, have suffered, lived, and died: to point the way Before him. Who seeks to turn him back, or stay him on his course, arrests a mighty engine which will strike the meddler dead; and be the fiercer and the wilder, ever, for its momentary check.   (Third Quarter)

As the Phantom implies, progress is not simply beneficial to human-kind, it is inherent in the nature of civilization. Progress brings with it the amelioration of the human condition, just as it increases human awareness of how and why things are, and how and why they can be improved. Any attempt to put the clock back, or to stay the inevitable movement of Time, is likely to occasion a terrible and undesired retribution.

It is not only Dickens's distaste for a sentimental view of the 'good old days' that dictates the Phantom's prophecy in *The Chimes*. The words are also haunted by Dickens's fear of a reprise of a violent social revolution akin to that experienced in France in the last decade of the eighteenth century. As Dickens perceived it, the root cause of the French Revolution lay in an abuse of monarchic and aristocratic power in the eighteenth century. Aristocratic privilege had expressed itself in social injustice; once the tables were turned, a new injustice, imposed in the name of 'the People', had led inexorably to a new kind of oppression. This, as we shall see later in this study, was the issue addressed in *A Tale of Two Cities* in 1859. Dickens's acute unease at the prospect of a future revolution from below was shared by many of his contemporaries, both liberal and conservative. It had provided much of the stimulus for constitutional reform in the Britain of the 1830s. The parliamentary debates that Dickens reported for the new political press had been accompanied by orchestrated riots and sporadic violence in the streets of several British cities. Although from a radical point of view not enough was actually achieved by the reforms of the first half of the nineteenth century, substantial changes to the creaking and unwritten constitu-tion of the United Kingdom were brought about. In 1828 the repeal of the seventeenth-century Test and Corporation Acts had opened up the everyday administration of the law and local government to non-Anglicans. In the following year the Roman Catholic Relief Act removed most civil disabilities from British and Irish Roman Catholics (though King George IV wept as he signed the Act, and the prime minister, the redoubtable Duke of Wellington, confessed that his only reason for granting emancipation was that he could not help it!).[19] This was the effective beginning of the idea of a 'plural' state, one in which no single cultural or religious 'establishment' was allowed to dominate civil life. It was also the beginning of the movement that led to the difficult passage through Parliament of the Reform Bill in the years 1831 and 1832 (the Bill was finally 'forced' through the recalcitrant House of Lords when King William IV offered to create sufficient new peers who would be sympathetic to the principle of Reform).

The acclaim for the redistribution of seats in the House of Commons and the moderate extension of the electorate (by the addition of a further 217,000 male voters) brought about by the 1832 Reform Act was widespread amongst those of a liberal persuasion. The City of London cast a bronze medal showing Liberty presenting a copy of the Act to a grateful Britannia. A new London club, the Reform, was opened in Pall Mall in 1834 with the condition of membership that all candidates should subscribe to the Act (Dickens was himself an early member). In Newcastle-upon-Tyne a handsome new street was named after the Whig prime minister and local grandee Earl Grey. At its climax a Doric column was erected bearing a statue of the Earl. The plinth of the column extols him as 'the Champion of Civil and Religious Liberty' and as a man who had 'safely and triumphantly attained . . . the great measure of Parliamentary reform'. In the summer of 1834 Dickens's first major assignment after joining the staff of the *Morning Chronicle* was to report a public celebration of Earl Grey in Edinburgh (Scotland's electorate had grown more substantially than that of England). The novelist's response to those who had resisted reform and who remained unhappy with its consequences can be gauged from his critical portrait of Sir Leicester Dedlock in *Bleak House*. Equally revealing is the article 'Snoring for the Million' which Dickens published in the *Examiner* in December 1842. Here aristocratic conservatives are caricatured as 'snorers':

There are not a few of this order who will not find it an unspeakable happiness to become oblivious of the Reform Bill, with its long train of ungenteel and revolutionary consequences, as exemplified in the increased and increasing audacity of the millions who demand to live.[20]

Sir Leicester Dedlock feared that 'any move in the Wat Tyler direction' would bring the end of the old order, but the process of

Reform, having been initiated, was to have long-term consequences to which the old order adjusted easily enough.

It was the resilience of the old order and the persistence of the old corruptions that seems to have vexed Dickens most. As a professed radical, he was to prove a singularly jaded observer of parliaments, parliamentary processes, and parliamentarians. On 16 December 1835, for example, he sent his fiancée, Catherine Hogarth, an alarming account of the rowdy proceedings during the campaign in the Northamptonshire borough of Kettering, an election which he had been sent to observe as a reporter for the *Morning Chronicle*:

We had a slight flare here yesterday morning, just stopping short of murder and a riot. Party feeling runs so high, and the contest is likely to be so sharp a one that I look forward to the probability of a scuffle before it is over. As the Tories are the principal party here, *I* am in no very good odour in the town ... Such a ruthless set of bloody-minded villains, I never set eyes on, in my life. In their convivial moments yesterday after the business of the day was over, they were perfect savages. If a foreigner were brought here on his first visit to an English town, to form his estimate of the national character, I am quite satisfied he would return forthwith to France, and never set foot in England again ... beastly as the electors usually are, these men are superlatively blackguards. Would you believe that a large body of horsemen, mounted and armed, who galloped on a defenceless crowd yesterday, striking about them in all directions, and protecting a man who cocked a loaded pistol, were *led* by Clergymen, and Magistrates? (*Letters*, i. 106–7)

This account can be roughly paralleled by the equally corrupt, but yet more ludicrous, electoral process in the fictional borough of Eatanswill described in chapter 13 of *Pickwick Papers*:

Horatio Fizkin, Esquire, of Fizkin Lodge near Eatanswill, presented himself for the purpose of addressing the electors; which he no sooner did, than a band employed by the honourable Samuel Slumkey, commenced performing with a power to which their strength in the morning was a trifle; in return for which, the Buff crowd belaboured the heads and shoulders of the Blue crowd; on which the Blue crowd endeavoured to dispossess themselves of their very unpleasant neighbours the Buff crowd; and a scene of struggling, and pushing, and fighting, succeeded, to which we can no more do justice than the Mayor could, although he issued imperative orders to twelve constables to seize the ring-leaders, who might amount in number to two hundred and fifty, or thereabouts.

What these two election scenes suggest is a continuity with the noisy, violent, and corrupt parliamentary politics of the pre-Reform era. Little has evidently changed since Dickens's beloved William Hogarth had painted his celebrated 'Election' series in the early 1750s. The novelist's play with the words 'eat' and 'swill' in the name of his fictional constituency might even be taken as a shorthand description of Hogarth's tavern scene. Dickens, who prominently hung engravings of Hogarth's work in his homes, would have despairingly recognized that bribery, disorder, and mindless inebriation continued to pose a challenge to the proper exercise of representative government in the new century.

Despite his self-evident, and oft-expressed, sympathy with the dispossessed, Dickens remained somewhat more ambiguous in his response to the disenfranchised. He was essentially a middle-class radical rather than a champion of the working-class claim to representation in parliament. His letters also suggest that he was no friend to Chartism. The 'People's Charter' had been drawn up in 1838 in response to calls for further advances in the democratic process, ones that would embrace the interests of working-class men. The Charter called for universal manhood suffrage, for equal electoral districts, for a secret ballot, for the payment of MPs, for the abolition of the property qualification for MPs, and for annual parliaments. The Chartists (as the adherents of the radical cause were known), initially attempted to persuade a series of governments of the justice of their claims by petitions, by lobbies of parliament, by mass meetings, and by a plethora of cheap journals, newspapers, and pamphlets emanating from a well-organized network of provincial and metropolitan groupings. Their public demonstrations, though ostensibly pacific in intent, occasionally spilled over into the kind of violence that an observer like Dickens most dreaded. The Charter was formally presented to Parliament in July 1839 and again in May 1842 and it was rejected on both occasions. In 1848, when much of continental Europe was shaken by revolutions, a great petition was driven to Westminster in a series of cabs following a 20,000-strong mass rally on Kennington Common. Its third rejection failed to inspire a revolution in England, and the ruling classes, Mr Podsnap amongst them, breathed a sigh of relief and proceeded to claim that the nation had been safeguarded by the merits of its existing constitution and by its unequalled prosperity.

Dickens's reactions to such manifestations of working-class radicalism are ambiguous. On 25 July 1842 he wrote a long and
detailed letter to the editor of the *Morning Chronicle* outlining his
concern at the prospect of the House of Lords wrecking a bill
aimed at alleviating the working conditions of miners and banning
the employment of women underground. The letter shows that he
was not simply determined to oppose the vested interests of mine-
owners, he also recognized that the noisiest defenders of the 'rights
of labour' were those Chartists who were associated with excess in
the public mind: 'When we talk of "rights of labour", do we picture to ourselves a hideous phantom whispering discontent in the
depths of pits and mines, sharpening the Chartist's pike by stealth,
and skulking from the farmer's rickyard?' (*Letters*, iii. 282.) One
suspects that Dickens was himself worried by this amorphous, but
nonetheless 'hideous', phantom, one stalking country and city,
mine and manor-house alike. When on 29 February 1848 he
rejoiced with other liberals at the fall of King Louis-Philippe's
regime in France he fretted both about the prospect of the King
winning support from the upper classes in England and about
any spillover of French revolutionary sentiment into English
proletarian radicalism:

I have never known anything at all like the sensation that is made here, by
the French Revolution . . . The aristocratic feeling of England is against it,
of course. All the intelligence and liberality, I should say, are with it, tooth
and nail. If the Queen should be marked in her attention to old Papa
Philippe, I think there will be great discontent and dissatisfaction
expressed throughout the country. Meantime, we are in a queer position
ourselves, with great distress in the manufacturing towns, and all sorts of
public bedevilments.   (*Letters*, iv. 254)

The 'public bedevilments' which worried Dickens were to manifest
themselves in riots in Glasgow and Manchester and in a mass dem-
onstration in Leeds at which the French tricolour was raised (still a
far more emotive flag than the red one). Once the great demonstra-
tion in London in April 1848 had appeared to have burnt itself out
without severe civil disruption, Dickens noted, somewhat disparagingly, that 'Chartist fears and rumours shake us, now and then'
and then added, with a further note of cynicism, that he suspected
that the Government would 'make the most of such things for their
own purpose' (*Letters*, iv. 342: 17 June 1848).

It has often been argued that the central theme of *Barnaby Rudge: A Tale of the Riots of 'Eighty* (1841) can be related to the contemporary spate of Chartist disturbances in British cities. There is no direct evidence for connecting this story, set at the time of the Gordon Riots in London in 1780, with urban mayhem in the early 1840s. Indeed, as the subject of the novel was first mooted in 1836, Dickens's interest in expressions of violent urban unrest may well stem from his knowledge of the Reform riots of the early 1830s. There is a far greater link with a single telling episode in *The Old Curiosity Shop*, which was serialized in *Master Humphrey's Clock* in 1840–1 immediately before *Barnaby Rudge*. In chapter 45 Little Nell and her grandfather shrink away in horror from the smoky ghastliness of an industrial town and from a group of sullen proletarian demonstrators. Poverty and disease are rife in the town, but as night falls there is a new danger evident on the streets:

bands of unemployed labourers paraded in the roads, or clustered by torch-light round their leaders, who told them in stern language of their wrongs, and urged them on to frightful cries and threats; when maddened men, armed with sword and firebrand, spurning the tears and prayers of women who would restrain them, rushed forth on errands of terror and destruction, to work no ruin half so surely as their own . . .

Here, as in *Hard Times*, the middle-class, liberal Dickens appears to balk at the advent of working-class demagoguery, a demagoguery which exploits the grievances of the poor for its own narrow, political ends. Dickens's acute lack of sympathy with those who seemed to be dangerously manipulating the oppressed, and giving voice to the inarticulate, was to culminate in the denunciations, the betrayals, the score-settlings, and the bloody vengeances of the Reign of Terror reimagined in the revolutionary Paris of *A Tale of Two Cities*.

What certainly would have struck Dickens as standing in marked contrast both to the debased process of electioneering in the 1830s and to the working-class demagoguery of Chartism was the orderly conduct of the great extra-parliamentary campaign against slavery which had begun in the closing decades of the eighteenth century. On 28 August 1833 Parliament passed an Act abolishing slavery throughout the British Empire. This was the culmination of a long-drawn-out campaign against a gross abuse of human liberty which had had William Wilberforce and Thomas Clarkson as its most powerful advocates. British participation in the slave trade had been outlawed in 1807 but the abolitionists had determinedly pursued their ultimate goal by means of a steady process of persuasion: moral, economic, and political. Public opinion was swung in their favour through a combination of rallies, prayer-meetings, sermons, speeches, sugar-boycotts, pamphlets, letters, and parliamentary lobbies. With the advent of the Reform Parliament, the anti-slavery movement recognized that the time was ripe to achieve its end: recalcitrant MPs were threatened with peaceful direct action in their constituencies, significant consciences were pricked, and slavery was finally outlawed in the British sphere of influence, notably in the West Indies, from 1 August 1834. Although the Act stipulated that provision should be made for the promotion of industry among the manumitted slaves, it also set aside the vast sum of £20,000,000 to be paid as compensation to former slave-holders. The passage of this Act rendered the continuance of slavery in the liberty-loving United States even more of an anomaly in the minds of liberals on both sides of the Atlantic. Dickens, who had doubtless been long influenced by Wilberforcean rhetoric, was to describe slavery to readers of *American Notes* as 'that most hideous blot and foul disgrace'. He was consistently affronted by the phenomenon and by the lingering racial prejudices associated with it. When he travelled through slave-owning states during his extended American visit in 1842 he professed to note 'an air of decay and ruin abroad' in them, a condition which he believed was 'inseparable from the system'. In chapter 9 of *American Notes* he described crossing the Potomac into Virginia. There was a separate 'negro car' on the train in which he travelled, a car which contained the miserable human purchases of a white slave-holder:

The children cried the whole way, and the mother was misery's picture. The champion of Life, Liberty and the Pursuit of Happiness, who had bought them, rode in the same train; and every time we stopped, got down to see they were safe. The black in Sinbad's Travels with one eye in the middle of his forehead which shone like a burning coal, was nature's aristocrat compared with this white gentleman.

One can almost hear the stinging note of cynicism with which Dickens himself might have pronounced the word 'gentleman'.

Matters had not improved much beyond a change in the federal law by the time he returned to the United States in 1867–8. When he gave one of his public readings in the church of the famous anti-slaver, the Revd Henry Ward Beecher, in Brooklyn in 1868, Dickens was appalled to find that even in so 'liberal' an atmosphere an upper gallery was reserved for 150 'Coloureds'. On the first night no one, whether black or white, entered it. When Dickens insisted that he would restrict the number of his readings unless it was filled, he was again shocked that one white ticket-holder complained that he had been seated 'next to . . . two Gord damned cusses of niggers'. The objector was sternly informed that 'Mr. Dickens would not recognise such an objection on any account, but he could have his money back if he chose'. The man took the ticket money (*Letters*, xii. 27–8: 30 Jan. 1868).

Dickens and Empire

Britain lost most of its first empire following its defeat at the battle of Yorktown in October 1781. It then proceeded to acquire a second empire, as has often been remarked, almost by default. The first empire was centred on the eastern seaboard of North America. America had become an English-speaking colony, settled by emigrants from the Old Country who had largely supplanted its aboriginal population. It had been governed for the most part by prosperous landowners, farmers, and urban tradesmen who believed in the broad principle of personal liberty enshrined in the laws and religious convictions that their forebears had brought with them across the Atlantic. The fact that slavery had not only survived the Revolution, but had increased as the southern United States expanded westwards, was the consequence of the constitutional insistence that the rights of the individual included the right to the unhindered possession of property. The glaring anomaly that that property might also be human, and be therefore denied rights, took time to sink in.

The second empire had India as its focus. India was, by contrast with America, a densely populated land, with a highly developed indigenous culture (or cultures) and with a Mogul imperial tradition the mantle of which Britain gradually assumed. It was initially a land for trade not for settlement. It was to remain both a vast market for British-produced goods and an object of a quasi-romantic fascination. Until after the suppression of the revolt of 1857–8 (the 'Indian Mutiny') the British possessions in the subcontinent were administered by the East India Company and disciplined by the Company's armies, armies made up of a high proportion of native soldiers. Only following the India Bill of 1858 was direct rule imposed and local armies were brought under crown control (with a proportionate increase of European to Indian troops). If the American colonies had represented an extension of English manners and English government, India was exotic, glamorous, different. In the mind of its colonial rulers the subcontinent took a romantic precedence over all other parts of the empire. Victoria may have been queen of Great Britain and Ireland, but when she was proclaimed empress of India in May 1876 she took her imperial title from an immense territory a third of which remained under the personal control of a succession of maharajas, rajas, nizams, and nawabs. In European terms her exotic imperial title rendered her the equal of the old-established emperors of Austria and Russia and the newfangled one of Germany. In Canada or Australia she was the queen of a European mother country to whom allegiance was due. In India, however, she was an empress, a supreme sovereign to whom other sovereigns owed homage.

For Dickens, as for many of his contemporaries, India held a fascination. Its exoticism, akin to that of *The Arabian Nights*, stirred his imagination, but it remained distant from the everyday realities described in his fiction. In his essay 'Gone Astray' (*Household Words*, Aug. 1853) he described his boyhood 'veneration' for the phenomenon represented by East India House in Leadenhall Street in the City of London, the building which housed the Honorable East India Company:

I had no doubt of its being the most wonderful, the most magnanimous, the most incorruptible, the most practically disinterested, the most in all respects astonishing, establishment on the face of the earth. I understood the nature of an oath, and would have sworn it to be one entire and perfect chrysolite.

Thinking much about boys who went to India, and who immediately, without being sick, smoked pipes like curled-up bell-ropes, terminating in a large cut-glass sugar basin upside down . . .[21]

Here is a colonial institution bringing the benefits of good government, trade, and Christian civilization to an alien world. It is the exotic ambience of the 'rich' East India House, rather than the opportunities it might offer to an ambitious boy, which informs the description of the establishment in the fourth chapter of *Dombey and Son*:

teeming with suggestions of precious stuffs and stones, tigers, elephants, howdahs, hookahs, umbrellas, palm-trees, palanquins, and gorgeous princes of a brown complexion sitting on carpets, with their slippers very much turned up at the toes.

This is nonetheless the India of economic potential, the place where the fortunes of adventurous nabobs were made. It is a sadder, distant, more dangerous India that has produced the melancholy Master Bitherstone whom we first meet, pining for his home, at Mrs Pipchin's establishment in chapter 8 of the same novel. Bitherstone, we later learn, was 'born beneath some Bengal star of ill-omen' and wishes to get his revenge on Dr Blimber by having him 'carried up country by a few of his (Bitherstone's) Coolies, and handed over to the Thugs' (ch. 41). A rather different menace informs the accounts of the relationship between the overbearing Major Bagstock and his much put-upon Indian servant ('the Native'). Bagstock appears to have served in an Indian regiment with Bitherstone's father ('Bitherstone of Ours'). 'The Native', who has doubtless been acquired in Bengal, has no particular name 'but answers to any vituperative epithet'. Dickens was to describe him to his illustrator, Hablot Browne, as 'evidently afraid of the Major and his thick cane', dressed 'in European costume', possibly with earrings, but looking outlandish and dark brown (*Letters*, v. 34, 35: 10 and 15 Mar. 1847).

In 1857 Dickens's fourth son, Walter, was nominated for a cadetship in the East India Company, though he was never to prosper there. Having been sent to a professor in the University of London to study Indian languages, and having passed the Company's examinations, the 16-year-old Walter was dispatched to Calcutta. He was to see action almost immediately after his arrival, distinguishing himself in the campaigns against the rebel sepoys during the Mutiny, and was to rise to the rank of lieutenant in the 42nd Highlanders. Dickens was to remain anxious about his son's health and well-being

in India. On 7 September 1858 he wrote to a friend whose son had
been taken ill as Walter had been:

Be of good heart about your brave boy. *My* boy was invalided long ago,
and carried in a litter God knows how far and how long. But he began to
get well, the moment he arrived at a Hill-Station, and his care now, in the
letters he writes home, is to get away from that east life and be on service
again. He had sun-stroke, a passing attack of smallpox, and smart Fever.
But he rallied, gaily.   (*Letters*, viii. 654)

Walter was not to remain as resilient. He was to die of an aneurism in
Calcutta in 1863, leaving his sorrowing father to pay his debts. Walter's experiences in India seem to have shifted Dickens's responses
to the country and its culture from the merely fascinated to the
appalled. Distance no longer added romance. On 4 October 1857,
soon after his son's arrival in Calcutta and as news of the nature and
scale of the revolt against the British spread, Dickens exploded with
intemperate rage at the atrocities committed by the rebels at Delhi,
Cawnpore, and Lucknow:

I wish I were Commander in Chief in India. The first thing I would do to
strike that Oriental race with amazement (not in the least regarding them
as if they lived in the Strand, London, or at Camden Town), should be to
proclaim to them, in their language, that I considered my holding that
appointment by the leave of God, to mean that I should do my utmost to
exterminate the Race upon whom the stain of the late cruelties rested; and
that I begged them to do me the favor to observe that I was there for that
purpose and no other, and was now proceeding, with all convenient dis-
patch and merciful swiftness of execution, to blot it out of mankind and
raze it off the face of the Earth.   (*Letters*, viii. 459)

As the editors of the Pilgrim edition of Dickens's *Letters* point out,
this kind of violent protestation was not uncommon at the time,
inexcusable as his words might seem to modern readers. When, however, in the Christmas number of *Household Words* for 1857 he
returned to the touchy subject of British garrisons threatened by
rebellion, incarceration, and bloodshed, he set the story on a tropical
island rather than in India. This was the tale entitled 'The Perils of
Certain English Prisoners' co-written with Wilkie Collins. It was,
Dickens claimed, going to light up 'all the fire that is in the public
mind at this time' and to commemorate 'without any vulgar catch-
penny connexion or application, some of the best qualities of the

English character that have been shewn in India' (*Letters*, viii. 482: 24 and 25 Nov. 1857). The story generally eschewed both horrors and cries for vengeance. Instead it celebrated personal heroism and self-sacrifice in a manner that prefigured the reconciliatory actions of Sydney Carton in *A Tale of Two Cities*.

Dickens was to remain as intolerant of anti-colonial rebellion abroad as he was afraid of the threat of revolution from below at home. Most famously in 1865 he was to join with Tennyson, Ruskin, and Carlyle in voicing his support for Edward John Eyre, the Governor of Jamaica, who had brutally suppressed an uprising on the island. Moves to prosecute Eyre for contravening the Colonial Governors Act of 1700 had proved unsuccessful, despite the publicly voiced offence his actions had given to such prominent liberals as John Stuart Mill and T. H. Huxley (though Eyre was finally dismissed from his governorship in 1866 following a Royal Commission of Enquiry). An outraged Dickens, perturbed by liberal apologists who took the side of the colonized against that of the colonial regime, exploded in a ranting letter to his friend W. F. de Cerjat :

The Jamaica insurrection is another hopeful piece of business. The platform—sympathy with the black—or the native, or the devil—afar off, and that platform indifference to our own countrymen at enormous odds in the midst of bloodshed and savagery, makes me stark wild. Only the other day, here was a meeting of jawbones of asses at Manchester, to censure the Jamaica Governor for his manner of putting down the insurrection! So we are badgered about New Zealanders and Hottentots, as if they were identical with men in clean shirts at Camberwell, and were to be bound by pen and ink accordingly . . . But for the blacks in Jamaica being over-impatient and before their time, the whites might have been exterminated, without a previous hint or suspicion that there was anything amiss. *Laisser allez*, and Britons never, never, never!—   (*Letters*, xi. 115–16: 30 Nov. 1865)

In this case Dickens seems to been most offended by liberal-minded missionaries who appeared to be more concerned with saving the souls of foreign nations than they were with attending to the social and spiritual darkness of contemporary Britain.

In his middle and later years Dickens seems to have become firmly persuaded that the highest degree of civilization was unique to

Europe and to those peoples of European stock. Imperialism, and particularly that practised by the British, was essentially a civilizing mission which would gradually spread enlightenment rather than corruption to the dark places of the earth. Yet again, such sentiments were not uncommon amongst his fellow Victorians, though they may unnerve us when expressed so earnestly by Dickens. Despite the offence represented by slavery, he often appears to be as much concerned with the moral depravity of the white slave-owner as with the condition of the black slave. Not for him the eighteenth-century idea of the 'Noble Savage'. Savages were savages *tout court*, regardless of colour and regardless of which continent they originated from. This he made plain in the forthright article on the subject that he published in *Household Words* in June 1853:

To come to the point at once, I beg to say that I have not the least belief in the Noble Savage. I consider him a prodigious nuisance, and an enormous superstition. His calling rum fire-water, and me a pale face, wholly fail to reconcile me to him. I don't care what he calls me. I call him a savage, and I call a savage a something highly desirable to be civilised off the face of the earth. I think a mere gent (which I take to be the lowest form of civilisation) better than a howling, whistling, clucking, stamping, jumping, tearing savage. It is all one to me, whether he sticks a fishbone through his visage, or bits of trees through the lobes of his ears, or birds' feathers in his head; whether he flattens his hair between two boards, or spreads his nose over the breadth of his face, or drags his lower lip down by great weights, or blackens his teeth, or knocks them out, or paints one cheek red and the other blue, or tattoos himself or oils himself, or rubs his body with fat, or crimps it with knives. Yielding to whichsoever of these agreeable eccentricities, he is a savage—cruel, false, thievish, murderous; addicted more or less to grease, entrails, and beastly customs; a wild animal with the questionable gift of boasting; a conceited, tiresome, blood-thirsty, monotonous humbug.[22]

No Rousseauistic sentiments, therefore, about purer, simpler forms of communal life away from the corruptions of European society. And nothing to hint that Dickens might have understood the delicate relationships between humankind and the natural world that twenty-first century anthropologists and ecologists so earnestly seek to preserve in the face of an encroaching 'civilization'.

For Dickens the civilizing mission of imperialism meant European colonization. Although he was rapidly disillusioned with the

American republic and with Americans during his visit to the United States in 1842, he seems to have held out high hopes for the future of Britain's slowly burgeoning colonies in Australia and New Zealand. His optimism may well have been based on the fact that he visited neither colony. He seems, though, to have toyed with the idea of emigration at regular intervals. John Forster reports that during a fit of acute restlessness in the years 1857–8 he returned to the idea of the 'convict run', his 'old notion of having some slight idea of going to settle in Australia' (*Life*, p. 639). The nearest he came to realizing this vague dream was in the second half of 1862 when he was offered £10,000 for an eight-month reading tour. The Civil War had closed America to him and he was tempted by the prospect of finding material for an 'Uncommercial Traveller Upside Down'. Nothing was to come of the planned readings, and the well-heeled originators of the scheme, the Australian entrepreneurs Spiers and Pond, went on instead to arrange the successful visit of a team of Aboriginal cricketers to England (the first ever Australian cricket tour). Nevertheless, Dickens was clearly haunted by the potential of the empty antipodes. Thither he sent his sons Alfred and Edward, and thither he sought to send the 'fallen women' whose redemption from a life in the streets of London he attempted to achieve at Urania Cottage. Emigration as a cure for the economic ills of the poor was enthusiastically endorsed in a series of articles in the opening numbers of *Household Words*. He was to insist to a prospective contributor to *All the Year Round* that the magazine's readers would show an exclusive interest in 'the Settler in Australia, and not in the least with the aboriginal inhabitant' (*Letters*, xii. 172: 24 Aug. 1868). Perhaps most significant is the relationship of his fictional characters to an imagined land of opportunity on the other side of the world. It is not only the 'fallen' Emily and Martha in *David Copperfield* who will find a new life and prosper. As Mrs Micawber puts it, her husband may be nothing in England, but in Australia he might wield 'the rod of talent and power'. She proves to be right. Mr Peggotty is later able to show David a paragraph from the 'Port Middlebay Times' describing 'the public dinner to our distinguished fellow-colonist, WILKINS MICAWBER, ESQUIRE, Port Middlebay District Magistrate'. As the newspaper also reveals, David's old teacher, Mr Mell, has also prospered at Port Middlebay. He has not only acquired a doctorate but he has risen to the headmastership of the 'Colonial Salem-House Grammar School'.

Mell's and Micawber's Australia appears to be a new land rapidly putting its history as a penal colony behind it. Elsewhere in Dickens's fiction that history is not so easily forgotten. The Artful Dodger in *Oliver Twist* is sentenced to be transported for life, and New South Wales also receives those other incorrigibles Wackford Squeers (*Nicholas Nickleby*), Alice Marwood (*Dombey and Son*), and Uriah Heep and Littimer (*David Copperfield*). The most celebrated of Dickens's convict transportees is of course Magwitch in *Great Expectations*. He is also the only one who seems to make a success of himself once he has crossed 'many a thousand mile of stormy water'. In Australia Magwitch has worked on a sheep-farm as an assignee, and, after obtaining his ticket-of-leave he has made his fortune as 'a sheep-farmer, stock-breeder, and other trades besides' (vol. 1, ch. 20). Despite his justified pride in what he has made of himself, Magwitch remains a disturbing character, one who has dreamed of making 'his boy' into a gentleman while he was 'a hired-out shepherd in a solitary hut, not seeing no faces but faces of sheep'. Having had neither freedom of action nor possessions he now distorts Pip's life by seeking to possess him. If Magwitch 'ain't a gentleman, nor yet ain't got no learning', he is content to remember that he is 'the owner of such'. Like the free Wilkins Micawber, the convict Abel Magwitch has taken the class assumptions of the old world with him to the new. Both, in their different ways, aspire to achieve what had been denied them in England, but they both look intently over their shoulders at English definitions of success. Despite its ability to make men, the distant, supposedly classless Australia of *Great Expectations* has the ability to reach out and enslave others.

Dickens and Women

Dickens could be as ambiguous in his attitudes concerning the position of women as he was in regard to other disadvantaged sectors of Victorian society. Despite his professed liberalism, he was no John Stuart Mill when it came to responding to the demands for women's equality with men being voiced by an increasing number of his female contemporaries. Indeed, he seems at times to have been actively disturbed by any threat to upset the social status quo. When, for example, the issue of women's property rights was being addressed by Parliament in 1868 one of his letters shows that he was basically sympathetic to the reform. Nevertheless, after token words of assent, he abruptly shifted his argument round to the issue of divorce and to the marital disadvantages experienced by both men *and* women:

There is a bill before Parliament . . . for enabling a married woman to possess her own earnings. I should much like to champion the sex— reasonably—and to dwell upon the hardships inflicted by the present law on a woman who finds herself bound to a drunken, profligate, and spend-thrift husband—who is willing to support him—does so—but has her little savings bullied out of her, continually . . . Grant what we are told by bishops, priests, and deacons about sanctity of marriage, indissolubility of marriage tie &c &c. Grant that such things *must be*, for the general good. Cannot we—and ought not we—in such a case as this, to help the weak and injured party? Reverse the case, and take a working man with a drunken woman saddled on him as long as he lives, who strips his house continually to buy drink. If he must not be able to divorce himself—for the general good—surely 'the general good' should in return, punish the woman. (*Letters*, xii. 127–8: 4 June 1868)

This would appear to be an *ad hominem* argument, though whether the man in question is the long-suffering Stephen Blackpool in *Hard Times* or Charles Dickens himself seems to be difficult to determine. Blackpool's poverty had denied him a divorce despite being 'saddled' with a drunken wife; Dickens, one suspects, had had to deny himself a divorce because his own wife was, despite his emotional misgivings in regard to her, totally faithful and upright. What this letter of June 1868 indicates, however, is that Dickens never really found himself able to commit to important aspects of women's rights or to women's social, educational, and professional aspirations.[23]

Perhaps the most unfavourable picture of an aspirant professional woman in Dickens's fiction is that of Mrs Jellyby in *Bleak House*. There are relatively few middle-class women with what one might loosely describe as 'professions' in his novels—though the shabby-genteel miniaturist Miss La Creevy in *Nicholas Nickleby*, Sally Brass 'the amazon at common law' in *The Old Curiosity Shop*, and Cornelia Blimber 'working in the graves of deceased languages' at her father's school in *Dombey and Son* are possible exceptions (the latter two being decided curiosities). The widowed Mrs Pipchin, the 'ogress and child-queller' in *Dombey*, runs a children's boarding house, while that other genteelly impoverished relict, Mrs Sparsit, acts as Bounderby's housekeeper in *Hard Times*. Other women characters of somewhat more doubtful or challenged social status are obliged to work in somewhat more demeaning capacities: Kate Nickleby and Amy Dorrit as seamstresses, Ruth Pinch as a governess in *Martin Chuzzlewit*, and Biddy as an assistant in the dame school where Pip receives his basic education in *Great Expectations*. The 'small, neat, methodical and buxom' Miss Peecher in *Our Mutual Friend* is one of a new breed of working-class women who have advanced their social position having trained as teachers in elementary schools.[24] Dickens's working-class women characters are, of course, obliged to work due to the force of economic circumstances.

Mrs Jellyby stands out from the majority of her working middle-class sisters in Dickens's novels in being both married and a mother. Therein lies the novelist's evident distaste for her: in order to pursue her professional interests she neglects what he and his narrator, Esther Summerson, seem to regard as her higher duty as a wife and a parent. Mrs Jellyby describes her work to Esther, Ada, and Richard in the fourth chapter of *Bleak House*:

'You find me, my dears, . . . as usual, very busy; but that you will excuse. The African project at present employs my whole time. It involves me in correspondence with public bodies, and with private individuals anxious for the welfare of their species all over the country. I am happy to say it is advancing. We hope by this time next year to have from a hundred and fifty to two hundred healthy families cultivating coffee and educating the natives of Borrioboola-Gha, on the left bank of the Niger . . . It involves the devotion of all my energies, such as they are; but that is nothing, so that it succeeds; and I am more confident of success every day. Do you know, Miss Summerson, I almost wonder that *you* never turned your thoughts to Africa.'

Given Dickens's enthusiasm for the civilizing mission of white colonialism in Australasia, readers might have assumed that Mrs Jellyby's coffee-cultivating project in West Africa was laudable in intent if impractical in fact. Esther's acute unease in her house is, however, indicative not of a lack of interest in Africa but of the degree to which her hostess has got her priorities wrong. Mrs Jellyby was modelled on Caroline Chisholm (1807–77) whose work in organizing the Family Colonization Loan Society had in fact been supported by Dickens (he not only subscribed to the Society in 1848, but also enthusiastically endorsed her scheme to assist emigrants to Australia in the article they jointly wrote for the first number of *Household Words*).[25] On 4 March 1850, however, he had occasion to complain to Angela Burdett Coutts of Mrs Chisholm's domestic failures shortly after visiting her in connection with the article ('I dream of . . . her housekeeping. The dirty faces of her children are my continual companions' (*Letters*, vi. 53)). The portrait of Mrs Jellyby appears to have affronted contemporary opponents of the slave-trade rather more than supporters of Mrs Chisholm or Victorian feminists. Having been attacked by Lord Denman for giving 'a disgusting picture of a woman who pretends zeal for the happiness of Africa, and is constantly employed in securing a life of misery to her own children', Dickens was stung into a self-defensive response:

Mrs. Jellyby gives offence merely because the word 'Africa', is unfortunately associated with her wild Hobby. No kind of reference to Slavery is made or intended, in that connexion. It must be obvious to anyone who reads about her. I have such strong reason to consider, as the best exercise of my faculties of observation can give me, that it is one of the main vices of this time to ride objects to Death through mud and mire, and to have a great deal of talking about them and *not* a great deal of doing—to neglect private duties associated with no particular excitement, for lifeless and soulless public hullabaloo with a great deal of excitement, and thus seriously to damage the objects taken up . . . and not least by associating them with Cant and Humbug in the minds of those reflecting people whose sympathies it is most essential to enlist, before any good thing can be advanced. I *know* this to be doing a good deal of harm . . . I invent the cause of emigration to Africa. Which no one in reality is advocating. Which no one ever did, that ever I heard of. Which has as much to do, in any conceivable way, with the unhappy Negro Slave as with the Stars. (*Letters*, vi. 825–6: 20 Dec. 1852)

It is interesting that Dickens describes Mrs Jellyby's great project as her 'wild Hobby' rather than as a dedication to a proto-profession. He portrays her as an enthusiast with tunnel vision and as one who is exemplary of an earnest but misplaced Victorian charity, a charity more concerned with the condition of Africa than with the condition of England. Nevertheless, what looks like the sharpness of Esther

Summerson's final comment on her seems scarcely conciliatory
either to anti-slavers or to champions of women's rights:

She has been greatly disappointed in Borrioboola-Gha, which turned out
a failure in consequence of the King of Borrioboola wanting to sell
everybody—who survived the climate—for Rum; but she has taken up
with the rights of women to sit in Parliament, and Caddy tells me it is a
mission involving more correspondence than the old one.   (*Bleak House*,
ch. 67)

Far-fetched and far off as the prospect of women MPs might have
seemed to many readers in 1852, it was a matter that was beginning
to be addressed both seriously and articulately. For Esther, though, it
appears that Mrs Jellyby is wasting not only her own time and
energy, but those of the nation as well.

   Esther Summerson, level-headed, practical, and thoroughly
domestic in her inclinations, is possessed of a character which agrees
more readily with Dickens's prejudices about women and their social
roles than does Mrs Jellyby's. Esther stands in a line with those other
admirable, family-oriented, unambitious, domestic angels, Florence
Dombey, Agnes Wickfield, and Amy Dorrit. Each of these women
exhibits a need to give and receive love, and each finds fulfilment as a
helpmate and companion to a deserving man. These women lack
neither intelligence nor integrity, but they do not look far beyond the
boundaries of marriage, home, and family life in order to explore
their identity and to forge their destiny. In creating them Dickens
was developing a stereotype of the virtuous wife and mother that
very many of his bourgeois contemporaries, both male and female,
cherished. According to this stereotype, a good woman was not only
to be prized above rubies, she was also the enhancer of her husband's
life and soul, the inspirer of his nobler thoughts, and the fosterer of
all that was best in his nature. When David Copperfield announces
his second marriage to readers, he pays fulsome tribute to his new
wife, Agnes:

Clasped in my embrace, I held the source of every worthy aspiration I had
ever had; the centre of myself, the circle of my life, my own, my wife; my
love of whom was founded on a rock!   (ch. 62)

She is, as David reiterates at the end of his narrative, the one face
'shining on me like a Heavenly light by which I see all other objects'.
David and Agnes are therefore presented ultimately as centred on

one another in a marriage of true minds. To David they appear to be bound up in one another's embrace, but, as we know, it is David, not Agnes, who has another focus to his life: his profession as a writer. Writing to Angela Burdett Coutts on 16 May 1849 Dickens was to describe the ideal home as a 'World, in which a woman's course of influence and action is marked out by Heaven!' (*Letters*, v. 542.) The distinction he fails to draw is that although the home could be pictured as an exclusive and fulfilling world for women, most men of his class were also able to move in an alternative and larger world of professions and vocations. For Dickens, home was vocation enough for women and those who sought to break out of the pattern of domestic responsibilities were somehow renegade and perversely eccentric. Criticizing the ambitions of that early pioneer feminist, the American Amelia Jenks Bloomer, in the *Household Words* essay 'Sucking Pigs' in 1851 Dickens conjured up the figure of an English disciple of hers whom he christens 'Mrs. Bellows'. She is the prototype of Mrs Jellyby, and like her the object of patronizing fun:

If there were anything we could dispense with in Mrs. Bellows above all other things, we believe it would be a Mission. We should put the question thus to Mrs. Bellows: 'Apple of our eye, we well freely admit your inalien-able right to step out of your domestic path into any phase of public appearance and palaver that pleases you best; but we doubt the wisdom of such a sally. Beloved one, does your sex seek influence in the civilised world? Surely it possesses influence therein to no mean extent, and has possessed it since the civilised world was. Should we love our Julia (assum-ing, for the sake of argument, the Christian name of Mrs. Bellows to be Julia)—should we love our Julia better, if she were a Member of Parlia-ment, a Parochial Guardian, a High Sheriff, a Grand Juror, or a woman distinguished for her able conduct in the chair? Do we not, on the con-trary, rather seek in the society of our Julia, a haven of refuge from Mem-bers of Parliament, Parochial Guardians, High Sheriffs, Grand Jurors, and able chairmen? Is not the home-voice of our Julia as the song of a bird, after considerable bow-wowing out of doors?[26]

Julia Bellows and her sisters are being advised that their mission was properly and essentially a domestic one. At home she could provide the 'haven of refuge' as a relief from the noisy world of men and here she could work a blessed, but essentially unseen, influence.

Three of Dickens's most distinctive female characters seem

variously determined to evade, challenge, and even upset this cosy
domestic ideal. Rosa Dartle in *David Copperfield* and Miss Wade in
Little Dorrit can seem thoroughly disconcerting, but with Madame
Defarge in *A Tale of Two Cities* readers are faced with a woman who
is uncomfortably vindictive and determinedly maleficent. David
Copperfield is disturbed by Rosa Dartle's mien and mannerisms on
his first acquaintance with her and he seems not to know what to
make of a woman who 'never said anything she wanted to say, outright; but hinted it, and made a great deal more of it by this practice'.
Rosa's physiognomy is equally unsettling:

a slight short figure, dark, and not agreeable to look at, but with some
appearance of good looks too, who attracted my attention: perhaps
because I had not expected to see her; perhaps because I found myself
sitting opposite to her; perhaps because of something really remarkable in
her. She had black hair and eager black eyes, and was thin, and had a scar
upon her lip. It was an old scar—I would rather call it, seam, for it was not
discolored, and had healed years ago—which had once cut through her
mouth, downward towards the chin, but was now barely visible across the
table, except above and on her upper lip, the shape of which it had altered.
I concluded in my own mind that she was about thirty years of age, and
that she wished to be married. She was a little dilapidated—like a house—
with having been so long to let; yet had, as I have said, an appearance of
good looks. Her thinness seemed to be the effect of some wasting fire
within her, which found a vent in her gaunt eyes.   (ch. 20)

David is, as ever, an acute observer of physical characteristics, but his
unease is evident in his searching for terms to describe her. Steerforth might insist that Rosa is 'restless' and 'all edge', but David
concentrates on the scar as if it were symptomatic of his own unease
with a mystery of a woman whom he cannot explain. When David
describes Rosa's fearful confrontation with the shamed and deserted
Emily in chapter 50, she retains much of her evasiveness, but
now she speaks 'outright' and with a passion. Both her words
and her actions now exhibit a quality that can only be described as
sadistic:

Rosa Dartle sprang up from her seat; recoiled; and in recoiling struck at
her, with a face of such malignity, so darkened and disfigured by passion,
that I had almost thrown myself between them. The blow, which had no
aim, fell upon the air. As she now stood panting, looking at her with the
utmost detestation that she was capable of expressing, and trembling from

head to foot with rage and scorn, I thought I had never seen such a sight, and never could see such another.

'*You* love him? *You?*' she cried, with her clenched hand quivering as if it only wanted a weapon to stab the object of her wrath. Emily had shrunk out of my view. There was no reply.

'And tell that to *me*,' she added, 'with your shameful lips? Why don't they whip these creatures! If I could order it to be done, I should have this girl whipped to death.'

Rosa is a bitter and disappointed woman, frustrated by Steerforth's disdain for her, and ill at ease with both men and women. She is clearly not designed as a 'haven of refuge' for any man, but she is truly fearsome when confronted by a female rival whom she despises and in whose humiliation she actively rejoices. Dickens appears to have been as mystified by her as David evidently is. The last we hear of her is that she is a 'dark, withered woman' still retaining the white scar on her lip, still the companion of Mrs Steerforth and seemingly reconciled to her edgy spinsterhood.

Miss Wade, the 'self-tormentor' of *Little Dorrit*, claims to bear 'the misfortune of not being a fool' and could have been 'habitually imposed upon, instead of habitually discerning the truth'. Or so she insists. She was born illegitimate and seems to cherish the chip she carries round on her shoulder. Significantly enough, readers who never learn her Christian name, are obliged to identify her by her spinsterly title. She is intelligent and articulate, but she is essentially a misfit and an outsider: awkward with others and unconventional both in her emotional life and her sexual inclinations. John Forster was manifestly uneasy with her character and her account of herself. He found her interpolated autobiography ('The History of a Self-Tormentor', bk. 2, ch. 21) the 'least interesting' part of *Little Dorrit* while admitting that the 'rare force of the likeness in the unlikeness' in the relationship Miss Wade forges with Tattycoram possessed 'much subtlety of intention' (*Life*, p. 625). She has, by her own and others' admission, 'an unhappy temper' which renders her a prickly and difficult employee and an even uneasier companion and lover. She interprets affection as condescension and entrapment. Having broken off her engagement to an officer in the East India Company, and having indulged in a strangely charged but doomed relationship with Henry Gowan, she takes up with the orphaned foundling Tattycoram, the sullen and much patronized maid of the Meagleses:

I found a girl, in various circumstances of whose position there was a singular likeness to my own, and in whose character I was interested and pleased to see much of the rising against swollen patronage and selfishness, calling themselves kindness, protection, benevolence, and other fine names, which I have described as inherent in my nature. I often heard it said too, that she had 'an unhappy temper.' Well understanding what was meant by the convenient phrase, and wanting a companion with a knowledge of what I knew, I thought I would try to release the girl from her bondage and sense of injustice. I have no occasion to relate that I succeeded.

We have been together ever since, sharing my small means. (*Little Dorrit*, bk. 2, ch. 22)

When Arthur Clennam visits the two women together in their lodgings at Calais, Dickens's account of the approach to the house is marked by the reiteration of a single adjective which seems to sum up Miss Wade's choices: the house is dead, the shrubs outside are dead, the wall is dead, the gateway is dead, and even the doorknocker produces 'a dead, flat, surface-tapping that seemed not to have depth enough in it to penetrate even the cracked door' (bk. 2, ch. 20). Arthur senses that the two women are unhappy and 'how each of the two natures must be constantly tearing the other to pieces'. The sterile relationship is not to last. Miss Wade may be a marginal character in *Little Dorrit*, but she is a disturbingly memorable one. She has disconcerted as much as she has fascinated critics of the novel. As Michael Slater shrewdly remarks: 'there seems to be a secret bond of sympathy between [Dickens's] imagination and the creature he is ostensibly encouraging us to view with hatred, fear or repulsion'.[27] Many readers are, however, left with the feeling that much as she quickened the imagination of her creator, she also mystified him.

Dickens's disturbance at the phenomenon of Thérèse Defarge in *A Tale of Two Cities* derives from a far more easily identifiable source. Madame Defarge is the product of desperately diseased times and she resorts to desperate appliances in order to relieve them. To her adoring husband she is 'a great woman . . . a strong woman, a grand woman, a frightfully grand woman' (bk. 2, ch. 16) and to her revolutionary admirers she is 'superb' and 'an Angel' (bk. 3, ch. 12). Her most famous declaration of intent—'tell Wind and Fire where to stop, but don't tell me'—does, however, suggest that her frightful grandness lies in the fact that she is essentially an Angel of Death. Her statement is also more than a little theatrical. Although Dickens gives her thirst for vengeance a proper foundation in what has happened to her and her family as a girl on the Evrémonde estates, she is more than just a child of *ancien régime* injustices and a victim of *ancien régime* privileges. She is in many ways a development of the calculatingly murderous Lady Macbeth. That is what Dickens most fears about her. She is 'unsexed' and has abandoned or suppressed all that he holds to be properly 'feminine'. She is, like Lady Macbeth, married but conspicuously childless (perhaps even worse in Dickens's eyes is the fact that she does not even have the memory of having given suck to toothless babes). Nothing softens her, nothing inspires her compassion, and nothing seems to hold her back from acting yet more bloodily than the male revolutionary mob that she inspires. She claps her hands 'as at a play' when Foulon is hanged from a lamp-post and it is she who, once the governor of the Bastille has been hacked to death, put her foot on his neck 'and with her cruel knife—long ready—hewed his head off' (bk. 2, ch. 21). It is she who is so determined to destroy the Evrémondes to the end of their blood line that she seeks out Lucie and her daughter ('the Evrémonde people are to be exterminated, and the wife and child must follow the husband and the father' (bk. 3, ch. 13)). Madame Defarge may personify the negative, self-destructive, undoing side of the French Revolution, but she is also a negation of the 'womanly'.

The one woman in Dickens's novels who manages to unite what the novelist would deem to be the 'womanly' with a determined independence is Betsey Trotwood. What may seem to prejudice a reader's full and appreciative view of her as a key figure amongst Dickens's women characters is her determined eccentricity. Her tetchy exit from chapter 1 of *David Copperfield* (having hit Mr Chillip over the head with her bonnet on hearing that the new-born baby is a boy rather than a girl) or her noisy antipathy to donkeys may take precedence in a reader's memory of her over her quite extraordinary daring in opening her home to Mr Dick and her later generosity in adopting David himself. She is neither particularly prepossessing in her appearance nor outwardly warm, as even David admits remembering his first acquaintance with her:

My aunt was a tall, hard-featured lady, but by no means ill-looking. There was an inflexibility in her face, in her voice, in her gait and carriage, amply sufficient to account for the effect she had made upon a gentle creature like my mother, but her features were rather handsome than otherwise, though unbending and austere. I particularly noticed that she had a very quick, bright eye. Her hair, which was grey, was arranged in two plain divisions, under what I believe would be called a mob-cap . . . Her dress was of a lavender color, and perfectly neat; but scantily made, as if she desired to be as little encumbered as possible . . . She wore a gentleman's gold watch . . . she had some linen at her throat not unlike a shirt-collar, and things at her wrists like little shirt-wristbands.   (ch. 13)

It is only gradually that we learn of the qualities which render her so truly admirable. She has taken in Mr Dick ('a sort of distant connexion') because his own brother, in whose care he had been left, sought to send him 'to some private asylum place'. She stoutly defends her action to the boy David:

'So I stepped in,' said my aunt, 'and made him an offer. I said, Your brother's sane—a great deal more sane than you are, or ever will be, it is to be hoped. Let him have his little income, and come and live with me. *I* am not afraid of him, *I* am not proud, *I* am ready to take care of him, and shall not ill-treat him as some people (beside the asylum folks) have done. After a good deal of squabbling,' said my aunt, 'I got him; and he has been here ever since. He is the most friendly and amenable creature in existence, and as for advice!—But nobody knows what that man's mind is, except myself.'   (ch. 13)

This is manifestly *not* the action of a mere eccentric. It is an act of uncommon courage, just as her resolve to take on David (on Mr Dick's 'invaluable' advice) is. For a single woman to have assumed such a double burden would be remarkable enough in our own time (regardless of the legal technicalities now involved); for a Victorian woman to have done so might even have been viewed as scandalous by Dickens's contemporaries. As we also learn, however, Betsey's ostensible prejudice against men is rooted in the fact that she is properly *not* a single woman, but a once ill-used married one, a sometime wife whose wayward and exploitative husband turns up periodically. Her tenderness, as much as her innate strength, is made clear to us when she reveals to David in chapter 54 her secret visit to her dying husband in hospital and when David observes her tears at the subsequent funeral ('After the relief of tears, she soon became composed, and even cheerful'). It is possible that some readers may feel inclined to see Mr Dick as a surrogate, but impotent, husband, and David as a surrogate child, but David's narrative surely persuades us that Betsey is instinctively generous in her emotional life as much as in her financial dealings. She may have proved unsympathetic to David's mother, but she proves to be splendidly supportive of David's 'child-wife', Dora. If she appears unconventional and highly individual in her decisions and opinions, she is also a central embodiment of what Dickens most treasured in women, the heaven-sent talent to make a 'haven' of well-run home.

Given the nature of Dickens's prejudices concerning their domestic role, it is unlikely that he would have wholeheartedly espoused the cause of women's political and social emancipation. Given his prejudices about the state of contemporary politics, it is highly improbable that he would have seen female suffrage either as a reasoned response to the disadvantages endured by women or even as a pressing social concern. Nevertheless, he remained a liberal when it came to most matters of public debate. When, some months before his death, he accepted the approbation of a friend following a particularly forthright speech that he had made in Birmingham, he affirmed that he had been 'determined that [his] Radicalism should not be called in question' (*Letters*, xii. 484: 2 Mar. 1870). In that speech he reaffirmed what he had famously defined as his political creed in September 1869: 'My faith in the people governing, is, on the whole, infinitesimal; my faith in The People governed, is, on the whole illimitable.'[28] Three months later he explained this creed to his Birmingham audience in more detail:

When I was here last autumn I made . . . a short confession of my political faith, or perhaps I should better say, want of faith. It imported that I have very little faith in the people who govern us—please to observe 'people' there will be with a small 'p', but that I have great confidence in the People whom they govern: please observe 'People' there with a large 'p'. This was shortly and elliptically stated; and was, with no evil intention I am absolutely sure, in some quarters inversely explained. Perhaps as the inventor of a certain extravagant fiction, but one which I do see rather frequently quoted as if there were grains of truth at the bottom of it, a fiction called 'The Circumlocution Office', and perhaps also as the writer of an idle book or two, whose public opinions are not obscurely stated—perhaps in these respects I do not sufficiently bear in mind Hamlet's caution to speak by the card lest equivocation should undo me.[29]

This is the Dickens who in 1868 had turned down the 'flattering' request that he should stand as a Member of Parliament for Birmingham with what he called his 'stereotyped phrase ... that no consideration on earth would induce me to become a candidate for representation of any place, in the House of Commons' (*Letters*, xii. 182: 13 Sept. 1868). He had no intention of joining the governing classes. The offer of a parliamentary candidacy had been made to him in the wake of the Second Reform Bill. The Bill, enacted by Disraeli's Conservative Government in 1867, had both redistributed and created new seats and had enfranchised all rate-paying householders in boroughs, whether they were house owners or not. Most significantly, it had increased the male electorate by nearly a million, most of these new voters being drawn from the urban working classes. For once in his life Dickens had been prepared to express a modest enthusiasm for what the 1867 reforms might achieve in the long run:

My own strong impression is that whatever change the new Reform Bill may effect, will be very gradual indeed and quite wholesome. Numbers of the middle class who seldom or never voted before, will vote now; and the greater part of the new voters will in the main be wiser as to their electoral responsibilities, and more seriously desirous to discharge them for the common good than the bumptious singers of Rule Britannia, Our dear old Church of England, and all the rest of it. (*Letters*, xii. 172: 24 Aug. 1868)

Here then was some hope for the political future. It was a hope which Dickens bedded in 'the People', men and (given the same 'wholesome' and 'gradual' process) perhaps even women who promoted steady progress and social evolution. These would be men and women who had no vested interest in maintaining the status quo exemplified by Chancery and the Circumlocution Office and who would probably take no delight either in backward-looking state funerals or in self-glorifying Great Exhibitions. These would be the men and women of the future who defined themselves both against the dead hand of tradition and the 'bumptious' Podsnappery that he had so consistently satirized in his work.

CHAPTER 3

THE LITERARY CONTEXT

In 1872 Dickens's erstwhile friend G. H. Lewes recalled his first meeting with the young author at his Doughty Street house some thirty-six years before. Lewes had written flatteringly about the recently completed *Pickwick Papers* and the proud author had asked him to call on him. While waiting for his host to appear, Lewes was horrified to observe only 'three-volume novels and travel books' on Dickens's bookshelves. He was still prepared to draw an unfavourable intellectual conclusion from this fact after Dickens's death:

A man's library expresses much of his hidden life. I did not expect to find a bookworm, nor even a student, in the marvellous 'Boz'; but nevertheless this collection of books was a shock. He shortly came in, and his sunny presence quickly dispelled all misgivings. He was then, as to the last, a delightful companion, full of sagacity as well as animal spirits; but I came away more impressed with the fulness of life and energy than with any sense of distinction.

When, some two years after their first meeting, Lewes visited Dickens at his new residence at Devonshire Terrace he again took a critical look at the now expanded library, and again linked it to its owner's character and cast of mind:

The well-known paper boards of the three-volume novel no longer vulgarized the place; a goodly array of standard works, well-bound, showed a more respectable and conventional ambition; but there was no physiognomy in the collection. A greater change was visible in Dickens himself. In these two years he had remarkably developed. His conversation turned on graver subjects than theatres and actors, periodicals and London life. His interest in public affairs, especially in social questions, was keener. He still remained completely outside philosophy, science and the higher literature, and was too unaffected a man to pretend to feel any interest in them.[1]

Lewes's sharply critical observation is that of an intellectual snob, one who was clearly determined to imply that Dickens's reading habits, both established and newly developed, were bland. We know from the surviving inventory of Dickens's library at Devonshire Terrace what kind of 'standard works' it contained and with this information we can begin to dispute the idea that his collection of books represented little more than 'a respectable and conventional ambition'.[2] Apart from reference works and encyclopaedias there was, as we might expect, a good deal of drama from the sixteenth, seventeenth, and eighteenth centuries, prominent among them being collections of the plays of Shakespeare and Jonson. The prose literature in Dickens's library included editions of Pepys's Diary, Bacon's essays, Clarendon's *History of the Rebellion*, Hume's and Goldsmith's histories of England, Gibbon's *Decline and Fall of the Roman Empire*, and a translation of Thiers's *French Revolution*. The 'standard' fiction which had replaced what Lewes had considered to be the 'vulgar' new three-decker novels, now included sets of the collected works of Scott, Fielding, Richardson, Goldsmith, Smollett, and Sterne, while the poetry embraced volumes of Spenser, Milton, Waller, Dryden, Pope, Chatterton, Crabbe, Cowper, Wordsworth, Coleridge, Byron, Southey, Thomas Campbell, and Thomas Moore. Works by Dickens's British and American contemporaries in the library included the 1843 collection of the poems of Tennyson, Longfellow's *Hyperion* of 1839, Lowell's *Offering* of 1842, and Emerson's *Essays* of 1841, as well as the major early works of Carlyle (including *The French Revolution*). There were also sixty-eight volumes of a seventy-volume set of the works of Voltaire in French. Despite the fact that there was little classical literature (apart from Ovid's *Metamorphoses*) and relatively little that might have been described at the time as 'philosophical' or 'scientific' literature (though Dickens owned Carlyle's translation of Goethe's *Wilhelm Meister* and a copy of Lessing's *Laocoön*), this is no mean collection. As to what Lewes calls the 'higher' literature, Dickens's notable intolerance of theory would probably explain the absence of anything with an English Benthamite tinge as well as of any volumes of what was once called the 'higher criticism' of the Bible associated with German universities. Again, given his religious prejudices, it is also most unlikely that any theology, church history, or controversy emanating from the Tractarian circle of Newman and Pusey would have found its way onto his shelves.

Given what we know from the fragment of autobiography of

Dickens's boyhood reading habits, from the call slips he used in the British Museum Library in the early 1830s, and from the list of books in his library in 1844, it is clear that he was, even by the demanding standards of his own time, a well-read man. Yet it is also clear that Lewes was right in concluding that Dickens was no bookworm and that he possessed no real inclination to be a scholar in the nineteenth-century sense of that term. His reading was substantially confined to the English literary tradition perhaps because his formal education had left him with little command, and possibly rather less love, of Latin literature. He may well have had no access at all to Greek. As a glance at the notes added by recent editors of Dickens's novels and letters serve to show, the allusions, echoes, quotations, and citations of a wide range of English classics indicate a considerable familiarity with the native literary tradition and particularly with the plays of Shakespeare. The notes to the World's Classics edition of *David Copperfield*, for example, reveal that the novel contains five quotations each from *Hamlet* and *Macbeth* and one each from *Othello* and *Julius Caesar*. *David Copperfield* also includes allusions to two poems by Burns, one to a poem (*The Lady of the Lake*) and one to a novel (*Rob Roy*) by Scott, three to poems by Moore, and one each to works by Addison, Johnson, Goldsmith, Watts, Dibdin, and Byron. There are also seven allusions to lines from the New Testament and two to lines from the Old Testament, and several to popular songs from the eighteenth century. Although there is one citation of Horace in the novel, here as elsewhere Dickens makes no attempt to parade his limited knowledge of Greek and Roman literature. On the one hand he clearly felt no need to show off, but we can also assume that he was not as well equipped as a contemporary such as Thackeray would be to allude to classical literature. Thackeray's thorough public school training in the ancient languages gave him an easy fluency of allusion that Dickens completely lacked (the notes to the World's Classics edition of *The Newcomes*, for example, show that there are no fewer than twelve citations in Latin of Horace, three of Virgil, two of Juvenal, and one of Ovid, as well as twenty-two Latin phrases or proverbs; there are also two allusions to Homer's *Iliad* and two uses of Greek phrases). That Dickens was perfectly adept at demonstrating his acquaintance with Latin literature is clear from the scenes in *Dombey and Son* set at Dr Blimber's school at Brighton. Blimber's school manages to get 'every description of Greek and

Latin vegetable ... off the driest twigs of boys'. Nevertheless, Dickens himself prefers to *suggest* the nature of these classical vegetables rather than to specify them. Although the classics were integral to the nineteenth century's understanding of the idea of learning, it is evident that Dickens was not especially concerned to prove himself a distinctly *learned* writer. Even the fact that he rarely resorts to Latin tags and phrases, beyond familiar or technical ones, may be an acknowledgement of the fact that only a limited percentage of his Victorian readers would have readily picked up more complex allusions. Dickens, who was particularly sensitive both to his readers and to his sales, would always have recognized that too exclusive a range of classical reference would probably have left many of his undereducated male readers, and virtually all of his women readers, floundering in a sea of incomprehension. Given the steady decline of classical education during the twentieth century his eschewal of such reference may well come as a moderate relief to many twenty-first-century readers.

Dickens the 'Post-Romantic'

Dickens remains both an extraordinarily allusive writer and one firmly rooted in the literary culture of his own times. He would, were he not most readily counted as a 'Victorian' writer, be properly described as a 'post-Romantic'. His earliest publications seem to chime in with the ebullient and restless mood of the mid-1830s, but the roots of that restless ebullience lie in a development of, and a reaction against, many of the leading preoccupations and ideas of the English Romantics. It is significant that by the time of the publication of *Pickwick Papers* the most prominent figures in British Romanticism were dead. Only the long-lived Wordsworth, who was to be appointed Poet Laureate in 1843 in succession to Southey, could still be described as 'flourishing'. When in 1844 the critic Richard Hengist Horne published his *A New Spirit of the Age* only four of the thirty-nine authors discussed in the two volumes could readily be classed as what modern critics would call 'Romantics'. The achievement of these four writers—Wordsworth, Leigh Hunt, Walter Savage Landor, and Mary Shelley—might indeed have then been summed up in the almost patronizing terms in which Horne describes Wordsworth and Hunt: 'laurelled veterans' whose work has been 'so long before the public . . . that it will, perhaps, at first impression, be considered that there was no necessity for including them in this work'.[3] Despite their eminence and influence, they are also somewhat *passé*. The subjects of the majority of the essays are new writers, some of whose reputations are nowadays largely forgotten and others who had only just begun to make a significant mark on public sensibilities. These include Tennyson, Macaulay, Carlyle, Bulwer-Lytton, Browning, Elizabeth Barrett, and Harriet Martineau. It is testimony to the degree to which Dickens seemed to be representative of this 'new' *Zeitgeist* that Horne placed him prominently as the subject of the lead essay in the first volume. Unlike the often rarefied work of the older poets he discusses, Horne detected a new directness in Dickens's fiction:

The true characteristics of Mr. Dickens' mind are strongly and definitively marked—they are objective, and always have a practical tendency. His universality does not extend beyond the verge of the actual and concrete. The ideal and the elementary are not his region.[4]

Unlike the Romantic poets, therefore, Dickens writes predominantly about everyday life, but, as Horne's essay implies, he is also capable of transforming that impression of urban reality through the startling originality of his imagination. The 'practicality' that he admires in Dickens's work is interpreted as part and parcel of a new way of looking at things, less strictly idealistic and individualistic and more responsive to a wide range of social sensations. Though rooted in a long fictional tradition, Dickens emerges as the exemplary artist of a new age, one who is both an 'instinctive' writer and one who exhibits 'a larger number of faithful pictures and records of the middle and lower classes of England of the present period, than can be found in any other modern writer'.[5]

Dickens's response to two of Horne's older writers, both of them on the fringes of what many modern readers might now assume forms the central canon of English Romantic writing, is particularly revealing. He was personally acquainted with both Walter Savage Landor (1775–1864) and James Henry Leigh Hunt (1784–1859) and was prepared to include fictional portraits of both in *Bleak House*. The portraits appear to have been recognized by their contemporaries, and Dickens himself slyly admitted to a correspondent on 6 May 1852 that Lawrence Boythorn was a 'most exact' representation of

Landor (*Letters*, vi. 666). He had met Landor in 1840 and had lodged with him in his house in Bath. It was in this house that Dickens is said to have first thought of the character of Little Nell, a fact that inspired Landor to proclaim that he would willingly have burned the house to the ground in order that 'no meaner association should ever desecrate the birthplace of Nell' (*Letters*, ii. 36: 1 Mar. 1840). It was perhaps this propensity for rash extravagance on Landor's part that influenced the fictional character of the man whom Mr Jarndyce describes as having been 'the most impetuous boy in the world, and he is now the most impetuous man. He was then the loudest boy in the world, and he is now the loudest man. He was then the heartiest and sturdiest boy in the world, and he is now the heartiest and sturdiest man' (*Bleak House*, ch. 9). This 'tremendous fellow' had also doubtless won Dickens's admiration (the novelist had named his second son, Walter, after him) but, as the novel suggests, impetuosity and loudness have their embarrassing drawbacks in a world in which a degree of polite tolerance might be expected. When Esther and Mr Jarndyce's party arrive at Boythorn's country estate, for example, their coach is greeted by their irate host's almost comic, but nonetheless intemperate, rage: 'By Heaven . . . this is a most infamous coach. It is the most flagrant example of an abominable public vehicle that ever encumbered the face of the earth. It is twenty-five minutes after its time, this afternoon. The coachman ought to be put to death' (ch. 18). It is this same irrational and provocative intemperance that so vexes Boythorn's aristocratic neighbour, Sir Leicester Dedlock. Landor's essential generosity of spirit may have got him off relatively lightly, despite Dickens's misgivings about his constitutional extravagance. The same cannot be said, however, of the thinly disguised portrait of Leigh Hunt as the contemptible dilettante Harold Skimpole. Readers first encounter Skimpole in chapter 6 of *Bleak House*. He is introduced to Esther by the hugely tolerant Mr Jarndyce as 'the finest creature upon earth—a child'. It is scarcely a helpful thing to say. Jarndyce explains that this 'child' is a grown-up who 'in simplicity and freshness, and enthusiasm, and a fine guileless inaptitude for all worldly affairs . . . is a perfect child'. At dinner Esther learns more about him from his own lips:

Mr. Skimpole had been educated for the medical profession, and had once lived, in his professional capacity, in the household of a German prince

. . . And he told us, with great humour, that when he was wanted to bleed the prince, or physic any of his people, he was generally found lying on his back, in bed, reading the newspapers, or making fancy sketches in pencil, and couldn't come. The prince, at last objecting to this, 'in which,' said Mr. Skimpole, in the frankest manner, 'he was perfectly right,' the engagement terminated, and Mr. Skimpole having (as he added, with delightful gaiety) 'nothing to live upon but love, fell in love, and married, and surrounded himself with rosy cheeks'.

Skimpole then proceeds to explain his philosophy of life. He is afflicted, he says, by two of the 'oldest infirmities in the world', having no idea of time and no idea of money:

Well! So he had got on in life, and here he was! He was very fond of reading the papers, very fond of making fancy sketches with a pencil, very fond of nature, very fond of art. All he asked of society was, to let him live. *That* wasn't much. His wants were few. Give him the papers, conversation, music, mutton, coffee, landscape, fruit in season, a few sheets of Bristol-board, and a little claret, and he asked no more . . . He said to the world, 'Go your several ways in peace! Wear red coats, blue coats, lawn sleeves, put pens behind your ears, wear aprons; go after glory, holiness, commerce, trade, any object you prefer; only—let Harold Skimpole live!'

Skimpole expects a living from the world without actually earning it, either in the gentlemanly professions or in trade. He is, as the developing plot makes plain, a man of consummate laziness and consummate selfishness, one whose professed ideals are undermined by his actions (notably the betrayal of the sick Jo to Inspector Bucket in exchange for money). The last we hear of him is from the evidently exasperated Esther who notes in chapter 61 that Skimpole has left a posthumous autobiography in which he 'showed himself to have been the victim of a combination on the part of mankind against an amiable child'. He has also described the charitable Mr Jarndyce as 'the Incarnation of Selfishness'.

Dickens was probably stung into his satirical portrait of Skimpole by the appearance of Leigh Hunt's *Autobiography* in 1850, a volume which had described a visit to Lord Byron in Italy in 1821 during which Hunt had begun to find Byron distinctly uncongenial company. The *Autobiography* had ostensibly regretted the vehemence of an attack on Byron that Hunt had published on his return to England, but it had also attempted to offer a good deal of self-justification for the attack. What Dickens seems generally to resent about Skimpole's character and attitudes was something that he may have associated with the writers who formed the loose circle around Byron in exile: their fecklessness, their élitism, and their lack of social responsiveness. Interestingly, having first given Skimpole the Christian name 'Leonard', Dickens changed it to Harold, almost certainly as an echo of the title of Byron's poem *Childe Harold's Pilgrimage* (1812). It was not just Hunt's ingratitude that he most readily linked with Byron's circle but a pervasive *childish* irresponsibility, partly cultivated, partly congenital. It was something he may also have linked to the aristocratic birth and aristocratic assumptions of both Byron and Shelley. Dickens was, as we shall see, generally convinced of the social virtues of work and particularly of the professional status that a modern writer properly earned through work. He was not sympathetic to an old, gentlemanly ethic of leisurely nonchalance, particularly if that nonchalance entailed banishing due earnestness. It is in fact in the earnestness of a writer's vocation that Dickens beds his own professed dedication to literature. This quality, which David Copperfield sums up as 'thorough-going, ardent, and sincere earnestness', is singularly lacking in Harold Skimpole. It is also something that the rash and intemperate Boythorn seems to have forgotten.

When Harold Skimpole speaks of being 'very fond of nature' and 'very fond of art' we may also detect something further in Dickens's ambiguity about certain leading aspects of Romantic thought. A comparison of the inventory of his Devonshire Terrace library in 1844 with the catalogue of books sold posthumously in 1870 suggests that the novelist owned, and therefore probably knew, a good deal of what we now assume to be the 'canonical' poetry written in the closing years of the eighteenth and in the first quarter of the nineteenth centuries.[6] He was therefore well equipped both to cite and, when the occasion arose, to disparage. In addition to the six volumes of Wordsworth's *Works* published in 1836 he also owned the 1850 edition of *The Prelude*. In addition to the collected poems of Coleridge, Burns, Scott, and Byron that he possessed in 1844, he had since acquired the three-volume edition of Shelley's poetry edited by the poet's widow in 1847, the 1844 edition of the *Poetical Works* of Leigh Hunt, and, belatedly, the 1868 collection of Keats edited by Lord Houghton. Conspicuously enough, Dickens seems never to have bothered to acquire any edition of the poetry of William Blake (though some critics have made much of parallels between the work of the two writers). We can therefore assume that he was reasonably well informed about the debates about the natural world and about the nature of the imagination which so preoccupied the first generation of English Romantics. Certainly his own preoccupation with 'fancy' and 'imagination' (though, unlike Coleridge, he does not distinguish between the terms) suggests a real debt to his literary predecessors. A lack of any imaginative alternative to a world-view determined by 'fact' is, of course, the fatal flaw that Dickens detects in the Utilitarian educational systems he describes in *Hard Times*:

'Fact, fact, fact!' said the gentleman. And 'Fact, fact, fact!' repeated Thomas Gradgrind.

'You are in all things to be regulated and governed,' said the gentleman, 'by fact. We hope to have before long, a board of fact, composed of commissioners of fact, who will force the people to be a people of fact, and of nothing but fact. You must discard the word Fancy altogether. You have nothing to do with it.'   (bk. 1, ch. 2)

The Dickens, who like David Copperfield, so fondly and earnestly recalled the awakening, and then the sustaining, of his own boyhood fancy through literature firmly trusted in the creative, even spiritual, power of that imaginative faculty. Although he could not have read it, Dickens would have been in full sympathy with the account offered by his contemporary John Stuart Mill of his spiritual awakening from the restrictions of the strict and factual Benthamite education his father had given him. In the fifth chapter of his *Autobiography* Mill describes his discovery of Wordsworth when in a state of profound emotional dejection:

This state of my thoughts and feelings made the fact of my reading Wordsworth for the first time (in the autumn of 1828), an important event in my life. I took up the collection of his poems from curiosity, with no expectation of mental relief from it, though I had before resorted to poetry with that hope. In the worst period of my depression, I had read through the whole of Byron . . . to try whether a poet, whose peculiar department was supposed to be that of the intenser feelings, could rouse any feeling in me. As might be expected, I got not good from this reading, but the reverse . . . His Harold and his Manfred had the same burden on them which I had . . . But while Byron was exactly what did not suit my condition, Wordsworth was exactly what did . . . In the first place, these

poems addressed themselves powerfully to one of the strongest of my
pleasurable susceptibilities, the love of rural objects and natural scenery
. . . But Wordsworth would never have had any great effect on me, if he
had merely placed before me beautiful pictures of natural scenery . . .
What made Wordsworth's poems a medicine for my state of mind, was
that they expressed, not mere outward beauty, but states of feeling, and of
thought coloured by feeling, under the excitement of beauty. They seemed
to be the very culture of feelings, which I was in quest of.[7]

Mill's phrase 'the very culture of feelings' precisely captures what
Dickens believed to be the essence of the imaginative sympathy
between writer and reader that books fostered. Although his own
boyhood imagination had been stirred primarily by prose fiction
rather than by poetry, he consistently maintained, as the afflicted
David Copperfield put it, that books 'had kept alive my fancy, and
my hope of something beyond that place and time'.

  Although Dickens may not have shared Mill's sense of disillusion
with the gloomy burden of Byron's heroes, we can certainly detect a
general suspicion of Byronic individualism and earnestlessness. Yet
he was also unlikely to have been especially stirred by Wordsworth's
poetry. There are indications of an undercurrent of suspicion concerning the Romantic enthusiasm for nature in his own work. Indeed
where Wordsworth claims to have found sustenance in recalling the
beauties of the Wye valley, Dickens insists that *his* comfort came
from an imaginative association with the characters of eighteenth-
century fiction. There is certainly a lack of direct sympathy with the
idea of nature as a 'law and impulse': an educator, healer, and
inspirer. The closest we get to a Wordsworthian sense of nature as a
consoler comes towards the end of *David Copperfield* when the narrator has retired to Switzerland following the death of Dora. The Alps
at first reflect his sense of loneliness:

If those awful solitudes had spoken to my heart, I did not know it. I had
found sublimity and wonder in the dread heights and precipices, in the
roaring torrents, and the wastes of ice and snow; but as yet, they had
taught me nothing else.

In the next two paragraphs, however, David recognizes a subtle shift
in his meditations. It is a 'classic' moment of Romantic inspiration,
where a charged landscape and an expectant and responsive observer
coincide:

I came, one evening before sunset, down into a valley, where I was to rest. In the course of my descent to it, by the winding track along the mountain-side, from which I saw it shining far below, I think some long-unwonted sense of beauty and tranquillity, some softening influence awakened by its peace, moved faintly in my breast. I remember pausing once, with a kind of sorrow that was not at all oppressive, not quite despairing. I remember almost hoping that some better change was possible within me.

I came into the valley, as the evening sun was shining on the remote heights of snow, that closed it in, like eternal clouds . . . In the quiet air, there was a sound of distant singing—shepherd voices; but, as one bright evening cloud floated midway along the mountain-side, I could almost have believed it came from there, and was not earthly music. All at once, in this serenity, great Nature spoke to me; and soothed me to lay down my weary head upon the grass, and weep as I had not wept yet, since Dora died! (ch. 58)

It is perhaps significant that, despite the fact that 'great Nature' seems to have spoken, it is a letter from Agnes that David is carrying with him that really proves the more eloquent speaker and instructor. Human voices rather than ethereal ones call him back to social contact and human responsiveness.

Dickens's descriptions of the Alps in his letters, his fiction, and in *Pictures from Italy* are particularly striking. Nevertheless he seems generally to have remained less enthused by landscape than he was by townscape. Even during his own extended sojourn in Switzerland, when he was writing *Dombey and Son*, he longed for the stimulus that London gave to his writing (*Letters*, iv. 612: 30 Aug. 1846). Where his descriptions of the open countryside, whether wild or cultivated, are commonly bland, his accounts of streets and street life have a special vividness. The confused ant-hill of London was to remain central to Dickens's imaginative and creative life. The more placid rhythms of rural life elude him as much as does an ability to observe and record the delicacies of a flower or the contours of a working landscape. Although he readily recognized the Romantic conventions of seeing Nature as the inspirer and the regenerator, few of Nature's voices echo directly in his novels. As a writer of fiction, Dickens generally remained distinctly unawed by its phenomena. One suspects that his satirical digs at Mrs Skewton's idle sentimentality about Nature in *Dombey and Son* may contain something of his own impatience with those who placed too high a store on being surprised by the joy occasioned by natural stimuli. When, for example, she has to be reminded of the name of the garden of Eden by her daughter, Mrs Skewton protests:

'I cannot help it. I never can remember those frightful names—without having your whole Soul and Being inspired by the sight of Nature; by the perfume,' said Mrs. Skewton, rustling a handkerchief that was faint and sickly with essences, 'of her artless breath . . .'

This calculatingly false old woman is presenting us with a travesty of Romantic passion, just as she overwhelms the natural with the artificial. She also emerges as a maintainer of an eighteenth-century, Marie Antoinettish escapism into a supposedly ideal world secluded from convention and fuss:

'I assure you, Mr. Dombey, Nature intended me for an Arcadian. I am thrown away in society. Cows are my passion. What I have ever sighed for, has been to retreat to a Swiss farm, and live entirely surrounded by cows—and china.' (ch. 21)

There is, of course, a real distinction between Mrs Skewton's artificial Swiss farm and David Copperfield's inspirational Swiss valley, but, as Dickens himself recognizes, both are distractions from the business of the real world of the mid-nineteenth century: the world of work, and the hum of urban life. It was to that world that he recalled David Copperfield and it was from that world that he dismissed Mrs Skewton's idle sentiments.

Dickens and his Contemporaries

In 1890 Alfred Tennyson recalled his friend R. C. Trench saying to him when both men were undergraduates: 'Tennyson, we cannot live in art.'[8] The poet claimed that Trench had stimulated him to write 'The Palace of Art' in response, a poem that embodied his own 'Godlike' belief that 'life is with man and for man'. Tennyson then quoted his own lines:

> Beauty, Good, and Knowledge are three sisters . . .
> That never can be sunder'd without tears.
> And he that shuts out Love, in turn shall be
> Shut out from Love, and on her threshold lie,
> Howling in outer darkness.

Given such positive sentiments on Tennyson's part, it is scarcely surprising that Dickens should have responded so readily to his verse. He owned a second edition of the poet's two-volume collection of 1843, volumes that brought together the earlier poems, such as 'The Palace of Art', with certain new poems, notably 'Ulysses' and 'Morte d'Arthur'. The posthumous catalogue of Dickens's library notes of these books that 'the numerous pencil marks made by Dickens against various Poems in these volumes show how attentively he had read them'.[9] He had been obliged to replace the first edition of these volumes because on 1 March 1844 he had sent the originals to a friend's daughter in the hope that they might prove 'acceptable to a mind such as hers'. As he helpfully told his correspondent:

I have marked with a pencil in the Index to each, those pieces which I should like her to read first—as being calculated to give her a good impression of the Poet's Genius. And will you say that I have sent her a copy which is not quite new, in preference to a new one; hoping that she might like it none the worse for having been my companion often, and for having been given to me by Tennyson himself? (*Letters*, iv. 58)

In Dickens's library at Devonshire Terrace there hung two proof-engravings in gilt frames, one showing Tennyson, the other Carlyle. Moreover, in April 1846, Dickens named his fourth son Alfred, in joint honour of the boy's godfathers, Tennyson and Alfred D'Orsay.

This personal and literary admiration for Tennyson stemmed not simply from an easy acceptance of his 'genius', but also from the direction that that genius had taken by 1840. In a singularly perceptive review of Tennyson's *Poems, Chiefly Lyrical* of 1830 his friend Arthur Hallam had related the volume to the 'melancholy' which, Hallam believed, so evidently 'characterises the spirit of modern poetry'. This Romantic 'melancholy' had, he went on to insist, determined 'the habit of seeking relief in idiosyncrasies rather than community of interest'. This had proved to be essentially an individualistic rather than a communal stimulus in modern literature, and it had inclined the modern writer towards isolation:

In the old times the poetic impulse went along with the general impulse of the nation; in these, it is a reaction against it, a check acting for conservation against a propulsion towards change ... Our inference, therefore, from this change in the relative position of artists to the rest of the community is, that modern poetry, in proportion to its depth and truth, is likely to have little immediate authority over public opinion.[10]

Hallam's untimely death in 1833 had been the cause of great private agony to Tennyson. It had also contributed to a new mood in his work. In the years after 1833 the poet had steadily weaned himself away from the 'melancholy' and occasional morbidity of his early verse into a much more positive address to questions of personal and social relationships. Gone were the agonizing loneliness of Mariana and the love-in-death of the Lady of Shalott, to be supplanted by the confident sweep of Ulysses' ambition 'to strive, to seek, to find, and not to yield' and the dying Arthur's consoling profession of faith in the perception that 'the old order changeth, yielding place to new'. Tennyson had effectively ceased both to 'live in art' and had moved beyond a poetry of lonely yearnings for extinction. Instead there had emerged something akin to a coincidence of the newly reasserted confidence of the poet with that of early Victorian England, a nation often carried away by Hallam's 'propulsion towards change'. This was the mood summed up in the famous assertion in 'Locksley Hall':

> Forward, forward, let us range.
> Let the great world spin for ever down the ringing grooves of change.
>
> Thro' the shadow of the globe we sweep into the younger day:
> Better fifty years of Europe than a cycle of Cathay.

Tennyson may have muddled his analogy with the railway (locomotives did not travel on grooved rails) but his espousal of a world of machines and heady speed is a good way away from the melancholy landscapes and creaking castles of his early verse. The sense of isolation, so prevalent in that early verse, had also been replaced by a fresh concern with human relationships, both private and public. Both themes would culminate in *In Memoriam AHH*, a poem that traces a movement away from a devastating grief to a joint celebration of love and evolutionary progress.

A picture of Dickens had appeared as the frontispiece to the first volume of Horne's *A New Spirit of the Age* in 1844, but one of Tennyson illustrated the second volume. It must have struck original readers that both men were particularly exemplary of the *Zeitgeist*. Dickens himself was probably aware of a tutelary presence informing that new mood of Tennyson's early Victorian poetry. Although,

as *In Memoriam AHH* of 1850 served to suggest, the guiding spirit of
Arthur Hallam had continued to inspire Tennyson's understanding
of an evolutionary process in human development, there are also
echoes of the earnest voice of the noisiest and most persuasive social
critic of the 1830s and 1840s: Thomas Carlyle. Dickens's display of a
portrait of Carlyle next to that of Tennyson in his library suggests
that he thought of the work of both writers as representative of the
best and most expressive literature of his own day. He was also
honoured by the friendship and regard of both men. What the early
Victorians most admired in Carlyle was his ability to disturb them. It
was he who seemed to have identified the nature of their restlessness
and who had put his finger on the racing pulse of the age. Horne
described this disturbance graphically:

Mr. Carlyle . . . has knocked out his window from the blind wall of his
century . . . We may say, too, that it is a window to the east; and that some
men complain of a certain bleakness in the wind which enters in at it;
when they should rather congratulate themselves with him on the aspect
of the new sun beheld through it, the orient of hope of which he has
discovered to their eyes.[11]

Carlyle was, and remains, an uncomfortable and disconcerting
writer: edgy, prickly, experimental, challenging. He seems, by turns,
to be persuasively sophisticated and provocatively direct. He was an
outsider to mainstream early Victorian culture in two ways: he had
been born in the same year as John Keats and was approaching 40
when he moved to London; he was also, by origin, a poor Scot who
had been educated at the University in Edinburgh which still basked
in the afterglow of the Scottish Enlightenment. Nevertheless, his
establishment of himself and his wife in London in 1834 coincided
with a widely perceived crisis in British political and social life in the
years following the Reform Bill, a crisis which he analysed in a series
of striking tracts. It was he who coined the term 'the Condition of
England' and it was he who pressed the English to come to terms
with the modern urbanized and industrialized novelty of their
condition.

In his essay *Signs of the Times* of 1829 Carlyle had characterized
the age in which he lived as 'the Mechanical Age', an 'Age of
Machinery, in every outward and inward sense of that word'. Ten
years later, in 1839, the long pamphlet entitled *Chartism* attempted

to address not simply the problem of working-class aspirations to political influence, but also the wider social ills afflicting the body politic. His rhetoric would find many echoes in the work of his contemporaries, and nowhere more so than in Dickens's novels and journalism:

'But what are we to do?' exclaims the practical man, impatiently on every side: 'Descend from speculation and the safe pulpit, down into the rough market-place, and say what can be done!'—O practical man, there seem very many things which practice and true manlike effort, in Parliament and out of it, might actually avail to do. But the first of all things . . . is to gird thyself up for actual doing; to know that thou actually either must do, or, as the Irish say, 'come out of that!'[12]

Carlyle consistently stresses the importance of individual effort and individual responsibility as a means of responding to social problems. Tutored by him, Dickens, who owned and avidly read most of Carlyle's major early works, would define his own sense of the importance of work and of the vocation of the earnest man to master unpropitious circumstances. He too would place great significance on an earnest response to the effervescence of the era in which they lived. Carlyle also seems to have confirmed his existing prejudices against Utilitarians, Parliamentarians, a 'do-nothing Aristocracy', and the pervasive spirit of 'Mammonism'. In *Chartism* the argument takes a sideswipe at the 'Paralytic Radicalism' of the Benthamites, a socio-philosophic system which 'gauges with Statistic measuring-reed, sounds with Philosophic Politico-Economic plummet the deep dark sea of troubles' and which yet ends up shrugging its shoulders in the belief that 'nothing can be done'.[13] In *Past and Present* of 1843 Carlyle cites Cromwell's famous words 'Ye are no Parliament. In the name of God,—go!' and then proceeds to damn the listless Reformed parliament of his day as little more than representative of the ills of the nation as a whole:

In sad truth, once more, how is our whole existence in these present days, built on Cant, Speciosity, Falsehood, Dilettantism; with this one serious Veracity in it: Mammonism! Dig down where you will, though the Parliament-floor or elsewhere, how infallibly do you, at spade's depth below the surface come upon this universal *Liars*-rock substratum! Much else is ornamental; true on barrel-heads, in pulpits, hustings, Parliamentary benches; but this is forever true and truest: 'Money does bring money's worth; Put money in your purse.' Here, if nowhere else, is the human soul still in thorough earnest; sincere with a prophet's sincerity: and 'the Hell of the English,' as Sauerteig said, 'is the infinite terror of Not getting on, especially Of not making money.' With results![14]

Past and Present contrasts the energy and certainty of a reforming medieval abbot with the lacklustre uncertainties of the 1840s. Although it looks back to the past with sympathy, in no way does it suggest that nostalgia for a lost past should inform the search for modern solutions to modern dilemmas. The study of history, Carlyle insists, is monitory. It provides warnings rather than examples. This principle was most forcefully outlined in his masterly *The French Revolution* of 1837, a book that Dickens once rashly claimed to have read five hundred times (*Letters*, vi. 452: summer 1851). This history, which dramatically and inventively recounts the events that marked the bloody downfalls of the French monarchy and of the Republic that succeeded it, is the key work that lies behind Dickens's own monitory novel about the period: *A Tale of Two Cities*.

Perhaps the most illuminating of Carlyle's works in terms of the literary culture of the first half of the nineteenth century is the series of lectures delivered in 1840, *On Heroes, Hero-Worship and the Heroic in History*. In the fifth lecture, given on 19 May, Carlyle took as his subject 'The Hero as Man of Letters'. The central issue that he addressed was the emergence of the modern writer, one whose address was to a wide public rather than to a coterie and one who earned his living from his books rather than relied on patronage. This kind of literary hero was innovative:

He is new, I say; he has hardly lasted above a century in the world yet. Never, till about a hundred ago, was there seen any figure of a Great Soul living apart in that anomalous manner; endeavouring to speak forth the inspiration that was in him by Printed Books, and find place and subsistence by what the world would please to give him for doing that. Much had been bought and sold in the marketplace; but the inspired wisdom of a Heroic Soul never till then, in that naked manner ... Few shapes of Heroism can be more unexpected![15]

The writers to whom Carlyle referred specifically in his lecture were Johnson, Rousseau, and Burns, but his words would have had major implications for his own literary contemporaries. They may well find a direct echo in David Copperfield's opening speculation as to whether or not he would prove the hero of his own life. They certainly formed the kind of declaration that reflected Dickens's insistence on his own professional status as a self-made, and self-maintained, man of letters.

It was this insistence on the professional status of the Victorian writer that formed a major bone of contention between Dickens and his sometime friend and great rival William Makepeace Thackeray. Thackeray who preferred to think of himself as a gentleman first and a writer second, tended to regard authorship as an occupation rather than as a sacred or professional vocation. Throughout his life he was to maintain this same casualness when it came both to defining and to exploiting his gifts. In 1847 he had quarrelled with John Forster over the issue of 'dignity of literature'. Dickens took Forster's side, writing in a particularly friendly letter to Thackeray of his own pride in what he had achieved:

I *do* sometimes please myself with thinking that my success has opened the way for good writers. And of this, I am quite sure now, and hope I shall be when I die—that in all my social doings I am mindful of this honour and dignity and always try to do something towards the quiet assertion of their right place. I am always possessed with the hope of leaving the position of literary men in England, something better and more independent than I found it.   (*Letters*, v. 227: 9 Jan. 1848)

He may, with mock modesty, have called this declaration 'a wild and egotistical fancy', but his words have a Carlylean earnestness about them.

Dickens wrote this letter at the time when he was publishing *Dombey and Son* and Thackeray had embarked on the successful serialization of *Vanity Fair*. The literary rivalry between the two men was new, but it was consciously pursued and was in many ways complementary. Dickens published in green-covered monthly parts; Thackeray in yellow. *Dombey and Son* was Dickens's seventh novel; *Vanity Fair* was Thackeray's first true full-length work of fiction, and it made him famous. Nevertheless, the consistently generous-minded Thackeray was prepared to concede not only that Dickens would outsell him, but that he could also outwrite him. His biographer, Gordon Ray, records a telling anecdote:

When the fifth number [*Dombey and Son*: Feb. 1847] appeared containing the death of little Dombey, Thackeray, with the part in his pocket, went down to the *Punch* office, and startled Mark Lemon by suddenly laying it before him and exclaiming, 'There! read that. There is no writing against such power as this no one has a chance. Read the description of young Paul's death; it is unsurpassed—it is stupendous.'[16]

Ray also records Thackeray bursting impulsively into Dickens's room, 'announcing how that some passage in a certain book had made him cry yesterday, and how that he had come to dinner, "because he couldn't help it," and must talk the passage over'.[17]

Although the friendly relationship between the two writers was to break down steadily and was to be severed completely in 1858, they were reconciled to one another shortly before Thackeray's death in 1863. Dickens was to write a heartfelt tribute to him in the *Cornhill Magazine* (formerly under Thackeray's editorship). Although he could not forbear to mention the fact that his erstwhile friend had 'feigned a want of earnestness' and made a pretence of 'under-valuing his art, which was not good for the art that he held in trust', Dickens went on to praise the special quality of that art, noting 'his refined knowledge of character . . . his subtle acquaintance with the weaknesses of human nature . . . his delightful playfulness as an essayist . . . and . . . his mastery of the English language'.[18] Dickens has succinctly identified the best elements in Thackeray's writing, his seriousness as much as his whimsy. He fails to note, however, that, unlike his own, it could be a singularly disconcerting mode of writing. Although both men delighted in the long fictional tradition in which they worked, and both acknowledged the primacy of Fielding in that tradition, their comedy is quite distinctive. Thackeray was recognized by his contemporaries, and notably by Charlotte Brontë, as a moralist, one sharply observant of human traits. He was also a novelist who shaped his narratives around the premiss that heroes and heroines, in the old sense of those words, were out of place in modern realistic fiction. His worldly-wise, amused, deli-cately cynical narrators observe characters in the round, identifying qualities that edify but which are muddied by foibles, peccadilloes, and, once in a while, mortal sins. There is little of the clear distinc-tion between good and bad, the admirable and the loathsome, the light and the dark, which pervades much of Dickens's work and which often seems to present readers with defined villains and earn-est would-be heroes. In a sense Thackeray is a far less *prejudiced* novelist than Dickens. He plays with the unexpected and the morally surprising where Dickens is far more inclined to exploit the uncanny and the defined. Finally, although Thackeray's fiction, like Dickens's, is primarily London-based, London emerges from his work as a setting and as a social focus rather than as the brooding, vivid, animated, but somehow inescapable metropolis of Dickens's novels.

Dickens's tendency to sway his readers with his own prejudices was noted with distaste by one of their contemporaries who was a dedicated admirer of Thackeray's art. Anthony Trollope characterized Dickens in *The Warden* (1855) as 'Mr. Popular Sentiment', a 'very powerful man' and a writer determined to set the world right 'by shilling numbers'. In the novel 'Mr. Popular Sentiment' works under the influence of a second reformer, 'Dr. Pessimist Anticant' (Carlyle), who has 'astonished the reading public by the vigour of his thoughts, put forth in the quaintest language'. But it is not 'quaint' language that appears to offend Trollope. Rather, it is the ease with which the fictional Mr Sentiment and Dr Anticant massage public opinion against the novel's unassuming central character in the name of popular reform and 'progress'. Sentiment has produced a propagandist tale called *The Almshouse*, but the mask of fictionality slips once Trollope's narrator damns a real Dickens with what must be seen as faint praise:

> Mr. Sentiment's great attraction is in his second-rate characters. If his heroes and heroines walk upon stilts . . . their attendant satellites are as natural as though one met them in the street . . . yes, live, and will live till the names of their calling shall be forgotten in their own, and Buckett and Mrs. Gamp will be the only words left to us to signify a detective police officer or a monthly nurse. (ch. 15)

This flattery serves as a makeweight to the complaint that Dickens has an unwarranted power over his readers. He amuses them, but he narrows their perspective on the social issues around which he based his novels. Trollope, a loyal and successful employee of the General Post Office, had been particularly offended by Dickens's attack on a creaking Civil Service as the Circumlocution Office in *Little Dorrit*. His own fictional explorations of his profession, in, for example, *The Three Clerks* (1858) and *The Small House at Allington* (1862–4), are singularly more benign.

Trollope's antipathetic view of Dickens as a novelist was tinged with professional jealousy. At no point in his own successful career as a novelist could he attempt to rival Dickens's sales. Nevertheless, in his various stabs at literary criticism, whether in his *Autobiography* (1883), in his biography of Thackeray (1879), or in his lecture 'English Prose Fiction as a Rational Amusement' (1870), he consistently places Dickens's art in a decidedly lower category than that of Thackeray and George Eliot. In the obituary he wrote for the *Saint Paul's Magazine* in 1870 he even ventured the snobbish opinion that Dickens's real skill had lain in exploiting 'the ever newly-growing mass of readers as it sprang up among the lower classes'.[19] He seems to have detected a steady note of vulgarity in Dickens's work which not only offended his own decidedly gentlemanly sensibilities, but also provoked his private distaste for the author himself. In February 1872, after reading John Forster's revelations about Dickens's boyhood, he wrote to George Eliot complaining of the self-indulgence and the self-pity he found in Forster's reproduction of the autobiographical fragment: 'Dickens was no hero; he was a powerful, clever, humorous, and, in many respects, wise man;—very ignorant, and thick-skinned, who had taught himself to be his own God, and to believe himself to be a sufficient God for all who came near him;—not a hero at all.'[20] Dickens was apparently too pushy, too emotional, too 'stagey and melodramatic' a novelist for his taste.[21] Trollope's own penchant for an exact and careful realism never seemed to find proper expression in Dickens's fiction.

Beyond Thackeray's novels, Trollope most admired the work of his friend, George Eliot. She too seems to have shared his distaste for Dickens's 'vulgarity', for his 'melodrama', and for his tendency to stress external traits rather than exploring the inner life of his characters. Eliot's admixture of praise and sharp criticism of Dickens's work first surfaced publicly in the essay on realism that she published in the *Westminster Review* in July 1856. The essay was something of a personal artistic credo, one defining her personal creative predilections before she had begun her own career as a novelist:

We have one great novelist who is gifted with the utmost power of rendering the external traits of our town population; and if he could give us their psychological character—their conceptions of life and their emotions—with the same truth as their idiom and manners, his books would be the greatest contribution Art has ever made to the awakening of social sympathies.[22]

The trouble for Eliot lay in the fact that Dickens seemed to be constitutionally disinclined from moving easily from the external to the internal ('he scarcely ever passes from the humorous and external to the emotional and tragic, without becoming as transcendent in his unreality as he was a moment before in his artistic truthfulness'). There seems to be more than a degree of aesthetic intolerance here, as much as there is an incomprehension founded on the belief that Dickens ought to be doing something other than what he did best as a novelist. Eliot wanted a 'truthful', modern, psychologically based fiction, one that had developed well beyond the models left by the eighteenth century, and Dickens was not going to give her the 'realism' that she craved. If to some twenty-first-century readers, Dickens is likely to seem the more inventive, the more flexible, the more experimental novelist, it is perhaps because Eliot's demands for a psychological realism appear to be trapped in a typically nineteenth-century aesthetic. Nevertheless, despite her strictures against him (of which Dickens was probably not aware as her essay was published anonymously), he was an enthusiastic reader of her early fiction once it began to appear in print. On 18 January 1858 he wrote perceptively to a 'George Eliot Esquire', praising the 'excellence' of *Scenes of Clerical Life*, and noting that he had been 'strongly disposed . . . to address the said writer as a woman', for he had observed in the narratives 'such womanly touches' that persuaded him that 'no man ever before had the art of making himself, mentally, so like a woman, since the world began' (*Letters*, viii. 506). When he read *Adam Bede* in July 1859 he wrote again (this time addressing his letter to a 'Dear Madam') proclaiming that the book had 'taken its place among the actual experiences and endurances' of his life. He had laid the book down 'fifty times', he said, in order to shut his eyes and think about it and he insisted that he knew nothing 'so skilful, determined, and uncompromising' (*Letters*, ix. 92–3: 10 July 1859). Dickens was rarely to praise any other contemporary writer quite so fulsomely. In this same letter he expressed the hope that should Eliot ever desert her publisher, Blackwood, and should she ever have 'the freedom and inclination to be a fellow labourer with me', he hoped she might want to serialize one of her novels in his journals. She was not to be so inclined.

The major contemporary woman novelist who *was* so inclined was Elizabeth Gaskell. On 31 January 1850 Dickens wrote to Gaskell announcing his plans for *Household Words*, 'a new, cheap weekly journal of general literature'. He wanted her to be a contributor because 'there is no living English writer whose aid I would desire to enlist, in preference to the author of Mary Barton'. *Mary Barton* had, he said, most profoundly affected and impressed him (*Letters*, vi. 22). What he admired in Gaskell was her self-evident concern for the state of industrial society as well as her delicate intensity in describing ordinary life. As his new journal was intended for the 'raising up of those that are down, and the general improvement of our social condition' she seemed to be the ideal collaborator. She was also one who might successfully add a northern English note to pages otherwise dedicated to predominantly metropolitan concerns. Gaskell, who was almost certainly flattered, accepted Dickens's invitation with some pleasure. Her first contribution to *Household Words* was the short story 'Lizzie Leigh', a story published serially in the first three issues of the journal. She was thereafter to contribute short fiction on a regular basis and in December 1851 began the publication of the interconnected tales which were eventually collected as *Cranford*. Gaskell's early collaboration with Dickens was generally a happy success as far as both authors were concerned. The major complication in their literary relationship arose over the serialization of the far more ambitious *North and South* in 1855. The problem appears to have had two roots. One was the fact that *North and South* followed on immediately from Dickens's own *Hard Times* in the pages of *Household Words* and the two novels had, given their original context, something of a symbiotic relationship. The second was the fact that her novel, unlike the short stories or *Cranford*, was not episodic and Gaskell had not hitherto been accustomed to writing for serialization. Although Dickens provided the title for the new novel and volunteered to divide her narrative up himself into convenient sections, she seems, quite properly, to have objected to much of his interference. She delayed agreeing to his suggestions and changes and thereby caused considerable vexation both to Dickens and to his sub-editor. On one occasion he was annoyed enough to write, half in jest, to Wills: 'Mrs. Gaskell, fearful—fearful. If I were Mr. G. O Heaven how I would beat her!' (*Letters*, vii. 699–700: 11 Sept. 1855.) Only when the serialization was complete could Dickens write, congratulating her on what he regarded as her supreme success. The end of her task, he told her, marked 'the vigorous and powerful accomplishment of an anxious labor', a labour in which the author had 'strided on with a force and purpose that MUST now give you pleasure' (*Letters*, vii. 513: 27 Jan. 1855). Pleasure there seems to have been, but the authorial problems over *North and South* had served to expose the real differences in style and working methods between Gaskell and Dickens. She was not to serialize any of her later novels in his journals.[23]

The refinement of Elizabeth Gaskell's work appealed both to Dickens's developed sense of a fiction which responded to the 'Condition of England' question and to his real appreciation of her faithful delineation of everyday things, actions, and emotions (the 'womanly touches' he was later to admire in George Eliot's work). The friction between the two was caused by the demands he made on his contributors. Not only did he demand artistic control, but he evidently supposed that his fellow writers worked with the same phenomenal energy and efficiency that he did. Dickens never seems to have been the easiest of colleagues or collaborators. He was long experienced in writing to time and in sections appropriate to monthly and weekly publication. But where he had been a pioneer in the field of serialization, Gaskell preferred to allow her narratives to expand and develop at a more leisurely pace. Dickens was to find two further contemporary authors, both of them personal friends, far more amenable as contributors to his journals.

Dickens first met Wilkie Collins in March 1851 when Collins, twelve years his junior, was offered a minor role in the performance of Bulwer-Lytton's *Not So Bad as We Seem* mounted by Dickens's amateur company. A good deal of the close literary co-operation between the two men was to remain a theatrical one and it was to culminate in the play *The Frozen Deep*, largely Collins's work but with substantial contributions from Dickens. The play was first performed in January 1857 and was both to provide a stimulus to *A Tale of Two Cities* and to open up Dickens's relationship with Ellen Ternan. Although Dickens and Collins became firm friends, especially in the years following the breakup of his marriage, there was initially much in their relationship that suggests that Dickens relished acting as a mentor to a younger and amenable protégé. Collins was taken on as a member of staff at the *Household Words* office in November 1856. Dickens had told Wills, his sub-editor, in the previous July that he hoped that a real collaboration might develop: 'He and I have talked so much within the last 3 or 4 years about Fiction-Writing, and I see him so ready to catch at what I have tried to prove right, and to avoid what I thought wrong, and altogether to go at it in the spirit I have fired him with, that the notion takes some shape with me' (*Letters*, viii. 159: 10 July 1856). The two men were to jointly compose the Christmas number of *Household Words* for 1856 (*The Wreck of the Golden Mary*). The jaunts around Britain and on the Continent that the two men took together were on one occasion to be marked by the appearance of a fictionalized account of a journey to north-west England known as *The Lazy Tour of Two Idle Apprentices* (1857). Collins's gradual declarations of artistic independence came with the serial publication of his two major novels, *The Woman in White* (1860) and *The Moonstone* (1868), in the pages of *All the Year Round*. Dickens complained to Collins of the earlier story that 'the great pains you take express themselves a trifle too much . . . I always contest your disposition to give an audience credit for nothing—which necessarily involves the forcing of points on their attention' (*Letters*, ix. 194: 7 Jan. 1860). He liked *The Moonstone* even less, finding its construction 'wearisome beyond endurance'. Herein lies the essential difference between the fiction of the two men. Collins had proved himself to be a master of intricate plots. Such plots were never a forte of Dickens's, with the possible exception of *A Tale of Two Cities*. Collins was also at the forefront of the school of so-called 'Sensation Novelists' of the 1860s. Dickens had probably influenced the development of the sensation novel through his own *Bleak House* but he was never to accentuate mystery and murder, crime and detection, madness and mayhem, with quite the alacrity of a Collins or a Braddon. If *The Mystery of Edwin Drood* may in its turn show the influence of the 'Sensation Novel' it is significant that Collins was to describe Dickens's unfinished story after his erstwhile mentor's death as a 'last laboured effort, the melancholy work of a worn-out brain'.[24]

Dickens's relationship with Edward Bulwer-Lytton was on a very different footing. Bulwer was eight years his senior and had published some thirteen novels before Dickens completed the run of *Pickwick Papers*. The friendship between the two novelists deepened during the 1850s when they jointly founded the Guild of Literature and Art, a charitable organization which aimed to establish pensions for indigent writers and to provide houses for those who could no longer support themselves independently. The scheme, for which Dickens worked enthusiastically, sprang from a mutual feeling that literature *was* a profession and that its professors deserved to retain their independence. The performances of Bulwer's comedy *Not So Bad as We Seem* in 1851 had become the initial means of raising money for the endowment. Despite the growing personal intimacy between the two men (Dickens's last son, who was born in March 1852, was to be named Edward Bulwer Lytton Dickens), their earlier literary relationship had been cordial if a little formal. Both writers exchanged books and compliments with one another. Bulwer praised *David Copperfield* and Dickens in his turn wrote glowingly to Bulwer thanking him for the gift of the epic poem *Arthur* which he claimed to have read with 'the deepest interest, admiration and delight'. He was proud, he said, to find the poem 'a very noble instance of the genius of a great writer of my own time' (*Letters*, v. 500: 23 Feb. 1849). What precisely Dickens found to admire in the poem will probably always elude us. In a similar manner it is hard to imagine Dickens actually discovering real pleasure in reading Bulwer's unwieldy novel *Harold: The Last of the Saxon Kings* (1848) on the beach at Broadstairs, though he claimed in a letter that he was about to embark on such a task (*Letters*, v. 383–4: 4 Aug. 1848). Despite Bulwer's forays into fiction with modern settings, and despite his avowed 'progressivism', he was most esteemed by his contemporaries as an earnest and scholarly historical novelist. He was particularly attracted to ancient and medieval subjects and latterly he had begun to show an informed interest in the occult. His work would thus seem not to be especially in tune with Dickens's known tastes and it is perhaps this clear distinction between their styles and subjects which made for such an amicable relationship. Dickens certainly seems to have both deeply respected and trusted Bulwer's literary judgement. The most spectacular instance of this is his willingness to change the end of *Great Expectations* on his friend's advice. Given his frequent prickliness over criticism and given his prevalent self-assurance as a writer, his openness to Bulwer's radical suggestion has surprised many commentators. What his friend seems to have done is to have instinctively understood Dickens's own uncertainties concerning a muted and melancholy denouement to his fiction. 'So I have done in as few words as possible,' he told Bulwer, 'and I hope you will like the alteration which is entirely due to you' (*Letters*, v.

428–9: 24 June 1861). Dickens further described the process to Forster on 1 July 1860:

You will be surprised to hear that I have changed the end of *Great Expect-ations* from and after Pip's return to Joe's, and finding his little likeness there. Bulwer, who has been, as I think you know, extraordinarily taken by the book, so strongly urged it upon me, after reading the proofs, and supported his views with such good reasons, that I resolved to make the change . . . I have put in as pretty a little piece of writing as I could, and I have no doubt the story will be more acceptable through the alteration. (*Letters*, ix. 432–3)

The process of revision and redrafting was one that both writers seem to have taken for granted at that particular juncture. The letter to Forster goes on to detail the changes that Bulwer himself had made to his *A Strange Story* which was being serialized in *All the Year Round* as *Great Expectations* reached the end of its run. It also describes the warmth and captures something of the easy communication between the two men:

He was in better health and spirits than I have seen him in, in all these years,—a little weird occasionally regarding magic and spirits, but always fair and frank under opposition. He was brilliantly talkative, anecdotal, and droll; looked young and well; laughed heartily; and enjoyed with great zest some games we played. In his artist-character and talk, he was full of interest and matter, saying the subtlest and finest things—but that he never fails in. I enjoyed myself immensely, as we all did. (*Letters*, ix. 433)

What Dickens seemed to respect most about Bulwer was not simply the offer of a vivid friendship with a literary aristocrat but the fact that this particular aristocrat believed in his vocation as an artist and that he wrote as a professional and not as a dilettante. While they did not share common concerns as writers, they coincided in their faith in the social relevance of literature and in the social benefits brought about by the practitioners of literature.

Dickens, the Novel Tradition, Serialization, and Illustration

When G. H. Lewes critically observed Dickens's book collection at Doughty Street, he sneered at the amount of recent fiction it contained. When he noted the changes in Dickens's reading and collecting habits two years later, he was prepared to concede that the young author seemed to be developing more demanding tastes. What he failed to note was that, as his library suggested, Dickens's art drew from two literary stimuli: the tradition he had inherited from the eighteenth century and the challenge presented by contemporary society. He read modern fiction in the 1830s because he needed to find his own way forward. He continued to read the eighteenth-century classics that he had discovered as a lonely boy because they enabled him to develop his own art within and beyond a tradition. Essentially, he adapted the forms evolved by Fielding and Smollett to meet the new demands presented by a new, urban, and industrialized society. Few of his contemporaries could rival him in this.

None of his contemporaries could, however, rival Dickens's sales as a serial novelist.[25] Most Victorian novelists either chose or were obliged to publish serially, whether in separate monthly or weekly parts or in journals, though with the rise of the circulating libraries from the 1860s onwards this form of publishing went into decline. But it was Dickens who took most easily to serialization, pioneered its use, and, thanks to his training as a journalist, responded most readily to the discipline of writing to time and to a given word limit. He was always the brightest star in the serial firmament, with only that relative latecomer to the art of the novel, Thackeray, getting near to rivalling his sales. The serial mode in which Dickens most commonly worked, the green paper-covered monthly instalment of some thirty-two pages illustrated with two engraved plates, was first evolved for the publication of *Pickwick Papers* in 1837 (though the first two numbers of that novel had only twenty-four pages). Each monthly part typically contained two or three chapters and was priced at one shilling. The completed novel ended with a double number (parts 19 and 20), priced at two shillings, which drew the complex strands of the plot together and gave readers an illustrated title-page, a frontispiece, and other preliminary material (sometimes including a preface). Although Dickens's publishers would then issue the novel as a single entity, the owner of the parts was also free to have them bound into a single fat volume with the illustrations falling appropriately. When Dickens published his later fiction in his weekly journals, as he did in the cases of *Hard Times*, *A Tale of Two Cities*, and *Great Expectations*, he was not happy with the limited

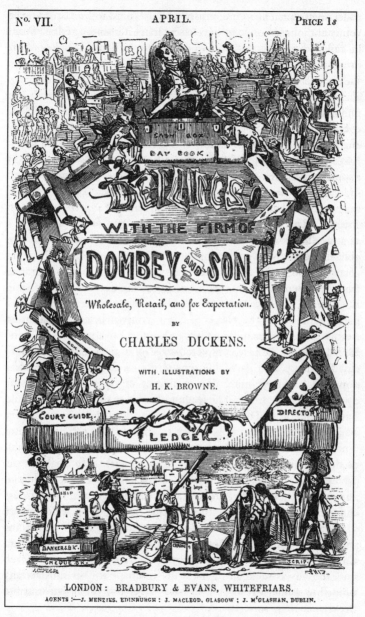

Cover design for the green wrapper of monthly parts for *Dombey and Son*.

space with which he found himself obliged to work (he disparagingly referred to these instalments as 'thimblefuls') and resorted to issuing *A Tale of Two Cities* both as a weekly serial in *All the Year Round* and as a monthly one in eight parts. The experiment was deemed to be a failure and was not repeated in the instance of *Great Expectations*.

The advantages of the serial form were multiple. Above all, the shilling monthly part rendered Dickens's novels hugely accessible to a broad section of the literate population. Evidence suggests that these monthly parts were read both communally and multiply. He was also always able to feel a special rapport with his readers, a rapport based on a cultivated interdependence. Unlike most writers, Dickens was able to experience an immediacy in his readers' responses to his work from month to month. Not only was his income related to his monthly sales rather than to the success of a completed narrative, but he also knew from those sales quite how responsive his wide readership was. Although, on occasion, he was inclined to respond to his audience's taste for a particular character (notably when it came to steadily accentuating the role of Mrs Gamp in *Martin Chuzzlewit*), by the middle of his writing career he had carefully planned the shape of his narratives before serialization began. Nevertheless, unlike George Eliot or Elizabeth Gaskell, who both preferred to have completed most of a given narrative before dividing it up into parts, Dickens wrote as he published, sending copy off to his printers only a matter of days before an issue appeared on the streets. The leading themes of the new novel would have been indicated on the cover on the monthly parts from the very beginning of its serial appearance (a particularly intriguing factor when it comes to puzzling out the possible development of the plot of the unfinished *The Mystery of Edwin Drood*). Like Shakespeare, whose plays he knew so intimately, Dickens knew how to play plot against sub-plot and how to integrate characters drawn from widely different social contexts into a shapely whole. It is testimony to Dickens's quite extraordinary aesthetic control that, despite the internal rhythm of each monthly part, and despite the tensions and the calculated element of suspense the novelist created between each one, the novels seem so thematically resonant and so substantially unified to modern readers who have rarely had the opportunity to experience them as serials.

The complex process of serialization, which Dickens so relished,

'I make myself known to my Aunt'. David Copperfield meets Betsey Trotwood in Phiz's illustration to the novel.

'Oliver's reception by Fagin and the boys'. Illustration by George Cruikshank to *Oliver Twist*.

also depended on the acquiescence and talent of his illustrators.[26] He was not the easiest of men to work with. The finest artist with whom he collaborated, George Cruikshank (1792–1878), was also the most demanding and exasperating (Cruikshank only worked on *Sketches by Boz* and, memorably, on *Oliver Twist*). Hablot Knight Browne (1815–82), who assumed the pseudonym 'Phiz' to complement Dickens's 'Boz', was far less of an individualist. He was also much more in awe of Dickens. It is easy enough to denigrate Browne's talent as an artist, but he proved to be an ideal collaborator with the novelist for a good deal of his career. He first worked on *Pickwick Papers*, though his services were dispensed with after the publication of *A Tale of Two Cities* in 1859. The greatest tribute that can be paid to Browne is that his visualizations of Dickens's characters have become fixed in the visual imaginations of generations of readers. Beyond Dickens's text, it is Phiz's Sam Weller, Phiz's Squeers, Phiz's Mrs Gamp, Phiz's Micawber, Phiz's Betsey Trotwood, and Phiz's Mr Chadband that film-makers and television directors most readily turn to for visual stimulus. The novel that Phiz was not called upon to illustrate, *Hard Times*, seems to be lacking in a vital visual resonance. Once Dickens had decided to work without Browne's services, he took time to find an appropriate successor. Due to its peculiar serial publication, *Great Expectations* went unillustrated. The masterly *Our Mutual Friend* has plates by Marcus Stone, a gifted-enough artist, but not an especially talented book illustrator. Only with *Edwin Drood* in 1870 did Dickens discover in Luke Fildes an artist worthy of the demands of his narrative. Alas, the collaboration was truncated by the novelist's untimely death. What probably stimulated the end of Dickens's working relationship with Browne was the shift in fashion in the mid-1850s away from steel engravings towards a revival of woodblock illustration. The novelist seems to have been slow in responding to this new fashion in book illustration (which had been triumphantly marked in an edition of Tennyson's *Poems* published in 1857 with plates designed, in part, by leading Pre-Raphaelites). Although Dickens had so distrusted the work of the Pre-Raphaelites in the early 1850s, it was ironically through the influence of John Everett Millais that the young Luke Fildes received the commission to illustrate *Edwin Drood*. Whereas Millais was asked by the novelist's family to record the face of the dead Dickens, it was Fildes who drew perhaps the most famous of contemporary tributes to him. This is the woodblock picture of 'The Empty Chair' which appeared in the *Graphic* in June 1870. It shows Dickens's study at Gad's Hill Place on the day after his death. The window is open to the summer weather, but the chair, pushed back from the desk, is empty, and the room itself seems drained of its creative purpose.

Significantly, Fildes's engraving was to prove a lasting influence on a particular admirer of Dickens's work, the young Vincent Van Gogh.[27]

Van Gogh seems to have readily recognized the extent to which Dickens was, like himself, a representative artist of his century. The cultural context in which Dickens worked demanded both a retrospect and a direct response to the multifariousness and disconnectedness of modern urbanized life. He took old narrative forms and traditional ways of presenting character and he steadily transformed them. Dickens the novelist worked as an assured, independent, and professional writer in a way that few writers of the previous century had been able to do. He keenly responded to the demands of his audience as much as he drew his material directly from the social conditions, the whims and the peculiarities of that audience. He dwelt habitually as he famously put it in the preface to *Bleak House* on the 'romantic side of familiar things', making fiction out of the raw material of the everyday, and vividly fixing what he had created in the imaginations of his readers.

CHAPTER 4

URBAN SOCIETY: LONDON AND CLASS

'THREE million five hundred thousand inhabitants; it adds up to twelve cities the size of Marseilles, ten as big as Lyon, two the size of Paris, in a single mass.' Thus, with a gasp that intermingles wonder and horror, the French critic Hippolyte Taine begins his account of mid-Victorian London. Taine, in common with many other visitors from abroad, could not get over the physical size of London, the greatest and most populous city of the nineteenth century. London was unprecedented. Once in its centre the encroaching city seemed to be inescapable. Taine had discovered that to reach open landscape one had 'to spend several days in succession in a cab, driving out north, south, east and west, for a whole morning, as far as those vague limits where houses grow scarcer and the country has room to begin'. He could only sum up the phenomenon that London represented with the reiterated adjective 'enormous, enormous'.[1]

Victorian London seemed somewhat less daunting to native Londoners and to seasoned British observers. The author of *Bohn's Pictorial Handbook of London*, a guidebook originally produced for the instruction of visitors to the Great Exhibition of 1851, expatiated on the city as an expression of national character rather than a stimulant to international *angst*:

London is the largest and wealthiest, as well as the most populous of the cities of the world. It is at once the centre of liberty, the seat of a great imperial government, and the metropolis of that great race whose industry and practical application of the arts of peace are felt in every clime, while they exert an almost boundless influence over the moral and political destinies of the world. About to become the theatre of an event of the highest moral importance, it is desirable that the stranger in our giant city should be made acquainted with its organization and structure—with its trade and commerce—with the sources of its social and political greatness—its many treasures hidden from the eye of the superficial observer.[2]

The difference between these two viewpoints is revealing. Essentially, London *needed* to be interpreted, but *how* it was interpreted depended on the sharpness and the quality of the axe that any given observer was grinding. What was the stimulus to one man's pride was the cause of another man's disconcertion. One man's concept of the city as the foster-mother of liberty could find its obverse in another man's fear of urban anarchy and social dissolution.[3]

Dickens's contemporaries were therefore divided both as to what the unprecedented phenomenon of London promised and as to what it threatened. Perhaps the most lastingly influential view of London as the quintessential metropolis of the industrial age was that expressed by Friedrich Engels in his *The Condition of the Working Class in England*, first published in German in 1845. Although Engels based most of his observations of urban life on Manchester, he opens his book with an account of his arrival in London by boat:

I know nothing more imposing than the view which the Thames offers during the ascent from the sea to London Bridge. The masses of buildings, the wharves on both sides . . . the countless ships along both shores, crowding ever closer together, until, at last, only a narrow passage remains in the middle of the river, a passage through which hundreds of steamers shoot by one another; all this is so vast, so impressive, that a man cannot collect himself, but is lost in the marvel of England's greatness before he sets foot on English soil.[4]

Engels, like Taine, rapidly loses his sense of wonder when the unease occasioned by London's street life supersedes it. The city becomes confusing, noisy, unfriendly, and threatening:

After roaming the streets of the capital a day or two, making headway with difficulty through the human turmoil and the endless lines of vehicles, after visiting the slums of the metropolis, one realizes for the first time that these Londoners have been forced to sacrifice the best qualities of their human nature, to bring to pass all the marvels of civilization which crowd their city . . . The very turmoil of the streets has something repulsive, something against which human nature rebels. The hundreds of thousands of all classes and ranks crowding past each other, are they not all human beings with the same qualities and powers, and with the same interest in being happy? . . . And still they crowd by one another as though they had nothing in common, nothing to do with one another, and their only agreement is the tacit one, that each keep to his own side of the pavement, so as not to delay the opposing streams of the crowd, while it occurs to no man to honour another with so much as a glance. The brutal indifference, the unfeeling isolation of each in his private interest becomes the more repellent and offensive, the more these individuals are crowded together, within a limited space.

Engels sees this process of the endless movement of crowds as emblematic of the dissolution of humankind into a race of monads, of individuals reduced to selfish atoms in a world of atoms.[5] The 'barbarous indifference' of Londoners towards one another seemed to have rendered London the apogee of the modern urban condition, a condition in which older, established patterns of human relationships had broken down to be replaced by an aggressive individualism. This individualism in turn manifested itself in economic exploitation. Engels's viewpoint, refined, expanded, theorized, and propagated by Marx, was to become an accepted way of interpreting and understanding not just the Victorian city but also the class systems and new class consciousness moulded by urbanization. The catastrophic breakdown of social relationships that Engels presumed that he had observed in the streets of London was taken to be the pattern for the future of urban civilization and the norm of the burgeoning cities of the newly industrial world.

Engels was a 24-year-old from the Rhineland when he wrote his book. As a provincial German he had little real experience of large cities, and even less of an appreciation of how a complex metropolis like London actually functioned. The essential flaw in the theoretical ramifications of his analysis lies in the fact that, as *The Condition of the Working Class in England* suggests, he spent insufficient time in exploring mid-nineteenth-century London. Engels also makes the assumption that the social condition and complexion of the capital paralleled that of the industrial Manchester where he had lived, worked, and formulated his ideas. Unlike Manchester, London was not a city with a single dominant manufacturing base, nor was it one where a clear social division between capital and labour, between mill-owner and mill-worker, or simply between haves and have-nots, could be taken as normative. The stark contrast between the standard of living enjoyed by the rich and the dire condition of the desperately poor in London was obvious to any observer, but so were the many social gradations which lay between these extremes, gradations which embraced both the modestly rich and the middlingly poor. It has since been estimated that, although four out of five inhabitants of mid-Victorian Britain were either manual workers, or the dependents of manual workers, in 1841 only one in five of these workers was employed in an industry that had been radically changed by the effects of the industrial revolution. Such workers exceeded a third of the workforce only in Lancashire.[6] London was not Lancashire, but nor was its economy rural. Given its distinctive history and geography, and given its complex demography and its political influence, the population of the capital, and the employment patterns of Londoners, posed quite distinctive questions to those Victorian commentators who attempted to make sense of them. The metropolis that Dickens had experienced since his boyhood, the physical city which he knew intimately and which he reanimated, described, and fictionalized, is not particularly susceptible to the theoretical assumptions about class struggle that are central to Marxian arguments and Marxian criticism. The lives, occupations, and the political consciousness of those manual workers who made up the real substance of Marx's dynamic working class figure only minimally in Dickens's fiction. There is in fact a multiplicity of worlds of work represented in Dickens's fictional London, but they are essentially dissimilar to the world of work described in his industrial Coketown in *Hard Times*. More to the point, Coketown has a marked rigidity in its social divisions, a demarcation between manufacturers and 'hands', that the London of Dickens's novels manifestly lacks.

Dickens and Class

Dickens's boyhood experience at Warren's blacking-factory gave him an active sympathy with the sufferings of the poor, but it also seems to have rendered him very wary of identifying himself with the urban working class. The contradictory pulls of his father's pretensions to gentility, and the threat of 'sinking' (as Dickens phrased it) into the companionship of Bob Fagin and his like, served to determine the representation of class relationships in his fiction. Dickens was born into the aspirant lower middle class, a class of clerks, tradesmen, owners of small workshops, and shopkeepers, which Marx rashly considered as likely to be subsumed into the working class by a process of historical evolution. It was a class that was in fact growing in numbers rather than shrinking in the middle

years of the nineteenth century. In some ways, though it would never
be prepared to admit it, it was to become a highly influential social
grouping whose manners, mores, and prejudices were pervasive by
the end of Dickens's century. The distinctive habits and morals, as
well as the equally distinctive insecurities, of the Victorian lower
middle class have been recently succinctly defined by K. Theodore
Hoppen:

Although the majority of the lower middle class shared many things with
manual workers—they went to the same schools, sprang from the same
parents, spoke (despite themselves) in much the same kinds of accent—
they, none the less, *felt* themselves to be very different indeed. Not only
that, but a nagging sense of insecurity and comparative marginality
rendered them perhaps the most concentrated repositories of so-called
'classic' Victorianism—a belief in respectability, merit competition,
money, hierarchy, privacy and success.[7]

This was a class that Dickens readily understood, though he was
happy enough to have escaped from its margins and limitations. His
rise to fame, fortune, and social status in early adulthood seem,
however, to have confirmed the justice of his and his father's early
social aspirations. They also set the seal on his escape from the social
marginalities and economic insecurities of his boyhood.

The fact that Dickens consistently took such pride in being an
earnest, self-made, professional man was part and parcel of his adult
claim to an established middle-class status. The Victorian middle
class to which he belonged was by the time of the 1841 census a
broadly based and generally prosperous 20 per cent of the nation.
Dickens's sense of detachment from the working classes, and from
the new, and often sporadic, kind of class consciousness of the industrialized regions of Britain is a significant aspect of his work as a
novelist and journalist. With the exceptions of *Oliver Twist* and
Great Expectations, none of his novels has a central working-class
hero or heroine. It is significant too that the orphaned Oliver, whose
life begins so unpropitiously in a workhouse, should turn out to be of
good middle-class stock, should be the heir to an inheritance
appropriated by his wicked brother, and should finally be adopted
into the safe bourgeois haven of Mr Brownlow's house. Philip Pirrip
may be unnaturally wrenched from his roots in a forge and rendered
a 'gentleman' by Magwitch's money, but, when that fortune

disappears, there is no question of 'Mr. Pip' reassuming an artisan trade, let alone languishing in poverty. Although Dickens seems to have been wary of taking manual workers as his central characters, certain of his snobbish Victorian critics were far more exercised by his supposed inability to catch 'a tolerable likeness of a man or woman whose lot is cast among the high-born and wealthy'.[8] Dickens, it was argued, could not describe a gentleman because, not being one, he knew 'nothing of their lives'.[9] What is certainly noticeable throughout his work is his middle-class distaste for the assumptions of the upper classes of his day. This upper élite, made up of the landed aristocracy and the old, generally country-based, gentry, had clung on to its ancient economic privileges and to a good deal of its political and social influence. Dickens's sense of his own hard-won professional status and economic independence gave him a profound distrust of aristocratic assumptions, rights, and privileges. He satirizes these assumptions through caricatures of predatory gentlemen such as Sir Mulberry Hawk and the foppish Lord Frederick Verisopht in *Nicholas Nickleby*, and through the more developed portrait of the would-be parliamentary power broker Sir Leicester Dedlock in *Bleak House*. He also associates aristocratic privilege with the corruptions, moral as much as polit-ical, of the eighteenth-century nobility in England (in *Barnaby Rudge*) and, more dangerously, in France (in *A Tale of Two Cities*). When Dickens was invited to meet Queen Victoria at Buckingham Palace three months before his death, rumours persisted that he either had been, or would be, offered a baronetcy. Dickens laid these rumours to rest in a letter of May 1870: 'You will probably have read before now that I am going to be everything the Queen can make me. If my authority be worth anything, believe on it that I am going to be nothing but what I am, and that includes my being as long as I live' (*Letters*, xii. 531: 20 May 1870). Proud as he was of having worked his way out of poverty he was quite deter-mined *not* to join the ranks of the old ruling classes, especially those associated with the inherited privileges and corruptions that he so despised. Dickens's egalitarian, but essentially middle-class, prejudices were founded on more than simply boyhood aspiration, boyhood degradation, and the achievement of adult self-sufficiency. The picture of class relationships in his fiction also suggests the degree to which he had been shaped by his experience of the distinctive class structures of London and by the complex patterns of work in London.

As we have seen, Dickens's extended trip to the United States in 1842 was, in part, a disillusioning experience. As he wrote to a friend in March 1842, with more than a touch of homesickness, he had 'a yearning after our English customs and english [*sic*] manners, such as you cannot conceive'. Although he could not quite put his finger on what made the America that he had experienced differ from his preconceived picture of it, at the end of his visit he found himself 'truly glad to leave it' (*Letters*, iii. 120: 12 and ?21 Mar. 1842). He may well have been missing the hum of city life amid the wide-open spaces of the expanding Republic, but he had also discovered that he was alienated by the sometimes raucously intrusive customs and manners of the Americans to whose supposedly classless society he had once been drawn. His statement that he much preferred 'a liberal Monarchy . . . to such a Government as this' also indicates that he had come to accept that British social gradations exercised a sway over his view of society which republican egalitarianism could not easily eradicate (*Letters*, iii. 156: 22 Mar. 1842). Easygoing America had not offered a feasible alternative to an older and hierarchical social system which served to stir both his wrath and his imagination. When he returned to the United States in 1867–8 he recognized '*great changes* for the better socially' but not necessarily politically. America, he believed, now resembled an 'England governed by the Marylebone vestry and the penny papers, and England as she would be after years of such governing' (*Letters*, xii. 13: 14 Jan. 1868). Post-Civil-War America therefore seemed to exhibit the worst kind of small-minded, lacklustre parochialism, but it had coupled it with a loutish popularism.

Dickens understood the British class system from the special perspective of a Londoner. As his most class-conscious novel, *Bleak House*, suggests, the social hierarchies of the capital did not consist merely of a sharp contrast between the rich and the poor or between haves and have-nots. London's social structure, as it is delineated in the novel, suggests that classes were interdependent, not in the old hierarchical manner of a stratified, deferential countryside, but in the sense that they live cheek by jowl, inhabiting the same spaces, sharing the same streets, and, more dangerously, the same urban diseases. His slum, Tom-all-Alone's, as Dickens's narrator darkly tells us, has his revenge, for fevers endemic amongst the poorest of the poor are communicated upward, polluting even the bluest blood (ch. 46). Between the Dedlocks in their fashionable West End mansion and the houseless Jo there is obviously a great social gulf, but that chasm between the extremes of riches and poverty is in fact bridged by an extraordinarily complex range of characters of a very varied social standing. Below the Dedlocks there are the lesser land-owners (Mr Jarndyce and the boisterous Lawrence Boythorn) and members of the older professions, lawyers such as Mr Tulkinghorn and Mr Vholes, and the doctor, Allan Woodcourt, who springs (as his mother proudly insists) from a distinguished and ancient Welsh family. Below them are the various representatives of the middling classes, both new and old: Mr Rouncewell, the northern ironmaster; the campaigning Mrs Jellyby, her long-suffering husband, and her chaotic family; the 'rapaciously benevolent' Mrs Pardiggle; the shabby-genteel dilettante Harold Skimpole; Mr Snagsby, the law-stationer; Mr Bagnet, the proprietor of a musical instrument shop; Mr Chadband, the oleaginous Dissenting minister; and those who are slightly more marginal such as the moneylender Mr Smallweed, the dancing-master Mr Turveydrop, and the pushy, upwardly mobile, law-clerk William Guppy and his friend Tony Jobling. Below them we have genuine marginals (at least in terms of Victorian class snobberies): Inspector Bucket, Mr George (Rouncewell) who runs a shooting gallery, the illiterate rag-and-bone dealer Mr Krook, and his lodger, Miss Flite. The novel's servants range from the superior housekeeper at Chesney Wold, Mrs Rouncewell, down through the lady's maids, Hortense and Rosa, and the largely silent servants of the well-to-do, to poor Guster the Snagsbys' maid of all work (who has been recruited from the workhouse and 'goes cheap with [an] unaccountable drawback of fits'). At the bottom of the social heap are Neckett, the sheriff's officer (whose young family is left destitute at his death); the novel's only manual workers, the sullen St Albans brickmakers and their families; and of course, the houseless, inarticulate crossing-sweeper, the monosyllabically named Jo. While Jo both lives and works on the streets, that conspicuously well-housed solicitor, Tulkinghorn, walks easily in one direction from his home in respectable Lincoln's Inn Fields to Snagsby's shop off Chancery Lane, and in another to the festering slum of Tom-all-Alone's. Although Lady Dedlock feels obliged to disguise herself as a servant in order to visit the graveyard where her former lover is interred, she, the denizen of the West End, comes on foot into territory exclusively inhabited by the poorest of the poor. It is London that brings them together. By means of the complex narrative structure of *Bleak House*, a fiction that Dickens claimed dwelt on the 'romantic side of familiar things', the novelist explores precisely those connections between characters drawn from radically different social classes, connections that a commentator like Engels assumed that metropolitan experience had irrevocably destroyed.

Dickens's Metropolis and Social Class: *Dombey and Son* and *Our Mutual Friend*

The emphasis *Bleak House* places on exploring the interconnection of the Dedlocks with those that they assume are their social inferiors renders it more concerned with the 'landed interest' than is true of most other Dickens novels. Two less 'aristocratic' but equally metropolitan novels, *Dombey and Son* and *Our Mutual Friend*, respectively from the middle and the end of Dickens's writing career, explore an exclusively urban social pattern. In *Dombey and Son* 'property' consists of commercial rather than landed wealth. Mr Dombey is a London merchant, the scion of a long-established City trading family, and the type of the 'old-fashioned' businessman, an importer and exporter who would be largely superseded with the triumphant arrival of joint-stock companies in the mid-century. As far as we can tell, the world which was made 'for Dombey and Son to trade in' is not yet a world of shares. It is not idly that Captain Cuttle associates Walter Gay's chance of an advantageous marriage to Dombey's daughter with the fortunes of that celebrated medieval City merchant, Dick Whittington, for Dombey and his firm embody old mercantile wealth and traditional methods of trading and profiting from trade. Mr Dombey is nevertheless the representative of an early nineteenth-century commercial ethic, a man of immense wealth and one intensely proud of his eminence in the established world of trade (though we never know precisely *what* he trades in). Despite his bourgeois self-assurance, the nature of his second marriage suggests that he also recognizes the social benefits of a distant connection to what was once regarded as more 'polite' society. Edith Granger is the widow of an army officer, the daughter of the Honourable Mrs

Skewton, and the cousin of Lord Feenix. Although she has no money of her own, as Major Bagstock remarks, she might have been married twenty times 'but for being proud'. Despite these links to the old but relatively impoverished aristocracy, most of the novel's other 'genteel' characters, and Mrs Skewton above all, have a distinctly shabby tinge to their gentility. The characters with real influence over events, such as Mr Dombey's sister and brother-in-law, the Chicks, and James Carker, 'the Manager', tend to wield that influence through their close connection with 'trade' embodied in the mighty and long-established City firm of Dombey and Son.

The distinction between James Carker and his elder brother, John ('the Junior'), is revealing. Both are essentially clerks, but clerks who work on utterly distinct levels, social as much as economic. John, the elder brother, has disgraced himself at some point in the past by embezzling funds. He has since been held back in a lowly position within the firm. James, by contrast, has risen to a heady eminence which serves to further emphasize the humiliation of his sibling. This kind of marked distinction between upper and lower clerical workers can be observed throughout Dickens's work and reflects the fact that, as the 1851 census revealed, white-collar workers numbered around 130,000, a preponderance of whom lived and worked in London. The London office environment, still largely free of labour-saving technology, made male clerks both an essential body of workers and an important economic presence.[10] Clerking had been Dickens's father's relatively humble job in the Navy Pay Office. Significantly enough, it was into the more distinguished upper reaches of office work that Dickens sent three of his own sons.[11] Reginald Wilfer in *Our Mutual Friend*, like Bob Cratchit in *A Christmas Carol*, is amongst the most typically clerkly of Dickens's many London clerks. But the placid, unambitious Reginald Wilfer is distinctive. He not only works in an office in a 'drug-house' in the neighbourhood of Mincing Lane, but he has sprung from a long and singularly undistinguished line of office workers:

the Reginald Wilfer family were of such commonplace extraction and pursuits that their forefathers had for generations modestly subsisted on the Docks, the Excise Office, and the Custom House, and the existing R. Wilfer was a poor clerk. So poor a clerk, through having a limited salary and an unlimited family, that he had never yet attained the modest object of his ambition: which was to wear a complete new suit of clothes, hats and boots included, at one time. (bk. 1, ch. 4)

Reginald Wilfer's 'majestic' wife in suburban Holloway tries, like Dickens's mother, to attract pupils to a girls' school that consists of little more than a brass-plate on her door. It is small wonder that R.W.'s daughter, Bella, is so determined to advance herself in a 'mercenary' manner and that she appears so ready to reject the tentative and, to her mind, the demeaning advances of the Boffins' 'mere' secretary, John Rokesmith.

The fictional worlds of both *Dombey and Son* and *Our Mutual Friend* are dominated by money made, remade, reinvested, or somehow recycled in Victorian London. The fact that the Boffins' inheritance consists of dust heaps does not seem to threaten the social status given them by their new and substantial wealth. Their entrée into 'Society' may be limited, but as Mr Boffin insists of his wife, the Harmon fortune has served to render her 'fashionable' and fashion entails moving 'into a nice house' and setting up 'a nice carriage'. Their 'nice' new house is advertised as an 'eminently aristocratic family mansion' and once established there they are beset by 'all manner of crawling, creeping, fluttering, and buzzing creatures, attracted by the gold dust of the Golden Dustman'. Money speaks, and it opens doors. Or at least, like so many things in *Our Mutual Friend* it *seems* to do so. That pair of self-deceivers, the quintessentially mercenary Alfred and Sophronia Lammle, act and find their being in a commercial world increasingly dominated by speculation, a world in which 'property' often seems to have no real substance:

The mature young lady is a lady of property. The mature young gentleman is a gentleman of property. He goes, in a condescending amateurish way, into the City, attends meetings of Directors, and has to do with traffic in Shares. As is well known to the wise in their generation, traffic in Shares is the one thing to have to do with in this world. Have no antecedents, no established character, no cultivation, no ideas, no manners; have Shares. Have Shares enough to be on Boards of Directors in capital letters, oscillate on mysterious business between London and Paris, and be great. Where does he come from? Shares. Where is he going to? Shares. What are his tastes? Shares. Has he any principles? Shares. What squeezes him into Parliament? Shares. Perhaps he never of himself ever achieved success in anything! Sufficient answer to all; Shares. (bk. 1, ch. 10)

This is a new world of appearances rather than of Dombeian

substance, a world in which money wipes out distinctions, but also one where the absence of money is the occasion of marginalization and dissension, even, as it proves, of social disgrace.

In both *Dombey and Son* and *Our Mutual Friend*, beneath the shifting and essentially *haut bourgeois* world of the City and its moneymakers and speculators, and beneath the established realm of the old professions (such as the law), other social worlds flourish and occasionally flounder. As we have seen, a large body of male clerks, both high and low, oil the workings of business. In both novels small shopkeepers are variously represented by the seemingly unviable finances of Sol Gills's maritime instrument shop in the City (a concern which seems to pick up, almost miraculously, by the end of the novel) and by Mr Venus's taxidermy and skeleton articulation business in Clerkenwell. Despite the fact that the profits of Venus's enterprise seem to be more than satisfactory, they are initially insufficient to attract the matrimonial attentions of Pleasant Riderhood, an independent woman who, as she informs the disconsolate Venus, does not 'wish to regard herself, nor yet to be regarded, in that bony light'. But then, the independent-minded Pleasant has her own business as an unlicensed pawnbroker in the East End.

The marginal lower middle classes are not only shopkeepers. To Dickens, the potentially unwelcome aspect of upward social mobility in *Our Mutual Friend* is edgily embodied in the lumbering pretensions of Bradley Headstone and his protégé Charley Hexam. Headstone, a 'highly certified stipendiary schoolmaster' has 'acquired mechanically a great store of teacher's knowledge'.[12] Dickens is not necessarily being snobbish about Bradley's rise from working-class respectability to 'decent', lower middle-class unease, but he is, in many senses, reversing the confident patterns of self-improvement evident in his early fiction. As early as *A Christmas Carol* Dickens had defined the twin evils besetting society as ignorance and want, but neither the schoolteacher nor his pupil suggest that ignorance has been properly or fittingly alleviated. Everything we learn about Bradley suggests the precariousness of his new-found status; everything we observe about Charley indicates the social threat that this ambitiously sullen, half-educated working-class boy betokens ('a curious mixture . . . of uncompleted savagery, and uncompleted civilisation'). Bradley and Charley are both socially and intellectually half-baked. More than undermining working-class aspiration from a bourgeois point of view, Dickens is in reality making a moral point about the variety of narrow, unimaginative educational curriculum offered by the kind of teacher-training establishment which produced Bradley and which is preparing Charley for his career. Headstone has risen from obscurity, but he has achieved little beyond mediocrity. The splendidly realized scene (bk. 2, ch. 6) which dramatizes the conflict between the gauchely posturing Headstone and the insultingly suave Eugene Wrayburn may still leave readers with something of a cringe of embarrassment:

Eugene looked on to Bradley Headstone. With consummate indolence, he turned to Mortimer, inquiring: 'And who may this other person be?'

'I am Charles Hexam's friend,' said Bradley; 'I am Charles Hexam's schoolmaster.'

'My good sir, you should teach your pupils better manners,' returned Eugene.

Composedly smoking, he leaned an elbow on the chimneypiece, at the side of the fire, and looked at the schoolmaster. It was a cruel look, in its cold disdain of him, as a creature of no worth. The schoolmaster looked at him, and that, too, was a cruel look, though of the different kind, that it had a raging jealousy and fiery wrath in it.

This is mutual class incomprehension and class antagonism. Despite Wrayburn's disdain, which is evident throughout the scene, Dickens never really seeks to counter it by justifying the schoolmaster either by action or word. Headstone is in fact to behave just as awkwardly and unprepossessingly when a man of much lower class, the brutish Rogue Riderhood, intrudes into his classroom. Bradley Headstone's real distinctiveness as a character lies not in his professional awkwardness, but in the violent and murderous inclinations that cannot be stifled by his outward respectability. Dickens may make it clear to readers as to why he is lacking as a teacher, but he makes it even clearer that Headstone is yet more deficient as a moral human being.

Working-class characters in both *Dombey and Son* and *Our Mutual Friend* are drawn from as wide a professional spectrum as the middle-class characters. Here again London's singular and varied patterns of employment can be said to have determined the distinctive nature, some might even see it as the eccentricity, of those patterns. Perhaps the least eccentric, and the most obviously 'new', of these jobs, is that of Mr Toodle in *Dombey and Son*. Toodle is that relative rarity in Dickens's novels, a man employed by a large concern, in this case a railway company. By his own account, he began his working life as some kind of navvy, labouring 'mostly underground', but he later resolved to move to 'one of these here railroads when they comes into full play' (ch. 2). By chapter 20, when he meets the bereaved Mr Dombey on the platform at Euston, he is 'a-doin pretty well' working as a stoker on the railway service running between London and Birmingham. The thoroughly respectable, but minimally comfortable, circumstances of the Toodle family, stand in stark contrast to that representative of the 'undeserving' poor in the same novel, 'Good Mrs. Brown', the petty thief and receiver of stolen goods who not only abducts and robs the child Florence Dombey of her clothes but, far worse, has effectively sold her own daughter into prostitution. In *Our Mutual Friend* the contrasts between the deserving and the undeserving, and between the upright and the criminally inclined, are less stark but no less revelatory. All are in their frugal way self-employed. Fanny Cleaver, known as 'Jenny Wren', survives as a dolls' dressmaker, while the widowed Betty Higden keeps herself out of the dreaded workhouse 'by dint of an indomitable purpose and a strong constitution'. Betty maintains herself as long as she can by means of her mangle and her 'Minding School' for three small children. Silas Wegg, the street-ballad seller, is of the type described by Henry Mayhew in the first volume of his *London Labour and the London Poor* (1861) as a 'Pinner-up' or 'Wall Song-seller'.[13] He has a fixed pitch in the West End and would probably, like other ballad-hawkers, have pinned printed songs 'to a sort of screen or large board' (and, if we believe Mayhew's testimony, he may have originally been a mechanic or porter before being 'reduced to struggle for a living' after the amputation of his leg). Despite the patronage of the Boffins, which takes him off the street, Wegg is readily drawn into the potentially more lucrative business of blackmail. In this seamier side to his commercial existence Wegg resembles the rival Thames watermen 'Gaffer' Hexam and 'Rogue' Riderhood. These two pursue a clandestine trade which intermingles working semi-legitimately as boatmen and, more lucratively, as scavengers (Dickens variously describes them as 'nightbirds of the Thames' and 'birds of prey'). They double as the dredgers-up and nefarious robbers of drowned corpses. Riderhood insists on his upright working-class credentials as 'a honest man, and sweating away at the brow as an honest man ought', but readers are readily led to presume that his honesty has its limits and that his brow is rarely even moist. As a waterman, and later as a lock-keeper, he has alternative, and distinctly illegitimate, sources of income which are clearly not related to honest sweat. The riverside types on whom Dickens based the characters of both Hexam and Riderhood are again usefully described by that most Dickensian of commentators, Henry Mayhew. Mayhew distinguishes between the 'licensed watermen' of his third volume, and the 'felonious' lightermen who figure in his fourth. This latter breed of petty criminal, which was on the decline thanks to the efforts of the police, had been accustomed to dredge the river for coals; to steal from barges, wharves, and docks; or, worst of all, to live by a kind of piracy based on boarding moored ships and mugging their drunken crews.[14] By these standards Rogue Riderhood's alternative earnings through blackmail seem almost refined. As *Our Mutual Friend* vividly suggests, the moral depravity of Dickens's London was by no means exclusively a matter of the exploitation of one social class by another.

'Those that *will* work . . . and those that *will not* work': *David Copperfield* and *Great Expectations*

As the first chapter of this study suggests, the central characters in Dickens's first three novels neither develop one from another, nor do they conform to what might be seen as an established pattern of fictional heroism. In terms of their social class they are, perhaps, even more interesting. As the rambling 'plot' of *Pickwick Papers* develops, Samuel Pickwick is almost imperceptibly edged upwards in a social hierarchy. Readers are first acquainted with him as a retired businessman resident in lodgings in a front pair of rooms in the unfashionable area of Goswell Street (a respectable enough, but decidedly dull, lower middle-class suburb north of the City of London). He is the chairman of a middle-brow, amateur antiquarian club of the kind that, even now, remains the butt of snobbish, higher-brow satire. As the narrative steadily advances, however, so does Mr Pickwick's social, moral, and even intellectual standing. Having acquired a manservant (Sam Weller) at an early stage in the novel, at the end of the narrative Pickwick retreats (with Sam) from his duties as general chairman of the Pickwick Club to a happy retirement in the desirably semi-rural suburb of Dulwich. The social advance of

Oliver Twist is at once far more unsteady and yet far more clearly determined. The boy may be born an orphaned pauper, one 'left to the tender mercies of churchwarden and overseers', but he will be fortuitously rescued from his poverty by Mr Brownlow and discovered to be the heir to respectable, though unmarried, parents. He was, as his accent and his innate uprightness may already have suggested to readers, a born gentleman despite the dire circumstances of his early existence (circumstances which could never be described as 'formative'). Nicholas Nickleby too is the son of a 'worthy gentleman', albeit an impoverished one who has lived on the small income from a particularly small Devonshire farm (which Dickens describes as being of the size of Russell Square). The farm and the income are lost before the narrative begins, thanks to an unwise speculation which has left the widowed Mrs Nickleby and her children destitute. It is Nicholas's uncle, Ralph, who has prospered having been 'placed' as a young man 'in a mercantile house in London' and having 'applied himself passionately to his old pursuit of money-making'. Nicholas may thus have been born into a landed inheritance of sorts, but once it is lost he is reduced to seeking the charity of an uncle in 'trade'. He will be obliged to make his own way in a world where his 'gentlemanly' status carries little weight.

The evidence of these first three novels suggests that as a young writer Dickens was more concerned with moral worth than with social status. Nevertheless, all three novels are rooted in values, moral as much as social, which could be most readily identified with the early Victorian middle classes. The worth and earnestness of this class of 'middling' men and women had been acclaimed in 1840 by a commentator who insisted that 'we do not believe that there is in the world a community so virtuous, so religious and so sober minded as the middle classes of England'.[15] The respectability of the middle classes was seen by many contemporary critics both as forming a buffer against the forces of revolutionary dissolution and as the true begetter and fosterer of Britain's commercial prosperity. But the supposedly benign social, economic, educational, and cultural influence of the middle classes over national life did not go unchallenged. It was their ungentlemanly education that was often regarded as defective, an education more generally typified by Salem House than by Dotheboys Hall. That scourge of middle-class philistinism, Matthew Arnold, was to recognize in 1881 that Dickens's work,

and *David Copperfield* in particular, contained within it representative pictures of both the strengths and the defects of the British
bourgeoisie. Arnold speaks as a man who knew a good deal about
Victorian schools:

Intimately, indeed, did Dickens know the middle-class; he was bone of its
bone and flesh of its flesh. Intimately he knew its bringing up . . . in this
country the middle class has no naturally defined limits . . . it is difficult to
say who properly belong to it and who do not . . . And therefore, for my
part, to prevent ambiguity and confusion, I have always adopted an educational test, and by the middle class I understand those who are brought
up at establishments which are more or less like Salem House, and by
educators who are more or less like Mr. Creakle . . . Our civilisation, as it
looks to outsiders, and in so far as it is a thing broadly communicable,
seems to consist very much in the Murdstonian drive in business and the
Murdstonian in religion, on the one hand, and in the Quinionian joviality
and geniality, on the other. Wherever we go we put forward Murdstone
and Quinion, and back up their civilisation all they can. But do what we
will, this civilisation does not prove attractive.[16]

Arnold's criticism is narrow and, despite its ostensible enthusiasm
for Dickens's work, it is ultimately highly unsympathetic to it. It
does, nevertheless, alert us to something of the immediacy of
Dickens's rapport with his middle-class Victorian readers. Although
Arnold may suspect that Dickens the artist was properly to be numbered amongst the very philistines from whose ranks he sprang, he
grants that the novelist was ideally equipped to delineate bourgeois
civilization because he was able to criticize it from an insider's point
of view.

     What Arnold signally failed to note in his short essay on *David
Copperfield* was the fact that it is Dickens's central character, rather
than the Creakles, the Murdstones, and the Quinions, who is the
true embodiment of Victorian middle-class values. Moreover, David
Copperfield's social success, and his eventual triumph over adverse
circumstances, is, by his own account, the result of self-discipline
and the encouragement of Dr Strong rather than the misguided
discipline of Mr Murdstone or the educational system of Mr
Creakle. In a famous passage in chapter 42 David expatiates on the
leading principles of his working life:

I have been very fortunate in worldly matters; many men have worked
much harder, and not succeeded half so well; but I never could have done

what I have done, without the habits of punctuality, order, and diligence, without the determination to concentrate myself on one object at a time, no matter how quickly its successor should come upon its heels . . . My meaning simply is, that whatever I have tried to do in life, I have tried with all my heart to do well; that whatever I have devoted myself to, I have devoted myself to completely; that, in great aims and in small, I have always been thoroughly in earnest . . . there is no substitute for thorough-going, ardent, and sincere earnestness.

Earnestness was a quality the mid-Victorians adulated above all others (which was precisely why Oscar Wilde was prepared to be so irreverent towards it in the 1890s). Throughout his writings Dickens reveals himself to be in real earnest when he addresses issues concerned with the ethical and social value of work. Work does not transform characters, nor does it necessarily mould them, but, as David Copperfield explains, it does serve to define them. Regardless of their class origins, class aspirations, or class allegiances, those male characters who do not work are generally presented as lacking moral fibre, a moral fibre that David recognizes as true 'earnestness'.

The contrast between the fortunes of David Copperfield and Philip Pirrip (Pip) in *Great Expectations* is therefore revealing. David is born into a leisured, if scarcely affluent, class but once his mother's annuity is lost with her death he is removed from school and is reduced by the Murdstones to the status of a wage-earning drudge. He is thus effectively de-classed and his only way back into the middle classes, where he feels he properly belongs, is by dint of personal effort, earnest struggle, and hard work. The pattern of Pip's development is radically different. Pip is born into an artisan family and is apprenticed to his brother-in-law in the useful and independent trade of blacksmithing. At no point in the story, therefore, is Pip set to be a drudge or a wage slave, though he has nothing of the gentleman about him. The glimpses of what he takes for gentility at Satis House, however, serve to skew his perceptions and to render him responsive to the terms of the mysterious benefaction which appears in the fourth year of his apprenticeship. As Mr Jaggers explains:

'he will come into a handsome property. Further . . . it is the desire of the present possessor of that property, that he immediately be removed from his present sphere of life and from this place, and be brought up as a gentleman—in a word, as a young fellow of great expectations.' (vol. i, ch. 18)

Where David's removal from 'his present sphere of life' had been a downward social move, Pip's is upward. David had been put to unworthy work; Pip is removed from the world of work altogether and placed in one of genteel idleness. David yearns to regain his lost 'sphere of life'; Pip readily relinquishes what he considers the economically and socially poorer sphere for the richer.

It is precisely this contrast which forcibly struck Bernard Shaw in his introduction to *Great Expectations* in 1937. His criticism has been much quoted:

David was, for a time at least, Dickens's favourite child, perhaps because he had used him to express the bitterness of that episode in his own experience which had wounded his boyish self-respect most deeply . . . we shall never know whether in that immensely broadened outlook and knowledge of the world which began with *Hard Times* and *Little Dorrit*, and left all his earlier works behind, he may not have come to see that making his living by sticking labels on blacking bottles and rubbing shoulders with boys who were not gentlemen, was as little shameful as being the genteel apprentice in the office of Mr. Spenlow, or the shorthand writer recording the unending twaddle of the House of Commons and the electioneering bunk on the hustings of all the Eatanswills in the country . . . Now contrast David with Pip; and believe, if you can, that there was no revision of his estimate of his favourite child David as a work of art and even as a vehicle of experience. The adult David fades into what stage managers call a walking gentleman. The reappearance of Mr. Dickens in the character of a blacksmith's boy may be regarded as an apology to Mealy Potatoes.[17]

Mealy Potatoes was the nickname of a boy with a 'pale or mealy' complexion with whom David Copperfield works at Murdstone and Grinby's warehouse. Mealy is the son of a Thames waterman, but his main claim to distinction in David's eyes is that this same waterman also works as a fireman in a London theatre where Mealy's sister 'did Imps in the Pantomimes' (ch. 11). One wonders why Shaw felt so strongly that Dickens needed to apologize to him, unless, of course, he was supposing that Mealy was modelled on the unfortunate and maligned Bob Fagin. Shaw is, however, rightly supposing that Dickens had been as humiliated by his time at Warren's Blacking as David is by his experience at Murdstone and Grinby's. But to presume that the Dickens who wrote *Great Expectations* was revising his earlier literary responses, was somehow reconciling himself to that dark period in his life, and was doing penance for his snobbery is surely mistaken. Shaw rashly wanted mid-twentieth-century readers of the later novel to regard all kinds of work as equally worthy in the sight of a classless society. He is, somewhat perversely, refusing to recognize that both for Dickens *and* for the vast majority of his contemporaries there was a real enough distinction between sticking labels on bottles and working as a parliamentary reporter. There was, too, a very real social and economic distinction between being apprenticed to a blacksmith and being apprenticed to an attorney. Shaw tellingly remarks towards the end of his introduction that 'as our social conscience expands and makes the intense class snobbery of the nineteenth century seem less natural to us, the tragedy of *Great Expectations* will lose some of its appeal'.[18] He has been proved wrong on both counts.

Pip was happy enough working as Joe's apprentice at the forge. It is very possible that he might have proved happy as an independent village blacksmith, but that readers can never know for certain. What we do know is that his social promotion as a consequence of the opening up of his 'great expectations' does not bring emotional fulfilment with it. Nevertheless, the history of Pip's progress does not form a persuasive apology to working-class boys such as Mealy Potatoes, nor does it present the life of a skilled artisan as far more life-enhancing than that of a gentleman. Pip's history is, if anything, a criticism of Magwitch's assumption that Pip can be made into a gentleman. The idea of such manipulation struck Dickens as 'grotesque' even when he was planning his novel (*Letters*, ix. 310: to John Forster, mid-Sept. 1860). The distortion seems to have been fixed in Magwitch's mind when his enemy, Compeyson, who had set himself up 'fur a gentleman' ('he'd been to a public boarding-school and had learning'), had received the lighter sentence on the presumption of his 'good character'. Magwitch's naïve but misguided benevolence removes Pip from a useful trade. It also temporarily renders him genteel but effectively *useless* in terms of the earnest world of work. He is taken from that world to one where he does not need to work. It is only when Magwitch's Australian fortune vanishes that Pip is obliged to take on a profession and, thanks to Herbert Pocket's offer, becomes a clerk in Clarriker and Co., the very firm in which Pip had earlier, and secretly, bought Herbert his own partnership. It is a thoroughly Dickensian move. By losing his private income and his 'expectations' Pip does not experience a drop in social status. Rather, in the novelist's eyes, he is enhanced by finding, and benefiting from, a useful, thoroughly middle-class occupation. As Pip himself notes of his business association with Herbert in the penultimate chapter of the novel, 'we were not in a grand way of business, but we had a good name, and worked for our profits, and did very well'. His eleven years in Egypt are no period of Israelite exile, but a period of consolidation which Pip's narrative passes over in relative silence. But the silence ought to be seen as speaking volumes. Few Victorian readers would have understood this period in Pip's life as representing defeat and disillusion. Pip, essentially like David Copperfield (though without his far more flamboyant career as a successful novelist), has found himself through earnest dedication.

Pip's wayward career has taken him from a village, to London, and to Egypt, but the crucial stage in his development is the one that is centred on London. In the metropolis he can be both gentleman and clerk, but in the country, given his humble origins and his lack of education, can really be neither. London first strikes him with much of the disturbing ambiguity with which it struck the commentators who were cited at the opening of this chapter:

We Britons had at that time particularly settled that it was treasonable to doubt our having and our being the best of everything: otherwise, while I was scared by the immensity of London, I think I might have had some faint doubts whether it was not rather ugly, crooked, narrow and dirty.   (vol. ii, ch. 1)

Here, rather than a splendiferous, well-planned city that proclaims its wealth on its streets, is a messy, untidy, money-grubbing place. It is characterized by the barely comprehensible hugeness that left the bemused Hippolyte Taine repeating the adjective 'enormous'. As ever in Dickens's fiction, it is full of milling, confusing crowds, but they are not Engels's directionless crowd of pushy monads. London, as Pip finds, will serve both to confuse class assumptions and then to redefine them according to new patterns of work. Although for that prototype of the commuting suburbanite, Mr Wemmick, it was a place where work was increasingly separated from a domestic environment, the complex nature of labour in London was moulded by its physical and economic geography. Dickens's London may be a city in which clerks and clerkships, trading firms and small shops, men of commerce and lawyers predominate, but this substantially middle-class vision of the urbanized nineteenth-century world has in fact proved largely prophetic of how modern urban society has since developed.

CHAPTER 5

UTILITARIANISM, RELIGION, AND HISTORY

THE first writer to figure in William Hazlitt's *The Spirit of the Age: or Contemporary Portraits* (1825) is the philosopher and economist Jeremy Bentham (1748–1832). He was thus presented to readers as a key figure in the culture of the opening years of the nineteenth century, though Hazlitt makes it plain that he was far from sympathetic to Bentham's philosophy and far from impressed by Bentham's character. He records one particularly revealing piece of hearsay:

Mr. Bentham, perhaps, over-rates the importance of his own theories. He has been heard to say (without any appearance of pride or affectation) that, 'he should like to live the remaining years of his life, a year at a time at the end of the next six or eight centuries, to see the effect which his writings would by that time have had upon the world.'[1]

The cynical Hazlitt feels constrained to add: 'Alas! His name will hardly live so long!' As history has shown, Bentham's direct influence was not to be felt even a hundred years after his death; and as far as we dare predict, it is unlikely to have much impact eight centuries later. Few readers, beyond scholars of the period, have returned to his work for instruction or guidance since. Historically minded economists and sociologists might refer to his achievement with modest respect, but few pure philosophers looking at their own tradition would give him so much as a nod. Even his contemporary, Hazlitt, regarded him as sadly deficient in innovative ideas:

Nor do we think, in point of fact, that Mr. Bentham has given any new or decided impulse to the human mind. He cannot be looked upon in the light of a discoverer in legislation or morals. He has not struck out any great leading principle or parent-truth, from which a number of others might be deduced, nor has he enriched the common and established stock of intelligence with original observations, like pearls thrown into wine.[2]

Nevertheless, in his time and in the years following his death, Bentham's intellect seemed to loom large. For John Stuart Mill, writing in 1838, he was both 'the father of English innovation, both in doctrines and in institutions' and 'the great *subversive*, or, in the language of continental philosophers, the great *critical*, thinker of his age and country'.[3] In early nineteenth-century Britain his influence and, perhaps more significantly, that of his disciples, proved to be pervasive. Bentham and the Benthamites were a particular bugbear of Dickens's.

The-once celebrated opening words of the *Introduction to the Principles of Morals and Legislation* (1789) outline the basic assumptions on which Bentham based his philosophical system:

Nature has placed mankind under the governance of two sovereign masters, *pain* and *pleasure*. It is for them alone to point out what we ought to do, as well as to determine what we shall do. On the one hand the standard of right and wrong, on the other the chain of causes and effects, are fastened to their throne.[4]

For Bentham the simple idea that humankind was motivated by the avoidance of pain and by the balancing search for pleasurable gratification was central to any legislative programme intent on improving the human lot. He also insisted on what he called the 'principle of utility' which he defined as

that principle which approves or disapproves of every action whatsoever, according to the tendency which it appears to have to augment or diminish the happiness of the party whose interest is in question: or, what is the same thing in other words, to promote or to oppose that happiness.[5]

It was from this principle that he and his followers derived the system of ideas known to posterity as 'Utilitarianism'. They also described themselves, somewhat self-righteously, as 'Philosophic Radicals'. By applying Bentham's assumptions about the motivation of individuals to society as a whole, they aimed to reform society by placing a new emphasis on the role of the enlightened administrator. Having dispensed with a set of ethical concepts ('Conscience', 'Principle', 'Moral Rectitude', 'Moral Duty') which Utilitarians regarded as masks for egotism or synonyms for the 'love of reputation', they went on to identify the enemies of benign social reform as the old obfuscating institutions: the Church, the Aristocracy, and the Law. By aspiring to facilitate general pleasure through legislation and by concomitantly minimalizing pain they hoped to bring about what Joseph Priestley famously summed up as 'the greatest happiness of the greatest number'. Seeking to proselytize, to retheorize, and to expound, they founded the *Westminster Review* in 1824 as a 'philosophic radical' alternative to the Tory *Edinburgh Review*.

Dickens and Utilitarianism

Although Dickens was generally a supporter of the reforming radicalism of the 1830s, and would have shared the Utilitarian distrust of the Church, the Aristocracy, and the Law, he had no real sympathy with the essence of the Benthamite programme. In 1838 John Stuart Mill put his finger on precisely what was humanly lacking in Bentham's philosophy and he thus helps us to understand what Dickens instinctively distrusted in it:

Man, that most complex being, is a very simple one in [Bentham's] eyes. Even under the head of *sympathy*, his recognition does not extend to the more complex forms of feeling—the love of *loving*, the need of sympathising support, or of an object of admiration and reverence. If he thought at all of any of the deeper feelings of human nature, it was but as idiosyncrasies of taste, with which neither the moralist nor the legislator had any concern.[6]

Mill's phrase concerning the motivation of Benthamite legislator almost exactly fits the complaint made against 'philosophers' throughout the early stages of *Oliver Twist* (Dickens refers in chapter 2, for example, to the board being constituted of 'very sage, deep, philosophical men'). Dickens had become aware of the guiding principles of Utilitarianism in the period when he had worked as a reporter on the *Morning Chronicle* in the early 1830s. Through its editor, John Black, the paper was a firm advocate and popularizer of social reform with a Benthamite tinge (and had been praised as such by Mill himself). Nevertheless, Dickens later claimed that he and Black had quarrelled many times about the effect of that cornerstone of Utilitarian legislation, the Poor Law Amendment Act of 1834 (Letters, ii. 275: 29 Apr. 1841). But it was not simply the Poor Law that offended Dickens's sense of humanity, it was the whole tenor of a philosophy, and by extension an economic system, which militated against the proper, and often spontaneous, practice of humane charity.

It could, on the one hand, be justly claimed that Dickens was reacting against a complex intellectual system, the full applications of which he had only barely grasped and to oppose which he too readily resorted to satire.[7] On the other hand, it can be argued with equal justice that he was intolerant of all formulas and all institutions which seemed to him to diminish or narrow human responsiveness. Utilitarianism, being the most prominent fomulaic social philosophy of his day, naturally attracted his antipathy. In one way, Benthamism represented a denial of the imagination. Just as it aimed to eschew what Mill called 'the love of *loving*', and to avoid the implications of 'the deeper feelings of human nature', so, for Dickens, it seemed to represent a rigid system which preferred statistics to souls and found heads more amenable than hearts. It is in this sense that he seems to refer to it when he describes Mr Dombey's complex feelings towards his son in the eighth chapter of *Dombey and Son*:

Some philosophers tell us that selfishness is at the root of our best loves and affections. Mr. Dombey's young child was, from the beginning, so distinctly important to him as a part of his own greatness, or (which is the same thing) of the greatness of Dombey and Son, that there is no doubt his parental affection might have been easily traced, like many a good superstructure of fair frame to a very low foundation.

Mr Dombey is a man with an *idée fixe*, a pride in himself and in the achievement of his inherited business. But he is also a man who has narrowed his perspectives and who proves to be incapable both of an imaginative leap beyond himself and of unselfish love. He is Benthamism in action. More pervasive, however, is the attack on 'the principle of utility' in all its aspects in *Hard Times*. Take, for example, the account Thomas Gradgrind seems to give of himself at the opening of book 1, chapter 2:

Thomas Gradgrind, Sir. A man of realities. A man of facts and calculations. A man who proceeds upon the principle that two and two are four, and nothing over, and who is not to be talked into allowing for anything over. Thomas Gradgrind, Sir—peremptorily Thomas—Thomas Gradgrind. With a rule and a pair of scales, and the multiplication table always in his pocket, Sir, ready to weigh and measure any parcel of human nature, and tell you exactly what it comes to. It is a mere question of figures, a case of simple arithmetic.

He is a man who has come to rely on statistics and on the undoubted rightness of his own opinions. When his son, Tom, reaches puberty, the narrator's comment on the event has a similar asperity: 'Time, sticking to him, passed him on into Bounderby's Bank, made him an inmate of Bounderby's house, necessitated the purchase of his first razor, and exercised him diligently in his calculations relative to number one' (bk. 1, ch. 14). The consequences of the educational system of which he so approves are finally brought home to Gradgrind in the penultimate chapter when Bitzer, 'true to his bringing-up' (as Dickens put it in his number plans), attempts to deliver the delinquent Tom over to the law. Bitzer is asked if he has a heart. He baldly insists in reply that 'the circulation . . . couldn't be carried on without one'. When further asked if his motive is self-interest, he produces a yet more slickly Utilitarian response:

I beg pardon for interrupting you, Sir, . . . but I am sure you know that the whole social system is a question of self-interest. What you must always appeal to, is a person's self-interest. It's your only hold. We are so constituted. I was brought up in that catechism when I was very young, Sir, as you are aware.

It is significant that Dickens entitled this penultimate chapter 'Philosophical'.

Dickens and Religion

If Dickens was generally intolerant of a 'philosophical' system that appeared to prefer heads to hearts, he was equally unsympathetic to many of the religious reformulations and redefinitions of his time. Yet again his antipathy seems to have been based on the assumption that any rigid interpretation of the letter of the Mosaic law implied a neglect of the spirit that gave life to that law. His distaste for the line of ranting Nonconformist preachers in his fiction, a line that begins with the 'prim-faced, red-nosed' Mr Stiggins in *Pickwick Papers*, is patent. It is a distaste which figures too in the pictures of those rigid, female, secular interpreters of the law: Miss Murdstone in *David Copperfield*, Miss Barbary in *Bleak House*, and Mrs Clennam in *Little Dorrit*. In each case Dickens seeks to suggest that the true spirit of the Christian gospel has been abandoned in favour of an unbending and intolerant Old Testament legalism. Mrs Clennam has a propensity for reading 'certain passages aloud from a book—sternly, fiercely, wrathfully—praying that her enemies . . . might be put to the edge of the sword, consumed by fire, smitten by plagues and leprosy. That their bones might be ground to dust, and that they might be utterly exterminated' (bk. 1, ch. 3). It is significant, too, that Miss Barbary is struck down in chapter 3 of *Bleak House* as Esther is reading the story of the woman taken in adultery to her (John 8: 3–7). Characteristically, instead of grasping the implications of the gospel of forgiveness, her last words are a monitory warning of the Second Coming: 'Watch ye therefore! Lest coming suddenly he find you sleeping. And what I say unto you I say unto all, Watch!' (Mark 13: 35–7). This perhaps formed a reminder to Victorian readers of the excesses of those religious millenarians who had proclaimed, by close reference both to Scripture and to the 'signs of the times', that the end of the world had been imminent in the 1830s.[8] Dickens's response to Scripture seems to have been conditioned by his own preference for the liberal interpretation rather than the literal. At the end of his will, reprinted as an appendix to Forster's biography, he exhorted his children 'to try to guide themselves by the teaching of the New Testament in its broad spirit, and to put no faith in any man's narrow construction of its letter here and there'. This injunction can be seen as deriving from a long-held antipathy to sectarianism and to strict Churchmanship, whether that Churchmanship were of the High, Middle, or Low variety (as contemporary Christians were wont to define such things). It is something that shines through the somewhat sentimental pages of the *Life of Our Lord* that he wrote for the use of his children in 1846. It was to bear a very different kind of fruit when for a period in the 1840s Dickens worshipped not as an Anglican but as a Unitarian.

Dickens's decision to rent a pew in a Unitarian chapel in 1843 was probably the result of his friendship with, and admiration of, prominent American Unitarians during his visit to the United States. American religious liberty, American tolerance of open-mindedness, and American social action were among the few aspects of American life for which he retained an unstinted respect. This flirtation with Unitarianism, which appears to have lasted until 1847, was also influenced by his feeling that the contemporary Church of England had shown more interest in addressing doctrinal issues than social ones.[9] He refers in a letter of 2 March 1843 to being 'disgusted with our Established Church, and its Puseyisms, and daily outrages on common sense and humanity (*Letters*, iii. 455). 'Puseyism' was the term regularly used by Dickens's contemporaries to describe the religious practices of growing numbers of Anglican clergy who associated themselves with the influential figure of the Oxford Professor of Hebrew, Edward Bouverie Pusey. Pusey had been, with John Henry Newman and John Keble, a leading influence on the development of the 'Oxford Movement'. This group of clergy had insisted on the need to restore a sense of catholic holiness to the Church of England of the 1830s and thereby to stress the Church's spiritual rather than its secular mission. They were also determined to resist the increasing influence of an avowedly reformist State, and of a radically Benthamite legislative programme. Through a series of provocative pamphlets, known collectively as the *Tracts for the Times*, they had sought to stir a sleepy Church into an awareness of the significance of its half-suppressed catholic tradition in the midst of a modern world obsessed with the virtues of change. The affairs of the Oxford Movement had reached a crisis point in the early 1840s with various diocesan bishops flounderingly attempting to counter and curb their influence. In March 1841 Newman had published *Tract XC*, presenting a careful reading of the formularies of the Church of England in an exclusively catholic manner. His tract was roundly condemned. A wounded Newman retired from his living at Oxford and in October 1845 he was received into the Roman Catholic Church, leaving Pusey as the effective leader of the 'party'.

For Dickens the teachings, arguments, and manoeuvres of the 'Puseyites' seem to have represented a dangerous diversion from the true mission of the Christian religion as he claimed to understand it. If the kind of strict reading of Scripture and scriptural law as practised by Evangelicals offended his liberal views, so, too, the extended debates about the niceties of creeds and rituals profoundly irritated him. Both were concerned with distracting moral and intellectual issues rather than with the broad sweep of a faith based on the exercise of charity. They placed ideas above action. On 13 March 1843 Dickens protested to a friend:

I find that I am getting horribly bitter about Puseyism. Good God to talk in these times of most untimely ignorance among the people, about what Priests shall wear, and whither they shall turn when they say their prayers.—They had better not discuss the latter question too long, or I shrewdly suspect they will turn to the right about: not easily to come back again. (*Letters*, iii. 462–3)

He sought a renewal of the Church's secular mission that he assumed the Puseyites had abandoned in favour of academic debate. His irritation stemmed both from a conviction that he was on the moral high ground and from a deep-seated distrust of intellectual nit-picking. In June of the same year he published in the *Examiner* a parody of a report of an enquiry into 'the Condition of Persons Variously Engaged in the University of Oxford'. Its irony is palpable:

It is unquestionably true that a boy was examined ... at Brinsley, in Derbyshire, who had been three years at school and could not spell 'Church' with great readiness, and, indeed, very seldom spell anything else. Whereas there is no doubt that, the persons employed in the University of Oxford can all spell 'Church' with great readiness, and, indeed very seldom spell anything else. But, on the other hand, it must not be forgotten that, in the minds of the persons employed in the University of Oxford, such comprehensive words as justice, mercy, charity, kindness, brotherly love, forbearance, gentleness, and Good Works, awaken no ideas whatever; while the evidence shows that the most preposterous notions are attached to the mere terms Priest and Faith.[10]

What Dickens appears to be attacking here is a propensity for definition which stands opposed to his own firmly held conviction that no further definition was required. If he was never the kind of fervent Protestant who assumes a total reliance on Holy Scripture, he was certainly the kind of progressivist Protestant who accepted the virtues of the Reformation as a liberation from superstition and an overweening and absolutist Church. For him the Oxford Movement represented an attempt to argue from tradition rather than from a pragmatic position informed by history. They looked backwards for evidence to support their case, not to present secular experience or to the supposed demands of the future. They sought to prove their points from the history of the Church, from ancient books and neglected documents, and not from what Dickens would have seen as the more pressing evidence of the streets and alleys of Victorian England. He refused to recognize that there might be a connection between the two, or that searching for the roots of holiness might stimulate social action. For him the study of history offered not a series of alternatives or examples, but dire warnings to the present.

Dickens was to remain intolerant of the Roman Catholic Church, its structures, its teachings, and its history, and he was to have even less time for those Anglican apologists for a Catholic understanding of the role of the Church of England. His rooted anti-Catholic prejudices were aired in public in *Pictures from Italy*, but his correspondents were frequently regaled with bitter asides and pointed observations about supposed Roman abuses. When he visited the Alpine abbey of Mont St Bernard in September 1846 the best he could find to say about the monks was that they were 'sheer humbug' and 'a lazy set of fellows; not over fond of going out themselves . . . the convent being a common tavern in everything but the sign (*Letters*, iv. 619: 6 Sept. 1846). He does not seem to have revised his opinion much, or to have shown much gratitude for the monks' hospitality, when he described the monastery again in *Little Dorrit* and in the *Household Words* essay 'Lying Awake' (30 Oct. 1852). While the monks struck him as essentially passive, he was yet more exercised about active Catholic influence. When he wrote to John Forster describing the aftermath of a minor political revolution in Geneva in 1846 he protested about what he saw was the pernicious interference of the Jesuits in Swiss affairs:

If I were a Swiss with a hundred thousand pounds, I would be as steady against the Catholic cantons and the propagation of Jesuitism as any radical among 'em: believing the dissemination of Catholicity to be the most horrible means of political and social degradation left in the world. (*Letters*, iv. 639: 20 Oct. 1846)

What Dickens appears to have disliked most about Roman Catholicism was the association between its rigidly enforced doctrines and its historic political aspirations. He reacted against it as an institution with an unbendingly dogmatic definition of itself. That dogmatic definition seems to have struck him as unscriptural over definition, an intellectual exercise which had developed into a rigid system of control. Like many British travellers in the nineteenth century he presumed that Protestantism, whether in England or Switzerland, encouraged progress, liberal thought, individual dignity, the work ethic, and high standards of personal hygiene. By contrast, Catholicism fostered political conservatism, mental enslavement, tyranny, laziness, and slovenliness. This attitude is particularly evident in the account of Dickens's visit to the former papal enclave of Avignon in

Pictures from Italy. He shows himself to be initially troubled by a series of modern ex-voto paintings in the cathedral, seeing the principle behind the idea of an ex-voto as some unhappy survival of paganism: 'Though votive offerings were not unknown in Pagan Temples, and are evidently among the many compromises made between the false religion and the true, when the true was in its infancy, I could wish that all the other compromises were as harmless.'

The Roman Church, the political and spiritual heir of pagan Rome, is therefore seen as having compromised with paganism long ago and to have continued to support practices unworthy of a matured understanding of the faith. As Dickens explores the neighbouring papal palace he sees evidence of an even worse perversion of ancient Roman polity. Here he was shown the tower where Cola di Rienzi, the fourteenth-century revolutionary who had attempted to re-establish a Roman republic, had supposedly been imprisoned (Rienzi had been the subject of Bulwer-Lytton's novel of that name published in 1835). But it is not simply the injustice meted out to a medieval radical that offends him, it is what was once supposed to be the prison of the Inquisition that most fascinates and appalls him. Dickens, who was doubtless following the grim description offered by Murray's *Hand-Book for Travellers in France* of 1843, claims that he was shown these cells by a 'little, old swarthy woman' whom he caricatures as the 'She-Goblin'. His description is appropriately Gothic in its tone:

I am gazing round me, with the horror that the place inspires, when Goblin clutches me by the wrist, and lays, not her skinny finger, but the handle of a key upon her lip. She invites me, with a jerk to follow her. I do so. She leads me out into a room adjoining—a rugged room, with a funnel-shaped, contracting roof, open at the top, to the bright day. I ask her what it is. She folds her arms, leers hideously, and stares. I ask again. She glances round, to see that all the little company are there; sits down upon a mound of stones; throws up her arms, and yells out, like a fiend, 'La Salle de la Question!' The Chamber of Torture! And the roof was made to that shape to stifle the victim's cries!

Although the presence of the histrionic 'She-Goblin' helps to render this passage almost melodramatic in tone, there is no escaping Dickens's own sense that only a perverted sense of religious authority could have established an Inquisition and employed torture to enforce its power. As Dickens's own account goes on to prove, this medieval oppression found its inevitable and unhappy response at the time of the French Revolution when priests were amongst the victims of a massacre by an Avignon mob in the same palace. As he would later do in *A Tale of Two Cities*, Dickens insists that old injustice breeds new injustice, and old oppression new oppression:

Was it a portion of the great scheme of Retribution, that the cruel deed should be committed in this place! That a part of the atrocities and monstrous institutions, which had been, for scores of years, at work, to change men's nature, should in its last service, tempt them with the ready means of gratifying their furious and beastly rage! Should enable them to show themselves, in the height of their frenzy, no worse than a great, solemn, legal establishment, in the height of its power! No worse! Much better. They used the Tower of the Forgotten, in the name of Liberty—their liberty; an earth-born creature, nursed in the black mud of the Bastille moats and dungeons, and necessarily betraying many evidences of its unwholesome bringing up—but the Inquisition used it in the name of Heaven.

Dickens is parading his self-righteous sense of Protestant offence, but he is also linking the Inquisition, and the religious mentality that spawned the Inquisition, to the autocratic system of government which was established by Louis XIV and which lurched into a bloody collapse under Louis XVI. Catholicism and autocracy, religion and politics seem to go hand in hand.

Dickens and History

The link Dickens makes between an oppressive ecclesiastical system and political tyranny may seem naïve, but it was a common-enough one in the nineteenth century. As his contemporary Thomas Babington Macaulay argued in his best-selling *History of England* (1849–61), the triumph of English liberty and constitutional government was rooted in the Reformation settlement, in the Civil War, and, above all, in the so-called 'Glorious Revolution' of 1688–9, the bloodless revolution which had ejected the 'tyrannous' Catholic James II and replaced him with a Protestant monarchy dependent on the goodwill of a Protestant parliament. This reading of British history has since been known as the 'Whig interpretation'. Dickens had a copy of the *History* in his library at the time of his death and it is possible that its arguments served to reinforce those long-standing historical, political, and religious prejudices that he expressed in simple terms in his own *A Child's History of England* (serialized in *Household Words*, 1851–3). Dickens brings his *Child's History* virtually to a close with an account of what he calls 'England's great and glorious Revolution'. The very brief last chapter merely allots paragraphs to subsequent reigns, pausing briefly over Jacobitism ('I think the Stuarts were a public nuisance altogether') and the loss of America under George III ('that immense country, made independent under WASHINGTON and left to itself, became the United States; one of the greatest nations of the earth'). Throughout Dickens seems to prefer anecdotalism to analysis and to reveal a penchant for snap judgements or for what would now be called 'sound bites'. Nevertheless, it should be remembered that the *Child's History* is precisely what it purports to be, a *child's* history: didactic, forthright, vivid, and entertaining. Beyond its determining political and religious prejudices we should not suppose that it represents Dickens's last word on the nature of British history or the development of Britain's political and religious institutions.

In the early 1940s the critic Humphry House somewhat scornfully wrote of Dickens's attitude to history:

It is curious that he, who was so scornful of the moral abuses of the times in which he lived, should have almost universally condemned the times before him. There is no trace of idealizing the past. When he writes of the Middle Ages, or even of the late eighteenth century, he does so with an amused contempt for their standards of life, which shows him as a proud Victorian conscious of living in a progressive age.[11]

House cites what he sees as evidence of this from Dickens's fiction and he refers tellingly to the series of joke titles that Dickens invented for the false book backs which decorated the door of his study at Gad's Hill Place. These titles are often whimsical ('Cat's Lives' is in nine volumes; 'Adam's Precedents' is in one); occasionally they are bitterly satirical and echo themes of the novels ('History of a Short Chancery Suit' is in nine volumes with an index, while 'Hansard's Guide to Refreshing Sleep' amounts to no less than thirty-two volumes). Most apposite are the series collectively entitled 'The Wisdom of our Ancestors', the volumes of which purport to deal with such issues as Ignorance, Superstition, The Block,

The Stake, Dirt, Disease, and The Rack.[12] Although these supposed repositories of ancient wisdom might seem to be echoes of the prejudices which Dickens expressed in his account of his visit to Avignon, it should again be recalled that they are essentially sardonic jokes. House is right, of course, about Dickens's general antipathy to anything to do with the Middle Ages and towards any latter-day apologist for things medieval, but he is far more blinkered when he seeks to suggest that the novelist was generally intolerant of the past and that he was ill-informed when it came to the study of more recent history. Dickens may sentimentalize the somewhat fussy rural gothic architecture which surrounds the dying Little Nell in *The Old Curiosity Shop*, but in *The Mystery of Edwin Drood* the cathedral city of Cloisterham seems to be pervaded by the dust of decay (the cathedral itself has an 'earthy odour'). Unlike Sir Walter Scott, or George Eliot, or his friend Edward Bulwer-Lytton, Dickens was never to set a historical novel in the Middle Ages or in the Renaissance. In not doing so, he was certainly indicating a lack of interest in the more distant past. Equally significantly, however, he was also pointing up the fact that he *did* choose to set two major works in the period of the late eighteenth century. It ought to be appreciated by his readers that both *Barnaby Rudge: A Tale of the Riots of 'Eighty* and *A Tale of Two Cities* suggest a far from shallow acquaintance with the culture and history of the period.

Sir Walter Scott's *Waverley* of 1814 is in many ways the *fons et origo* of the nineteenth-century historical novel. It not only established many aspects of the model on which Scott would shape his subsequent historical fictions, it provided a vivid example of how a later novelist might seek to explore the leading social issues which moulded the generation of his or her grandparents. The subtitle to *Waverley* (''Tis Sixty years Since') would provide cues for writers as diverse as George Eliot, Gaskell, Hardy, and Tolstoy. History and the study of history mattered acutely to nineteenth-century thinkers and readers, and the history of the period 1780–1815 was to have a particular resonance for them, marking as it did a transition between a predominantly aristocratic world dominated by the monarchic principle and a bourgeois world in which issues of representative government and social mobility were keenly debated. Dickens, in particular, was the heir to the kind of progressivist historical arguments developed during the period of the Enlightenment (he owned the histories of England written by Hume and Smollett). If for Scott, that other heir of the Edinburgh Enlightenment, progressive, modern Scotland seemed to have emerged in the aftermath of the defeat of Jacobitism in the mid-1740s, so, for his English successors, the period of the Revolutionary Wars against France seemed to mark a turning point in social and political history. Although to some observers the French Revolution may have seemed to be a disruption of the steady evolution of constitutional government, to others it represented the climax of the Enlightenment campaign to establish the principles on which human rights were to be based in future. In Britain the years 1780–1815 also saw the gradual triumph of the industrial revolution as much as they witnessed the success of British arms. The growth of the influence of major cities and provincial towns ran concurrently with a shift of power away from country landowners to urban manufacturers and tradesmen. These social developments brought with them an appetite for political change, one which culminated in the pressure for steady parliamentary reform in the 1830s. The period presented fertile ground for those novelists who sought to use their art as a means of exploring both how change came about and how it shaped the lives of private individuals. As Macaulay was amongst the first to recognize, Scott had not simply changed the way in which history could be written by a new generation of historians, he had also stimulated a new appetite for history among the reading public.

We cannot be certain when Dickens first became acquainted with Scott's work. He certainly owned an incomplete set of the novels in 1844 (six volumes of a forty-eight-volume set appear to have been missing, though they had been replaced by the time of his death). He was, however, both through his wife's family connections and through his general acquaintance with modern literature, acutely aware of the nature of Scott's achievement as a writer. Dickens was not much given to theorizing about literature and the nature of his own art, but one letter of his gives an indication of the extent to which he had learned from the manner in which Scott balanced fictional figures against historical ones, and especially from the fact that he weighted his fictions towards an exploration of the experiences, insights, and dilemmas of imagined, rather than documented, characters. Like Scott, he believed that fiction was freer in its analysis of a given historical situation than was a history book. Much of the quality of this analysis derived from an imaginative recreation of dramatic events and a presentation of particularly charged situations. In November 1841, the painter and engraver John Landseer had written to him asking why he had not introduced the celebrated John Wilkes, who was a London magistrate at the time of the Gordon Riots, as a character in *Barnaby Rudge*. Dickens's reply tells us much about how he thought of his own historical novel:

I determined . . . not to notice [Wilkes] in Barnaby, for this reason.— It is almost indispensable in a work of fiction that the characters who bring the catastrophes about, and play important parts, should belong to the Machinery of the Tale,—and the introduction towards the end of the story, where there is always a great deal to do, of actors until then unheard of, is a thing to be avoided, if possible, in every case. Now, if I had talked about Wilkes, it would have been necessary to glance at his career and previous position . . . and if I had stopped to do that, I should have stopped the riots which must go on to the end headlong, pell mell, or they lose their effect . . . I need not tell you who are so well acquainted with 'Art' in all its forms, that in the description of such scenes, a broad, bold, hurried effect must be produced, or the reader instead of being forced and driven along by imaginary crowds will find himself dawdling very uncomfortably through the town, and greatly wondering what might be the matter. In this kind of work the object is,—not to tell everything, but to select the striking points and beat them into the page with a sledge-hammer . . . my object has been to convey an idea of multitudes, violence, and fury; and even to lose my own dramatis personae in the throng, or only see them dimly, through the fire and smoke. (*Letters*, ii. 417–18: 5 Nov. 1841)

Dickens, the novelist, is therefore showing himself as determined to write fiction rather than documentary, to place 'art' over the demand for a record. As his letter reveals, he realized that a novel like *Barnaby Rudge* had a particular dynamic derived from the motives and actions of his fictional characters ('the Machinery of the Tale'). Equally significantly, he knew that his central concern demanded that these same fictional characters should be subsumed in historical events over which they exercised no real control. The anti-Catholic riots of 1780 were a matter of mobs, not of individual motives; of generalized 'fury' and mindless violence, not of considered action. The account of this 'fire and smoke' is perhaps the finest thing about the often-neglected *Barnaby Rudge*, something that remains

powerfully in a reader's mind long after the whims, gestures, eccentricities, and idioms of minor characters have receded in the memory. Dickens was clearly both disturbed and inspired by this recall of
mob rule and urban violence, and the vividness of his imaginative
account of it was intended both to shock and to inform his readers.
The riots may have been inspired by the deranged, ranting, obsessive
Lord George Gordon, but, as Dickens's account shows, they easily
degenerate into the uncontrollable, undirected misrule of the mob.
Readers are made aware of multiple motives, of the working-out of
numerous petty grudges and tensions, and, above all, of a general
penchant for gratuitous violence on the part of a mob which is only
rarely individualized.

In *Barnaby Rudge* Dickens had, however, been careful to suggest
that the cause of much of this violence lay in the social conditions
which he believed pertained in the London of June 1780 (just over
'sixty years since' in 1841). To quell the Gordon Riots some 11,000
militiamen and a further 1,000 officers had been drafted into
London. But what troubled Dickens was both the root cause of this
popular discontent and the arbitrary and ruthless 'justice' imposed
on the city once public order had been restored. The novel explores
the nature of a severely stratified society in which political power,
privilege, and influence still lay in the hands of the landed class, a
class which provided government ministers, militiamen, judges,
magistrates, and even jurymen. Dickens takes the odiously snobbish,
scheming Sir John Chester as representative of this class (and
Chester in his turn expresses himself with much of the smugness of
that great bugbear of Dickens's, Lord Chesterfield). The dispossessed, the urban underclass, may have no particular grudge against
Catholics, but they have a motive in seeking a redress of their many
grievances. The looting of Catholic property in London proves to be
symptomatic of a wider malaise. Dickens seeks to relate two kinds of
mental disturbance (Gordon's and Barnaby's) to a larger social propensity for recklessness and destruction, but he was also determined
to demonstrate that eighteenth-century England possessed a cruel
and repressive legal code and was governed by a cynical aristocracy who used that legal code for their own ends. As a young man
Dickens had seen the number of capital offences on the statute book
considerably reduced during Sir Robert Peel's tenure of the office of
home secretary (1824–9). His retrospect on the England of George

III is, however, informed by a horror at the old 'Bloody Code'. This horror is most clearly expressed in the blackly comic, self-justifying declarations of Ned Dennis, the public hangman. Dennis is particularly forthcoming to George Gordon's secretary, Gashford:

Parliament says this here—says Parliament, 'If any man, woman or child, does anything which goes again a certain number of our acts'—how many hanging laws may there be at this present time, Muster Gashford? Fifty? . . . Well, say fifty. Parliament says, 'If any man, woman or child does anything again any one of them fifty acts, that man, woman or child shall be worked off by Dennis . . . I got Mary Jones, a young woman of nineteen who come up to Tyburn with a infant at her breast, and was worked off for taking a piece of cloth off the counter of a shop in Ludgate Hill, and putting it down again when the shopman see her; and who never done any harm before, and only tried to do that, in consequence of her husband having been pressed three weeks previous, and she being left to beg, with two young children—as was proved upon the trial. Ha, ha!—Well! That being the law and practice of England, is the glory of England, aint it, Muster Gashford.

The case of Mary Jones, to which Dennis refers, was a real one. His relish for his grim trade is only slightly tempered by the fear that, if Catholicism were to triumph, 'boiling and roasting' might supersede good old Protestant hanging. What Dickens is suggesting here is that violence breeds violence, and that the 'Bloody Code' merely sows the seeds of a more pervasive lust for blood. When the law breaks down, as it does during the 'Riots of Eighty', the lust for bloody vengeance thrives in its temporary demise. As the novel suggests, however, the reimposition of the rule of law required the restoration of this same 'Bloody code' and a process of bloody retribution as the rioters are pursued, tried, and executed. Here, yet again, Dickens is attempting to demonstrate his theory that history is a pattern of causes and effects, of repression which breeds further repression and oppression which fosters worse oppression.

This uncomplicated, even unsubtle, theory of history would bear its richest fruit in *A Tale of Two Cities*. Here Dickens was to explore both a contrast between the affairs of England and France in the eighteenth century and the traumatic impact of the French Revolution on private lives. He was thus able to investigate the interrelationship of past and present, and the interconnection between memory and the consequences of remembering, in both public and the private realms. Even the shapely plot of his novel (of which Dickens was inordinately proud) served to emphasize these inter-connections and consequences. Dr Manette, the victim of the arbi-trary injustice of the *ancien régime*, is obliged to live through the consequences of the curse he placed on his persecutors when he learns that his own daughter has married into the aristocratic family that he had once cursed. For Dickens, history has both an in-exorability and an arbitrariness. Only human action, individual relationships, and private commitments made in the present can serve to counter the social divisions and the political hatreds inherited from the past. His formula is neat, but it is not simplistic: the French Revolution came about as the inevitable consequence of the exercise of tyranny and injustice, but the tyranny and the injustice which the Revolution introduces in *its* turn are given a perspective by individual decisions, by private changes of heart, and by the triumph of human love which is prepared to give its self utterly and selflessly.

Despite Dickens's basically optimistic Enlightenment-influenced view of the historical process, the composition of *A Tale of Two Cities* was most influenced by the often contorted and ambiguous philosophy, and the vividly inspirational prose, of Thomas Carlyle. At the opening of his novel Dickens sees the Revolution as growing out of historic circumstances, just as the trees that were to be cut down to make the guillotine and the farm carts that were to bear the guillotine's victims to their deaths were part of an established and inevitable order of things. So too in the second chapter of his *French Revolution* Carlyle recognizes a more complex evolutionary process at work in the natural world, a process which is echoed in the workings-out of human fate:

For ours is a most fictile world; and man is the most fingent plastic of creatures. A world not fixable; not fathomable! An unfathomable Some-what, which is *Not we*; which we can work with, and live amidst,—and model, miraculously in our miraculous Being, and name World.—But if the very Rocks and Rivers (as Metaphysic teaches) are, in strict language, *made* by those outward Senses of ours, how much more, by the Inward Sense, are all Phenomena of the spiritual kind: Dignities, Authorities, Holies, Unholies! Which inward sense, moreover, is not permanent like the outward ones, but forever growing and changing. (vol. i, bk. 1, ch. 2)

The natural world changes and a various human perception of it

changes too, but what the historical figures at the opening of
Carlyle's narrative fail to perceive is that their own hold on power
and their ability to control events has slipped away from them. Their
titles, their influence, and their claims to dignity and honour are now
precarious. One King Louis dies and is succeeded by another Louis,
but the France bequeathed by the dying Louis XV to his heir is, as
Carlyle sees it, gripped by an unreal perception of itself. It is a
perception variously fed by what Carlyle sees as a dilettante, do-
nothing culture infected by a casually sceptical 'Philosophism':

In such a France, as in a Powder-tower, where fire unquenched and now
unquenchable is smoking and smouldering all round, has Louis XV laid
down to die. With Pompadourism and Dubarryism, his Fleur-de-lis has
been shamefully struck down in all lands and on all seas; Poverty invades
even the Royal Exchequer, and Tax-farming can squeeze out no more;
there is a quarrel of twenty-five years' standing with the Parlement;
everywhere Want, Dishonesty, Unbelief, and hotbrained Sciolists for
state-physicians: it is a portentous hour.
    Such things can the eye of History see in this sick-room of King Louis,
Which were invisible to the Courtiers there.

Carlyle, the historian, seeks to observe the France of the *ancien
régime* drifting towards its bloody destiny with 'the eye of History'.
For Dickens, that view was to be additionally determined by the eye
of fiction.

Dickens used the plot of *A Tale of Two Cities* as a means of
suggesting to his readers that individuals possessed the power to free
themselves from historical conditioning and from an imposed uni-
formity of response. He sought, on the one hand, to re-emphasize in
his last chapter that Sydney Carton's fate is the result of past political mistakes and that those mistakes are repeatable mistakes ('Crush
humanity out of shape once more, under similar hammers, and it
will twist itself into the same tortured forms'). But as this last
chapter also reveals, he placed his final emphasis on Carton's dying
prophecies. These prophecies are as much private as public. Carton
has saved the life of his one-time rival, Charles Darnay, and, through
Darnay, he has enhanced the future of the Darnay family. There will
be a son born who will bear Sydney's now-honoured name and who
will redeem Sydney's professional and personal sins of omission.
This son will not only administer proper justice, but he will also visit
a Paris freed of the 'disfigurements' of the Revolution. It is not

simply the physical 'disfigurement' of the guillotine, it is also a 'disfigurement' of minds and attitudes. For readers Carton's sacrifice of himself emerges as an affirmation not a negation, and Dickens has carefully placed it within a Christian context. *A Tale of Two Cities* is, in its distinctive way, as pointed a critique of Benthamism as *Oliver Twist* and *Hard Times*. Only the most perverted of Utilitarians could have regarded Carton's sacrifice as predicated by pleasure-seeking or self-gratification. Instead of the 'principle of utility' Dickens appears to be suggesting that neither love nor moral rectitude had been negated in his own theory of human action. By exploring the vital interconnection of the private and the public, the personal and the social, in fiction he was attempting to suggest that even history itself was subject to a greater law than that of utility.

CHAPTER 6

SCIENCE AND TECHNOLOGY

WHEN Dickens first visited Rome in 1845 he claimed that he could never see enough of the Coliseum (*Letters*, iv. 288: 26 Mar. 1845). In *Pictures from Italy* he famously described his fascination with the great ruin:

It is the most impressive, the most stately, the most solemn, grand, majestic, mournful sight, conceivable. Never, in its bloodiest prime, can the sight of the gigantic Coliseum, full and running over with the lustiest life, have moved one heart, as it must move all who look upon it now, a ruin. GOD be thanked: a ruin!

The Coliseum was magnificent in its ruin and its redundancy, but this same redundancy seemed to render the ruined arena especially haunting. When he returned to Rome in 1853, however, he noted with relish one significant change that seemed to enhance the deep impression the Coliseum had formerly made on him: 'The Electric Telegraph shoots through the Coliseum like a sun-beam—in at one ruined arch, and out at another' (*Letters*, vii. 193: 14 Nov. 1853). What might have struck an antiquarian observer as an example of the highest and most intrusive philistinism, is seen by Dickens as evidence of progress. The electric telegraph seems to him to be testimony to a civilization that has advanced so far beyond gratuitous bloodshed that it can happily embrace a new era of enlightened technology.

Dickens was never one to dwell longingly or nostalgically on the achievements of the past. As we have seen in the previous chapter, Dickens preferred to see history as offering a warning to the present rather than setting an example to it. Like Mr Boffin in *Our Mutual Friend*, shocked by the 'confounding enormities' described in Gibbon's *The Decline and Fall of the Roman Empire*, he saw the pages of history as being substantially peopled by 'scarers'. Precedents were tutelary, rarely occasions for reverence. Soon after the novelist's death that great expounder of the moral message of architecture,

John Ruskin, complained to an American friend that he found Dickens too much bound up with the economic and technological achievements of his own time to be bothered with the civilization of his ancestors:

Dickens was a pure modernist—a leader of the steam-whistle party *par excellence*—and he had no understanding of any power of antiquity except a sort of jackdaw sentiment for cathedral towers . . . His hero is essentially the ironmaster . . . he has advanced by his influence every principle that makes them harder—the love of excitement, in all classes, and the fury of business competition, and the distrust both of nobility and clergy which, wide enough and fatal enough, and too justly founded, needed no apostle to the mob, but a grave teacher of priests and nobles themselves, for whom Dickens had essentially no word.[1]

This is generally perceptive and justified criticism. We shall return to the issue of Dickens and the 'steam-whistle party' later in this chapter, but it is Ruskin's contention that the essential Dickensian hero is the ironmaster that is worth exploring here.

Dickens and the Industrial Revolution

It is true, as we have already seen, that Dickens's perception of social class stems from his essential allegiance to the productive, urban middle classes, the class of self-made men amongst whom he counted himself. He was a ready distruster of the aristocratic and clerical old order, an old order which he had seen as challenged in history by the principles of the Reformation and latterly by the libertarian and egalitarian aspirations of the American and French Revolutions. The England in which Dickens grew up was one in which commerce, manufacture, and technology had steadily shifted power away from the old landowning classes. If political influence all too often remained in the hands of landowners, the cultural and economic energy of the nation was now predominantly bourgeois. Nevertheless, that typical product of the industrial revolution, the 'ironmaster' whom Ruskin identifies as a normative Dickensian hero, only actually figures in one of Dickens's novels: *Bleak House*. Here Sir Leicester Dedlock, the Lincolnshire baronet and controller of pocket-boroughs, represents the old order. The man identified as his most likely social antagonist is Mr Rouncewell, the son of his house-keeper and a manufacturer in 'the iron country farther north' who has conspicuously named his son 'Watt'. Dickens's choice of names is indicative. Sir Leicester and his kind hold the nation in a 'dead-lock', a position that inhibits both movement and escape. This same Sir Leicester assumes that Watt Rouncewell has been provocatively named after the medieval 'arch-rebel' Wat (or Walter) Tyler, the leader of the Peasants' Revolt who had been killed in 1381. He has in fact been christened in honour of the great engineer James Watt (1736–1819), the perfector of the steam-engine, the pioneering sur-veyor of canals and harbours, and the projector of the idea of the screw-propeller. Watt Rouncewell's father had, as a young man, built himself a model of a power-loom and he has gone on to establish himself in the industrial north of England, a place which Sir Leicester darkly assumes is peopled by 'some odd thousand conspirators, swarthy and grim, who were in the habit of turning out by torch-light, two or three nights in the week, for unlawful purposes' (ch. 7). Rouncewell may be a new man with new, and perhaps radical, ideas (he is even proposing to send his daughter and daughter-in-law to Germany for 'a little polishing up in her education') but he is no Chartist. Nor does he seem to be the kind of man to employ or encourage Chartists. When he is sought out by Trooper George in chapter 63 of the novel he is discovered in 'a busy town, with a clang of iron in it'. Rouncewell's factory is typified by its seemingly random energy:

A great perplexity of iron lying about, in every stage, and in a vast variety of shapes; in bars, in wedges, in sheets, in tanks, in boilers, in axles, in wheels, in cogs, in cranks, in rails; twisted and wrenched into eccentric and perverse forms, as separate parts of machinery; mountains of it broken up, and rusty in its age; distant furnaces of it glowing and bubbling in its youth. Bright fireworks of it showering about, under the blows of the steam-hammer; red-hot iron, cold-black iron; and iron taste, an iron smell, and a Babel of iron sounds.

This is an England of furnaces and smoke-stacks, not of country houses and rolling agricultural estates. This may not be the England that Dickens knew best, but it was certainly one that stimulated and fascinated him. When, for example, in September 1858 he gave a reading in the small cathedral city of Durham he complained of the 'local bores' in his audience and found the city 'not large enough' for his tastes. As an alternative, he happily walked across the thirteen miles of scarred landscape that separated Durham from the industrial town of Sunderland, making 'a little fanciful photograph' in his mind of the pit-country (*Letters*, viii. 669: 24 Sept. 1858). Medieval Durham does not seem to have satisfied Dickens's 'jackdaw sentiment for cathedral towers', but the road to Sunderland stirred him with its untidy evidence of industrial energy and noisy creativity.

The picture of a manufacturing town and of the mindsets of those who ran the local economies of industrial northern England is far less benign in *Hard Times* of course. As Dickens wrote to Elizabeth Gaskell on 21 April 1854, his novel was to deal with 'the monstrous claims at domination made by a certain class of manufacturers, and the extent to which the way is made easy for working men to slide down into discontent under such hands' (*Letters*, vii. 320). In *Hard Times* he seems not to be directing his attack against machinery but against what Carlyle would have seen as a machine-like mentality. Gradgrindian principles are reductively Benthamite, not a celebration of industrial prowess and technological achievement. Dry statistics are seen as destroying both the imaginative faculty and the human delight in invention. In *Little Dorrit*, the novel that succeeded *Hard Times*, however, Dickens presents his readers with an inventor frustrated by government paper work and official indifference. We first encounter Daniel Doyce as a man humiliated by the tergiversations of the Circumlocution Office. Mr Meagles introduces him to Arthur Clennam as

a smith and engineer. He is not in a large way, but he is well known as a very ingenious man. A dozen years ago, he perfects an invention (involving a very curious secret process) of great importance to his country and his fellow creatures. I won't say how much money it cost him, or how many years of his life he has been about it, but he brought it to perfection a dozen years ago. (bk. 1, ch. 10)

In those dozen years Doyce has been systematically ignored by the very government that he sought to benefit by his invention. In book 1, chapter 16 we learn much more about his history as a technological innovator. He is

a man of great modesty and good sense; and, though a plain man, had been much accustomed to combine what was original and daring in conception with what was patient and minute in execution, to be by any means an ordinary man ... it appeared that he was the son of a north-country blacksmith, and had originally been apprenticed by his widowed mother to a lock-maker; that he had 'struck out a few little things' at the lock-maker's, which had led to his being released from his indentures with a present, which present had enabled him to gratify his ardent wish to bind himself to a working engineer, under whom he had labored hard, learned hard, and lived hard, seven years. His time being out, he had 'worked in the shop' at weekly wages seven or eight years more; and had then betaken himself to the banks of the Clyde, where he had studied, and filed, and hammered, and improved his knowledge, theoretical and practical, for six or seven years more. There he had had an offer to go to Lyons, which he had accepted; and from Lyons he had been engaged to go to Germany, and in Germany he had had an offer to go to St. Petersburg, and there he had done very well indeed—never better. However, he had naturally felt a preference for his own country, and a wish to gain distinction there, and to do whatever service he could do, there rather than elsewhere. And so he had come home. And so at home he had established himself in business, and had invented and executed, and worked his way on, until, after a dozen years of constant suit and service, he had been enrolled in the Great British Legion of Honour, the Legion of the Rebuffed of the Circumlocution Office, and had been decorated with the great British Order of Merit, the Order of the Disorder of the Barnacles and Stiltstalkings.

The main thrust of this paragraph is Dickens's complaint against a self-satisfied and self-perpetuating Civil Service. The story of Doyce's career consequently appears to be more exemplary of disappointment than of actual achievement. Nevertheless, what Dickens wants his readers to understand is how a talented contemporary engineer's career might indeed have developed. Like Rouncewell, Doyce is a great self-improver. Unlike Pip, who in *Great Expectations* is removed from the smithy and given gentlemanly pretensions, Doyce never quite relinquishes his artisan roots and never seems to worry about getting his hands dirty on the shop floor. He remains ungenteelly linked both to metals and to steam-driven machines. His time on the banks of the Clyde may indeed associate him not only with Clydeside's great tradition of shipbuilding and engineering but also with James Watt who had famously thought of the idea of the separate condenser for the steam-engine while walking on Glasgow Green. His period in Lyons is doubtless linked to the city's famous silk manufacturing and his profitable sojourn in St Petersburg probably re-establishes his primary interest in metallurgy (though it is unclear whether or not Russia is to be identified with the 'barbaric Power with valuable possessions on the map of the world' that tempts Doyce abroad again). Doyce is perhaps Dickens's quintessential man of science, a 'useful' man who is both practical and inventive. It is, however, indicative of Dickens's ignorance of engineering that the nature and quality of his great invention is never actually spelled out to readers.

Dickens and Victorian Science

We cannot be certain as to how informed Dickens was when it came to the drift of scientific thought in the nineteenth century. As a young man he had certainly exhibited a marked intolerance towards contemporary experimental science in two lengthy articles published in *Bentley's Miscellany* in October 1837 and September 1838. Both articles describe meetings of 'The Mudfog Association for the Advancement of Everything' and both satirize the British Association for the Advancement of Science, a body founded in 1831 with the laudable intention of promoting 'the intercourse of those who cultivate science with each other'. The Association had held its inaugural meeting in York in 1831 and had met annually thereafter (most recently at Liverpool in 1837 and at Newcastle in 1838). Dickens had invented the name 'Mudfog' in February 1837 for the benighted town in which Oliver Twist had the misfortune to be born. In its creator's eyes, therefore, Mudfog's 'Association for the Advancement of Everything' was most unlikely to advance anything but obfuscation. It bears a closer relationship to Jonathan Swift's picture of the deranged academicians of Laputa in *Gulliver's Travels* than it does to the proceedings of the real British Association. As readers of *Bentley's Miscellany* were to discover, however, visitors to Dickens's fictional scientific assembly included the aptly named Professors Snore, Doze, Wheezy, Muff, and Nogo, men who presided over learned papers on such things as 'The Industrious Flea', on a 'cauliflower somewhat larger than a chaise-umbrella which had been raised by no other artificial means than the simple application of highly-carbonated soda water as manure', and on the last moments of a learned pig called Solomon who unhappily expired due to the effects of a cold. In the Anatomy and Medicine Section Dickens has his Professor Muff explain an experiment with infinitesimal doses of drugs, noting in particular the case of a publican who was rendered drunk by drinking three drops of rum in a bucket of water. As we might expect, given Dickens's contempt for Benthamite methods, the Statistics section is presented with some 'curious calculations' by a Mr Slug concerning dogs'-meat barrows in London and with a paper by a Mr X. Ledbrain which proves by calculation that a quarter of the population of a Yorkshire town either had no chairs to sit on or were obliged to use boxes in their stead. When Professor Nogo exhibits a model of a safety fire-escape to the section dealing with Mechanical Science, he explains that the contraption cannot be fixed in less than half an hour, but that it has been proved to work perfectly well when there is no fire. A similar vein of heavy-handed cynicism is evident in the second article. Here the learned professors are joined by Messrs. Muddlebranes, Drawley, Misty, Purblind, Rummun, and the Honourable and Reverend Mr Long Ears. At the end, the cerebrations and entertainments of the Mudfog Association are summed up by a 'talented' but toadying correspondent who has witnessed the proceedings:

I cannot close my account of these gigantic researches and sublime and noble triumphs without repeating a *bon mot* of Professor Woodensconce's, which shows how the greatest minds may occasionally unbend when truth can be presented to listening ears, clothed in an attractive and playful form. I was standing by, when, after a week of feasting and feeding, that learned gentleman, accompanied by the whole body of wonderful men, entered the hall yesterday, where a sumptuous dinner was prepared; where the richest wines sparkled on the board, and fat bucks—propitiatory sacrifices to learning—sent forth their savoury odours. 'Ah!' said Professor Woodensconce, rubbing his hands, 'this is what we meet for; this is what inspires us; this is what keeps us together, and beckons us onward; this is the *spread* of science, and a glorious spread it is.'[2]

With this rather painfully strained joke the account concludes.

What is evident from the two reports on the Mudfog Association is that the young Dickens viewed a good deal of scientific enterprise in the same light as the theoretical propositions of the Utilitarians. The difference lay in the fact that the Benthamites were prepared to apply their theories to society while, to Dickens's mind, most scientific enterprise was impractical, airy-fairy, arrogantly esoteric, and effectively useless. During the 1840s, however, a significant change came over him. He seems to have acquired, or at least read,

Robert Chambers's highly influential book on geology, *Vestiges of the Natural History of Creation*, first published in 1844. Although no copy of the book is listed either in the catalogue of Dickens's library in 1844 or in the list of books he possessed at the time of his death in 1870, he refers to Chambers's work, with what looks like deep approval, in his most direct treatment of modern science, a long review of Robert Hunt's *The Poetry of Science* which appeared in the *Examiner* in December 1848. Chambers, like Hunt after him, was a gifted interpreter of the drift of modern geological science for the intelligent general reader. He had outlined the principle of evolutionary development from a geological perspective, and, although he had not moved towards Darwin's idea of natural selection, he had anticipated many of the leading ideas now associated with Darwin's name. Chambers had also attracted the antipathy of both clerical critics and of many fellow scientists. Nevertheless, as Dickens insisted, Chambers's work had done society a considerable service in rendering 'the general subject popular, and awakening an interest and spirit of inquiry in many minds, . . . not exclusively scientific or philosophical—to whom such offerings can be hopefully addressed'.[3] Chambers's book was therefore to be classed as 'useful' and instructive rather than airily speculative. It has been argued not only that Dickens knew Chambers's arguments well, but also that his reading of *Vestiges* had turned him into 'a decided evolutionist about a dozen years before the *Origin of Species*'.[4] It was therefore in the light of his appreciation of the benign influence of *Vestiges of the Natural History of Creation* that Dickens outlined the general argument of Hunt's book to the readers of the *Examiner*. Hunt, he believed, had revealed that

in every forest, in every tree, in every leaf, in every ring on every sturdy trunk, a beautiful and wonderful creation, always changing, always going on, always bearing testimony to the stupendous workings of Almighty Wisdom, and always leading the student's mind from wonder on to wonder, until he is wrapt and lost in the vast worlds of wonder by which he is surrounded from his cradle to his grave.

This revelation was deemed to be 'worthy of the natural philosopher, and salutary to the spirit of the age'.[5] What Dickens seems to have most admired in Hunt's work was an alertness to the 'poetry' of science, a poetry which fired the imagination rather than deadened it. This was not an unweaving of rainbows or a clipping of angels' wings: rather, it was an inspired exploration of a divine mystery in Nature, one which suggested new wonders in the systematic discovery of formerly unrecognized rhythms and patterns. Although Dickens was clearly worried by Hunt's implied criticism of Chambers's work, he was generally impressed by the fact that both men had articulated grand scientific principles in a manner which appealed to an imaginative and liberal Christian believer.[6] Both men seemed to be offering an assuring revelation rather than unsettling bewilderment.

As Tennyson was influentially to suggest in *In Memoriam AHH* (1850), the pre-Darwinian understanding of the processes of mutability and development in Nature, or 'evolution', could legitimately be associated with a poetry which sought to explore a mystery at the heart of creation and to assert the ultimate benevolence of the evolutionary process. Dickens's own enthusiasm for this demystifying kind of geological science is forcefully expressed in his review:

Science has gone down into the mines and coal-pits, and before the safety-lamp the Gnomes and Genii of those dark regions have disappeared. But, in their stead, the process by which metals are engendered in the course of ages; the growth of plants which, hundreds of fathoms underground, and in black darkness, have still a sense of the sun's presence in the sky, and derive some portion of the subtle essence of their life from his influence; the histories of mighty forests and great tracts of land carried down into the sea, by the same process which is active in the Mississippi and such great rivers at this hour; are made familiar to us. Sirens, mermaids, shining cities glittering at the bottom of the quiet seas, and in deep lakes, exist no longer; but in their place, Science, their destroyer, shows us whole coasts of coral reef constructed by the labours of minute creatures; points to our own chalk cliffs and limestone rocks, as made of the dust of myriads of generations of infinitesimal beings that have passed away; reduces the very element of water into its constituent airs, and re-creates it at her pleasure. Caverns in rocks, choked with rich treasures shut up from all but the enchanted hand, Science has blown to atoms, as she can rend and rive the rocks themselves; but in those rocks she has found, and read aloud, the great stone book which is the history of the earth, even when darkness sat upon the face of the deep.

This is Dickens, informed by the language of the Bible and by the magical wonder of *The Arabian Nights*, rejoicing in the liberating, imaginative power of scientific knowledge.

Dickens's ostensible enthusiasm for geology and palaeontology, and for what was known in his time as the 'Theory of Development', may well have rendered him more sympathetic to Darwin's ideas than has often been supposed. He acquired a copy of the second edition of *On the Origin of Species by means of Natural Selection, or the Preservation of Favoured Races in the Struggle for Life* in 1860, and this copy remained in his library until his death. As editor of *All the Year Round* in 1860 and 1861, he also printed three post-Darwinian articles by unidentified authors which discussed 'Species', 'Natural Selection', and the 'Transmutation of Species'.[7] Whether or not Dickens *understood*, let alone actually *read*, Darwin's work remains open to speculation.[8] He certainly does not seem to have been as troubled by its intellectual ramifications or by its sapping religious implications as were his more receptive, or susceptible, contemporaries such as George Eliot or Thomas Hardy. As his review of Hunt's *The Poetry of Science* suggests, he was probably more open to Chambers's conclusions about fossil evidence and geological strata than he was to more abstract biological arguments. He told his friend W. W. F. de Cerjat in 1863 that he found more pleasure in geological speculation than he did in a literal interpretation of the Old Testament:

It is contended that the science of geology is quite as much a revelation to man, as books of an immense age and of (at the best) doubtful origin, and that your consideration of the latter must reasonably be influenced by the former. As I understand the importance of timely suggestions such as these, it is, that the Church should not gradually shock and lose the more thoughtful and logical of human minds; but should be so gently and considerately yielding as to retain them, and, through them, hundreds of thousands . . . Nothing is discovered without God's intention and assistance, and I suppose every new knowledge of His works that is conceded to man to be distinctly a revelation by which men are to guide themselves. (*Letters*, x. 253: 28 May 1863)

Despite such frank and even radical open-mindedness, Dickens's novels, letters, and journalism indicate that he responded more readily to advances in medicine, manufacturing, and technology, for which there was tangible evidence, than he did to scientific theory, however 'poetically' that theory might be expressed. His grasp of the steadily advancing scientific thought of his time probably went no further than that of an intelligent general reader. This was the kind of reader who took pleasure in Henry Morley's whimsical popularization of the discoveries of the geologist William Buckland and the naturalist Richard Owen in the article 'Our Phantom Ship on an Antediluvian Cruise' which Dickens published in *Household Words* on 16 August 1851, shortly before he began work on *Bleak House*. It is very likely that Morley's description of a megalosaurus ('thirty feet long, with a big body, mounted on high thick legs') contributed to the playful reference to the forty-foot monster which might have been found waddling up a muddy Holborn Hill in the opening chapter of the new novel. Here at least, any fear of biological regression is held in check by a trust that, as in Morley's article, Time fosters an evolutionary process that could be observed moving progressively and inexorably forwards. Or, as Morley put it, in a final extension of his extended boating analogy, with a 'long pull, and a strong pull' human enterprise and human achievement would be shown to be the decisive forces in evolutionary development.

Dickens's publication of three articles about Darwinian theories in the 1860s suggests that he was anxious to encourage a wide and open discussion of science on an accessible level. He seems, however, to have been equally determined to balance Darwinian theory with confident assertions of the divine nature of creation elsewhere in the pages of *All the Year Round*. He was clearly not prepared to threaten the theological status quo and chose to offer an interpretation of the geological evidence read in the light of the book of Genesis rather than vice versa. The religious sensibilities of his readers were evidently not to be ruffled unduly. This scruple probably stems from the fact that Dickens had always been somewhat ambiguous about the intellectual aspirations of readers of his journals. Although he had boasted to Sir Edward Bulwer-Lytton in 1860 that *All the Year Round* had 'the largest Audience to be got that comprehends intelligence and cultivation' (*Letters*, ix. 281: 3 Aug. 1860), he noted a year later of his assistant editor, W. H. Wills, that Wills was 'sufficiently commonplace to represent a very large proportion of our readers' (*Letters*, ix. 415: 15 May 1861). Dickens was careful to write in as direct and easy a manner as possible and he encouraged his contributors to do likewise. As he wrote to Henry Morley on 31 October 1852, what was required was 'the devising of some pleasant means of telling what is to be told' in order 'to get the publication down into the masses of readers' (*Letters*, vi. 790). Both *Household Words* and

All the Year Round offered 'commonplace' readers a considerable variety of 'scientific' articles, articles which covered aspects of astronomy, physics, chemistry, and geology, as well as medicine and technology. Where *Household Words* picked up on public interest in, for example, comets, *All the Year Round* explored lunar and solar eclipses.[9] What runs through both journals, however, is a strong sense that scientific innovation should not only be communicable but should also ideally have immediate and explicable social applications. Dickens's respect for those who contributed to the advance of knowledge and to technological progress is clear throughout his work. He also seems to have been anxious that men of science should be honoured by their country rather than neglected and ignored as Daniel Doyce was ignored. In 1851, for example, he wrote to W. H. Wills proposing a *Household Words* article on the subject of 'the distribution of Titles'. The article would not only expose the unworthiness of present holders of titles, it would also go on to advocate a true meritocracy and a proper acknowledgement of the place of applied research in national life:

It would be a very remarkable thing to take the list of the House of Peers, the list of Baronets and Knights, and (without personality) divide the more recent titles into classes and ascertain what they were given *for*. How many chemists, how many men of science, how many writers, how many aldermen
How much intellect represented.
How much imagination.
How much learning.
How much expression of the great progress of the country—
How much of Railway construction, of Electric Telegraph discovery, of improvements in Machinery, of any sort of contribution to the happiness of mankind.   (*Letters*, vi. 467–8: 22 Aug. 1851)

Dickens's article, which finally emerged as 'Proposals for Amusing Posterity' on 12 February 1853, was whimsically explicit in what it suggested, shockingly radical though the 'proposals' might have seemed to the contemporary political establishment. The new titles that Dickens put forward included a 'great Jenner or Vaccination Dukedom', a 'Watt or Steamship peerage', an 'Iron-Road Earldom', a 'Tubular Bridge Baronetcy', a 'Faraday Order of Merit', and an 'Electric Telegraph Garter'.[10] The cynical Dickens knew that such things were not to be envisaged within his century or even beyond.

As Esther Summerson was to remark in chapter 53 of *Bleak House*, 'it was not the custom in England to confer titles on men distinguished by peaceful services, however good and great; unless occasionally, when they consisted of the accumulation of some very large amount of money'. Despite the advances of the iron road into rural Lincolnshire and the industrial prowess of the Rouncewell ironworks, Sir Leicester Dedlock and his peers had no real need to quake in their velvet slippers at the prospect of parvenu intellectuals and upstart inventors.

Dickens and the Railway

Of all the scientific and technological innovations of his time it was the railway, the 'Iron Road', that most fascinated and impressed Dickens. It was also the one great technological advance of the nineteenth century that had a singular impact on his fiction and on his occasional writing. Although he was to be involved in a series of serious railway accidents, including the major disaster at Staplehurst in June 1865, to Dickens's mind the railway exemplified benevolent change. He saw it as combining usefulness with enchantment. In 'A Flight', a *Household Words* essay of August 1851, he wrote in terms of magic of an overnight excursion to Paris on the South Eastern Railway's 'Double Special Express Service'. In a letter to John Forster he had described his twelve-hour journey prosaically enough as 'astounding—marvellously done' (*Letters*, vi. 118: 24 June 1850). In the essay, however, the trip took on something of an *Arabian Nights* adventure and a theatrical transformation scene. The second chapter of *A Tale of Two Cities* captures something of the attendant problems of road travel in the late eighteenth century, many of which had been smoothed out in the opening years of the succeeding century, but Dickens long remembered the inconveniences of his earliest journeys to Paris. What had once been a gruelling stage-coach journey to Dover, an unsettling sea-crossing by a sailing ship dependent on winds and tides, and finally a tiresome, dusty overland journey to the capital by French diligence was, by the 1850s, a matter of smooth transition from train to steamship to train. In the essay Dickens the traveller finds himself bewitched by the novelty of it all:

So, I pass to my hotel enchanted; sup, enchanted; go to bed, enchanted;

pushing back this morning (if it really were this morning) into the remoteness of time, blessing the South Eastern Company for realising the Arabian Nights in these prose days, murmuring, as I wing my idle flight into the land of dreams, 'No hurry, ladies and gentlemen, going to Paris in eleven hours. It is so well done, that there really is no hurry!'[11]

This delight in the speed of railway travel is reflected in another of the *Household Words* essays, 'Railway Dreaming' of May 1856. Here the sensation of rapid, easy, progressive movement seems to lull the narrator into free, imaginative speculation:

I am never sure of time and place upon a Railroad, I can't read, I can't think, I can't sleep—I can only dream. Rattling along in this railway carriage in a state of luxurious confusion, I take it for granted I am coming from somewhere, and going somewhere else. I seek to know no more. Why things come into my head and fly out again, whence they come, and why they come, where they go and why they go, I am incapable of considering. It may be the guard's business, or the railway company's; I only know it is not mine. I know nothing about myself—for anything I know, I may be coming from the Moon.[12]

The narrator then proceeds to speculate as the train speeds from Paris to London as if he indeed *did* come from the Moon.

It is hard for twenty-first-century readers to appreciate quite how radically railway travel changed human perceptions of time and place. Although the narrator of 'Railway Dreaming' purports to be caught up in his own fantasies, fantasies which erode the barriers between fact and fiction, the more practical and quotidian Dickens, who needed to travel between A and B for professional reasons, seems to have rejoiced in the sheer speed and convenience of the nineteenth-century railway. What probably struck the pioneer railway travellers of the 1830s as extraordinary soon became commonplace to mid- and late-Victorians. This was advanced technology responsive to the demands of a new age, the age Carlyle had dubbed 'the Age of Machines'. Having reached a peak of efficiency during the first third of the century, the network of stage-coach routes that had criss-crossed the island of Britain rapidly fell into a state of decay. Old perceptions of speed were radically changed, distances lost both their mystery and their ancient inconvenience, and provinces proud of their distinctive differences were tied into a metropolitan whole by iron and steam. In 1829 Stephenson's *Rocket* had been able to reach speeds of between 25 m.p.h. and 35 m.p.h.; by the late 1860s average speeds had risen to around 70 m.p.h. Those Victorians who rejoiced in statistics could relish the expansion of the system. In 1843 there were 1,775 miles of track in England and Wales; by the time of Dickens's death there were 11,662. In 1845 33,791,253 railway journeys were made; by 1870 the number had risen to 330,162,801.[13]

As we can readily appreciate, Dickens was quick to appreciate both the innovation and the convenience of railway travel. Having spoken metaphorically of 'getting his steam up' in November 1835, he travelled north on the new London–Birmingham line three years later, only two months after the line had opened to the public, and then extended his journey from Birmingham to Liverpool on the Grand Junction Railway (finished in 1837). Nevertheless, it might seem remarkable that Dickens's earliest novels, and *Pickwick Papers* in particular, seem to be stuck in the stage-coach era and that that inveterate coach-driver, Tony Weller, should dismiss the railway as 'unconsitootional' and as an 'inwaser o' priwileges' (though this particular Wellerism comes from *Master Humphrey's Clock* of 1840 rather than from *Pickwick Papers*). Tony and the peripatetic Pickwickians are relics of a dying age. Like the foot-slogging Nell and her Grandfather, or Nicholas Nickleby on the snowbound coach to Dotheboys Hall, they are trapped in a slower-paced age which is occasionally, but never consistently, glimpsed in a rosy light. It was a nostalgia that the restless, older Dickens, a man decidedly wedded to innovation, quickly dispelled. If his later characters, such as David Copperfield and Pip, travel on carriers' carts or stage-coaches, it is because both men, as first-person narrators, look back from their adulthoods to the lost age of their boyhoods. For many Victorian readers of the 1850s the very mention of older means of transport would have reminded them of a distinct demarcation between childhood and maturity, between then and now, between the eras of the Prince Regent and Victoria. It was a demarcation famously described by Thackeray in his essay 'De Juventute' in 1860:

We who have lived before railways were made, belong to another world. In how many hours could the Prince of Wales drive from Brighton to London, with a light carriage built expressly, and relays of horses longing to gallop the next stage? . . . It was only yesterday; but what a gulf between now and then! *Then* was the old world. Stage-coaches, more or less swift, riding-horses, pack-horses, highwaymen, knights in armour, Norman invaders, Roman legions, Druids, Ancient Britons painted blue, and so forth—all these belong to the old period.[14]

Thackeray gives an impression of history receding, at first rapidly and then with greater and greater strides. He moves his readers from the remembered, from the once familiar and tangible, into a realm known only through written records or recovered artefacts. The stage-coach represents the past; the railway, the technological present which is rapidly evolving into the future. For Pip the coach journey to London at the end of the first volume of *Great Expectations* is similarly marked by a sense of transition as the horses are changed at each stage, the mists rise, 'and the world lay spread before me'.

The advent of the railway marked more than just the collective consciousness of Victorian Britain. It physically changed the landscape as well, and with it the economic fortunes of the provinces. In chapter 55 of *Bleak House*, for example, Sir Leicester Dedlock's Lincolnshire is about to be stirred out of its rural and feudal seclusion by the noisy, populist disruption of a new railway:

Railroads shall soon traverse all this country, and with a rattle and a glare the engine and train shall shoot like a meteor over the wide landscape, turning the moon paler; but as yet, such things are non-existent in these parts, though not wholly unexpected. Preparations are afoot, measurements are made, ground is staked out. Bridges are begun, and their not yet united piers desolately look at one another over roads and streams, like brick and mortar couples with an obstacle to their union: fragments of embankments are thrown up, and left as precipices with torrents of rusty carts and barrows tumbling over them; tripods of tall poles appear on hilltops, where there are rumours of tunnels; everything looks chaotic, and abandoned in fell hopelessness.

Dickens's gloomy description of the suspended railway works forms part of the account of the night-time search for Lady Dedlock in the highways and byways of her husband's ancestral shire. The account, like the search for the missing wife, seems to be full of uncertainties and dead ends. Essentially, it suggests much of the ambiguity attendant on progress where gains have to be balanced against losses and the old order must reluctantly, and sometimes painfully, yield to new. The landscape is left scarred and soiled, but it is also about to be energized, just as the ironmaster has energized the site of his foundry elsewhere in the novel. It is perhaps significant that in this passage from *Bleak House* Dickens sees the coming railway train as a meteor, that natural phenomenon which was anciently taken to portend radical change, but one which could also be observed moving steadily, unstoppably, and blazingly by the unsuperstitious eye. The steam-engine moving inexorably forwards seems to represent not just a harnessing of natural energy by science, but also a quintessential expression of that energy.

A similar mood of anticipation and excited disturbance pervades Dickens's extended celebration of the railway in *Dombey and Son*. Having travelled on the new London–Birmingham line in 1838 he introduces a description of the construction works for the railway's approach to its metropolitan terminus in chapter 15 and a rhythmical account of the bereaved Mr Dombey's jaded train journey to Leamington in chapter 20. The section dealing with the momentous reconstruction attendant on the progress of the line into its London terminus has a double significance, one that was both private and, on a more public level, imaginatively liberating. For Dickens the man, the works near Mornington Crescent had occasioned the demolition of familiar landmarks, and most notably, of his old schoolroom. For Dickens the novelist, however, the disappearance of the straggling suburb of Staggs's Gardens represents the opening-up of new opportunities. His upbeat account of the reconstruction temporarily dispels the gloom surrounding the death-bed of Little Paul Dombey, and it effectively counters a series of negatives with a singularly positive delight in progressive technological and economic change:

There was no such place as Staggs's Gardens. It had vanished from the earth. Where the old rotten summer-houses once had stood, palaces now reared their heads, and granite columns of gigantic girth opened a vista to the railway world beyond . . . The old by-streets now swarmed with passengers and vehicles of every kind: the new streets that had stopped disheartened in the mud and waggon-ruts, formed towns within themselves, originating wholesome comforts and conveniences belonging to themselves, and never tried nor thought of until they sprung into existence . . . The carcasses of houses, and beginnings of new thoroughfares, had started off upon the line at steam's own speed, and shot way into the country in a monster train.

This 'monster train' has also served to transform the industry, the trade, and the daily life of the neighbourhood:

There were railway patterns in its drapers' shops, and railway journals in the windows of its newsmen. There were railway hotels, office-houses, lodging-houses, boarding-houses; railway plans, maps, views, wrappers, bottles, sandwich-boxes, and time-tables; railway hackney-coach and cab-stands; railway omnibuses, railway streets and buildings, railway hangers-on and parasites, and flatterers out of all calculation. There was even railway time observed in clocks, as if the sun itself had given in.

This last reference to the standardization of time throughout Britain as a result of the new railway timetables is telling. Little Paul Dombey had been born to the sound of the ticking watches of his father and his mother's doctors; at school he had been fascinated by the clock at Dr Blimber's academy; now, as one kind of time ushers him out of this world, another concept of the measurement of time seems to master even the sun. Humankind may be frail, but the reference here to the application of human science allows it to appear mighty.

The account of Mr Dombey's railway journey in chapter 20 is ostensibly far more ambiguous. As Dombey and Bagstock prepare to depart, they encounter Mr Toodle who now works as a stoker and professes to be 'doin' pretty well' in 'a worldly way'. But if Toodle's working life life has been enhanced by the railway, for Dombey the train journey merely represents an extension of his obsessional private grief. The train is little more than 'a type of the triumphant monster, Death'. As Dickens's account makes clear, however, Dombey is signally failing to recognize the thrill of speed, the aggressive but regular, rhythmical energy of the steam-engine, and the opening vistas of a Britain being gradually transformed by industry which are glimpsed from the carriage windows:

Breasting the wind and light, the shower and sunshine, away, and still away, it rolls and roars, fierce and rapid, smooth and certain, and great works and massive bridges crossing up above, fall like a beam of shadow an inch broad, upon the eye, and then are lost. Away, and still away, onward and onward ever; glimpses of cottage-homes, houses, mansions, rich estates, of husbandry and handicraft, of people, of old road and paths that look deserted, small and insignificant as they are left behind . . .

Away, with a shriek, and a roar, and a rattle, plunging down into the earth again, and working on in such a storm of energy and perseverance, that amidst the darkness and whirlwind the motion seems reversed, and to tend furiously backward, until a ray of light upon the wet wall shows its surface flying past like a fierce stream. Away once more into the day, and through the day, with a shrill yell of exultation, roaring, rattling, tearing on, spurning everything with its dark breath, sometimes pausing for a minute where a crowd of faces are, that in a minute more are not; sometimes lapping water greedily, and before the spout at which it drinks has ceased to drip upon the ground, shrieking, roaring, rattling through the purple distance.

Dickens's prose is exhilarating, suggesting something of the excitement of his own response to a phenomenon to which Mr Dombey declines to respond. The machine moves steadily and inexorably through cutting and tunnel, over viaducts and under bridges, exultantly ignoring sun and storm alike. A relentless monster, and a leveller like Death itself, but one which Dickens sees here as changing lives rather than terminating them. Like the water and sea metaphors which equally pervade *Dombey and Son*, the railway gives life as much as it takes it away. The grinningly villainous Mr Carker may finally fall victim to an advancing railway train, but the train speeding its passengers forward has no purposeful business with a dazed man who stands in its way. As the author of *Dombey and Son* almost certainly recognized, the water that elsewhere provided him with so many useful images of human transformation, has in the case of the railway engine become the steam which drives the pistons of the shrieking, roaring, rattling monster.

Dickens was to remain, as Ruskin posthumously categorized him, 'the leader of the steam-whistle party *par excellence*'. He was an enthusiast for science applied, for steam-trains and electric telegraphs, but he was generally as wary of scientific theory as he was alienated by Benthamite statistics. He preferred to see the created universe as tidy and divinely disciplined rather than replete with uncertainties, speculations and evolutionary doubts. As his novels suggest, he retained a belief in the order of creation, an essentially comic vision which looked for resolutions and, ultimately, for the realization of a God-given justice. But Dickens was no social or intellectual conservative; he disliked pious platitudes and he was only rarely given to restatements of traditional ways of seeing and to reiterations of conventional arguments. Some nine months before he died, he addressed the annual inaugural meeting of the Birmingham and Midland Institute of which he had recently been elected president. The Institute had first been projected in 1852 in order to provide enhanced educational facilities and opportunities for working men. In late December 1853 Dickens had given two public readings of *A Christmas Carol* in Birmingham Town Hall in order to raise funds for the project. In September 1869, however, he was less inclined to sound seasonal and diverting and his presidential address was suitably earnest in tone. The propriety of fostering a broadly educated general public figured prominently in a speech in which Dickens referred to the mathematician Charles Babbage's *Ninth Bridgewater Treatise* of 1839 and, less directly, to Sir David Brewster's astronomical treatise *More Worlds than One* of 1854. These references are brief, and substantially general, but they seem to be designed to suggest a man *au fait* with the drift of modern scientific thought.[15] Central to his address, however, is an argument against the proposition that he and his audience lived in a narrowly material age dominated by a mechanically applied science. Dickens's argument was typically pragmatic and typically devout:

Has electricity become more material in the mind of any sane, or moderately insane man, woman, or child, because of the discovery that in the good providence of God it was made available for the service and use of man to an immeasurably greater extent than for his destruction? Do I make a more material journey to the bedside of my dying parents or my dying child, when I travel there at the rate of sixty miles an hour, than when I travel thither at a rate of six? Rather, in the swift case, does not my agonized heart become over-fraught with gratitude to that Supreme Beneficence from whom alone can have proceeded the wonderful means of shortening my suspense. What is the materiality of the cable or the wire, compared with the immateriality of the spark?[16]

Dickens was insisting that the study of Science was not merely an integral element in human progress; it also explained how evolutionary progress was natural and inevitable and why it should not be impeded by human ignorance. Despite the cavils of blinkered divines, he implies, whatever God had given to be known should be known, and, despite the protests of those scientists given to abstract theorizing, what God had given to be used should be used for the benefit of human life. What Dickens is suggesting is that Science without God is bad Science, but that Science without any benign human application is even worse Science. In both cases 'enchantment' goes hand in hand with knowledge, and both offer freedom.

CHAPTER 7

RECONTEXTUALIZING DICKENS

IN the early years of the twentieth century the Royal Doulton factory issued a commemorative plate showing the head and shoulders of a benignly bearded Dickens against a background of London with St Paul's looming over the novelist's right shoulder. The rim of the plate shows the heads of eleven characters from Dickens's novels arranged in the manner of a wreath or a nimbus. With the exception of the head of Little Dorrit, all of the characters come from novels published in the first half of Dickens's writing career. Two (Pickwick and Sam Weller) are from *Pickwick Papers*; a second two (Fagin and Sykes) are from *Oliver Twist*, and there is a pair (Pecksniff and Mrs Gamp) from *Martin Chuzzlewit*. The other four heads represent Barnaby Rudge, Little Nell, Captain Cuttle, and Uriah Heep. There is thus a mixture of the comic and the tragic, the virtuous and the villainous, the young and the old, the male and the female. Most of the heads derive from the original illustrations to the novels by George Cruikshank and H. K. Browne ('Phiz'). The presence of Barnaby Rudge and the absence of Sydney Carton might perhaps have surprised some original purchasers of the plate, given the popularity of *A Tale of Two Cities* in comparison to Dickens's earlier historical novel. The fact that no character from *Hard Times* or *Great Expectations* appears may well be put down to the fact that neither novel was illustrated when it first appeared, but the neglect of *Bleak House* and *Our Mutual Friend* is almost certainly due to the fact that Dickens's later fiction was generally regarded by readers as gloomy and lacking in the comic vitality of his early work.

The Doulton plate can be seen as reflecting much of the popular perception of Dickens's art in the first half of the twentieth century. The fact that it remained in production for many years is not just a testimony to the novelist's continuing appeal to readers and collectors alike, but also an indication of the understanding of the kind of novelist that Dickens was. Although his work was widely under-rated, or even dismissed, by highbrow critics until the 1950s, he had retained a ready popular appeal, and his characters were familiar to a broad range of readers in a way that Thackeray's, or Trollope's, or George Eliot's, or even Hardy's were not. They lived in readers' imaginations independently of the green paper covers of the monthly parts or the covers of the many thousands of cheaply bound editions that succeeded the original serial issues. Dickens's first illustrators had certainly helped fix visual images of his creations in people's minds, and his own public readings had dramatically animated his texts for his contemporaries, but the immediate rapport that Dickens the writer had with his original audience seems to have been passed on from generation to generation. That special rapport is still effective at the beginning of the twenty-first century. No other English novelist carries with him quite so much popular baggage. The scene of Oliver Twist asking for more is perhaps the most familiar, and most commonly reproduced in cartoon form, in any English novel (the first such cartoon version, by John Leech, appeared in *Punch* in March 1844). The idioms of a Micawber, a Heep, or a Scrooge possess a ready familiarity and quotability. Even the shorthand term 'Dickensian' has achieved a unique and unrivalled breadth of application, whether that application refers to snowy Christmases or to decaying schools or failing hospitals. Having been photographed many times in his life, and having had those images widely circulated as popular Victorian cartes-de-visite, the everyday currency of Dickens's face reached its apogee when in 1992 the Bank of England issued a new ten pound note showing the maturely bearded novelist together with a representation of the cricket match at Dingley Dell from *Pickwick Papers*. Dickens was replaced on the ten pound note by an equally hirsute Charles Darwin in 2000 (beards being reputed to be a deterrent to would-be forgers). He had thus joined a very select band of historical figures on banknotes. Dickens is to date one of only two representatives of English literature to be so honoured (the other was Shakespeare).[1]

The First Biographies

We cannot tell if Dickens himself would have deemed his appearance on a banknote a signal honour. In his will, printed posthumously as an appendix to John Forster's biography, he expressed the hope that his claim to national remembrance would rest solely on his published works. He sought neither public monuments nor biographical tributes. By destroying his correspondence on a series of large bonfires he had attempted to confound the labours of any potential biographers (though he was only able to destroy letters sent *to* him rather than *by* him; these latter were generally treasured and preserved by their recipients and have been published in twelve fat volumes). Thanks to public pressure for such a tribute, Dickens's friend, John Forster, was moved to publish his fine three-volume *Life of Charles Dickens* between 1872 and 1874. This was effectively the first study to suggest that the novelist's published works did not exist in a biographical vacuum or as an entity utterly divorced from the facts of Dickens's life. Although Dickens's sister-in-law, Georgina Hogarth, believed that Forster's biography had left 'nothing to be said ever more' she was prepared to publish an edited selection of the novelist's letters as 'a sort of supplement' because the biography 'was universally felt to be incomplete as a *Portrait*'.[2] With Wilkie Collins acting as an adviser, Georgina and Dickens's daughter Mamie saw three editions of letters through the press, the first, in two volumes, of 1880 being followed by a third volume in 1882. Also in 1882 they pruned and rearranged the published letters in a two-volume edition ('cut and condensed *remorselessly*').[3] A one-volume edition followed a year later.[4] Since then, Dickens has rarely escaped the attentions of biographers, some of whom have delighted in casting him in a less than favourable light. In 1883 Robert Langton published *The Childhood and Youth of Charles Dickens* in a small subscription edition published in Manchester (it was reissued in an enlarged and revised trade edition in 1891). Langton was amongst the last who had the advantage of being able to interview surviving friends, acquaintances, and colleagues of Dickens's and he expressed himself confident that his work would 'confirm ... the close connection between ... the works of Charles Dickens and his own LIFE ... especially ... how his earlier experiences and surroundings, were coloured and reflected in his books'.[5] Georgina Hogarth's edition of the letters, and Forster's and Langton's biographies, typified the reverent, semi-revelatory accounts of Dickens's life which held sway until the appearance in 1928 of a novel published by Mills and Boon under the suggestive title *This Side Idolatry*. The novel, ascribed to one 'Ephesian' (in fact Carl E. Bechhoffer Roberts), offered an unflattering picture of Dickens as a vain man and a singularly inconsiderate husband. It was also the first printed work to mention the darker and, to date, the most secretive aspect of Dickens's later life, his relationship with the actress Ellen Ternan. The old image of Dickens, fostered by his surviving family, as a benign paterfamilias and as a man piously wedded to Victorian domestic virtues was thus tarnished. Although *This Side Idolatry* was dismissed as scandal-mongering by Dickens's most devoted admirers, its seemingly unsupported insinuations were strikingly justified in April 1934 by an article published in the *Daily Express* by the minor writer Thomas Wright. Wright claimed that Ellen Ternan had 'confessed' to a now-deceased clergyman that she had been Dickens's somewhat reluctant mistress. Wright reasserted his claims a year later in his *Life of Charles Dickens*, a work otherwise remarkable only for its insistence that the later novels should be read in the light of the novelist's illicit relationship with a younger woman. Questions concerning Dickens's once carefully concealed liaison with Ellen were raised again in 1939 by Gladys Storey in her *Dickens and Daughter*. The book claimed to be based on intimate conversations with Dickens's younger daughter, Kate Peruguni, and the book stands in marked contrast to the adulatory account of their father offered in 1885 by Kate's elder sister, Mamie.[6] Although Kate asserted that her father was 'a wicked man' and that Ellen had borne him a short-lived infant, she was elsewhere prepared to be more conciliatory. 'I know things about my father's character that no-one else ever knew,' she confided to Gladys Storey: 'he was not a good man, but he was not a fast man, but he was wonderful! He fell in love with this girl, I did not blame *her*—it is never one person's fault.' The real fault, she claimed, was funda-mental to Dickens's complex character: he 'did not understand women'.[7] The exact nature of Dickens's intimacy with Ellen Ternan will never be properly known, though it continues to fascinate both denigrators and admirers of Dickens. The novelist's acquaintance seems to have readily acquiesced to his insistence on discretion and secrecy and no letters exchanged by him and Ellen survive. There is certainly no record of the birth of an illegitimate child. Although Dickens's most recent biographers have been prepared to accept an open verdict on the affair, Ellen became the subject of a full-length biography by Claire Tomalin in 1990.[8] What is certain is that the Ternan affair has little relevance to a reader's appreciation of those 'published works' on which Dickens hoped that his true reputation would rest.

Dickens in Art

In his will Dickens instructed his executors that his tombstone should simply bear his name 'without the addition of "Mr." or "Esquire"'. He was also particularly insistent that his heirs should 'on no account . . . make me the subject of any monument, memorial or testimonial whatever'. In accordance with this instruction no statue of him has been erected in London, the city with which his work is most associated (though there is a bronze bust of him by his friend, Percy Fitzgerald, on the site of his first home at Furnival's Inn in Holborn). There is also a stone bas-relief, showing the novelist with certain of his characters, on the site of another former home, 1 Devonshire Terrace. Though there have been occasional moves to remedy what some suppose to be a slight on Dickens's memory, the only large-scale sculptural commemorations of Dickens are outside Britain. There is a bronze of the seated novelist, with Little Nell at his feet, in Clark Park in Philadelphia in the United States, and a marble statue of him was formerly in Centennial Park in Sydney, Australia. The lack of public memorials was to some degree countered after Dickens's death by a surprising range of porcelain representations of the novelist and his characters designed for domestic display. These range from spill-jars and jugs with Dickens's profile in high relief to somewhat more refined busts in Parian china, the smallest being 20 cm in height, the largest 48 cm.[9] One such model was issued to the public within a month of the novelist's death. Dickens was also commemorated by a variety of china figurines representing his most popular characters, most of them again drawn from his earlier rather than his later novels.[10]

Although Dickens was a close friend of two fine, though scarcely pre-eminent, Victorian artists, Daniel Maclise (1807–70) and Clarkson Stanfield (1793–1867), and intimate with several others (notably Edwin Landseer (1802–73), William Powell Frith (1819–1909), and Augustus Egg (1816–63)), neither he nor his characters figure prominently as subjects in English nineteenth-century painting. Unlike the other great urban writer of the period, Charles Baudelaire, who can be glimpsed as a quizzical observer of Parisian life in Edouard

Manet's painting *Music in the Tuileries Gardens* of 1862, Dickens was not at the forefront of contemporary visual art, either as a critic or as a patron. He owned pictures by his friends, and his novels were illustrated by talented and, occasionally, highly original graphic artists, but, when it came to contemporary art, his own tastes appear to have been conventional, even staid. As his travel book *Pictures from Italy* (1846) suggests, however, he had a keen eye for painting coupled with certain iconoclastic prejudices which he readily imparted to his readers.[11] His forthright attack on the young John Everett Millais's Pre-Raphaelite painting *Christ in the House of his Parents*, which appeared in *Household Words* in June 1850, also suggests the extent of his intolerance of a style and of a subject he found offensive to both his eye and his intelligence. The major portraits of him painted in oils by Maclise (1839, National Portrait Gallery) and Frith (1859, Victoria and Albert Museum) were both the work of friends who were not primarily portrait painters. The earlier pastels of Dickens and his young wife by Samuel Laurence (1837, National Portrait Gallery; Dickens House) are typical of the kind of conventional portrait that an up-and-coming writer might have commissioned in an age before photography.

Given the nature of Dickens's fiction, and given the fact that the majority of that fiction was illustrated as an integral part of its original serial publication, it is not surprising that it is easier to find parallels to Dickens's art in contemporary painting rather than direct derivations from it. In an important way the novels in their illustrated monthly parts effectively pre-empted the work of other artists. The work of the best Victorian genre painters, and notably the two major paintings by Frith—*Derby Day* (1858, Tate Gallery) and *The Railway Station* (1862, Royal Holloway College)—seem closer to the spirit of Dickens's novels than do the generally dull attempts at interpreting subjects derived from the novels themselves by other painters. Frith's two large canvases, for example, possess an intensity of detailing, a Hogarthian delight in characterization, and an acute sense of dramatic incident, which certainly helps to illuminate a Dickensian 'moment' in English culture. Painters of subjects from Dickens's novels tended, by contrast, to choose images of characters rather than incidents. William Holman Hunt's early *Little Nell and her Grandfather* (1845, Sheffield City Art Gallery) is painted in his pre-Pre-Raphaelite manner and shows the old man

and the girl pausing during their flight from a London which looms
smokily in the distance.[12] It is a poignant-enough image of youth and
age, and is an interesting expression of the contemporary urge to
seek a rural refuge as an alternative to the encroaching city, but it is a
painting which lacks both flair and dramatic resonance. In 1842
Dickens himself had commissioned two watercolours of scenes from
The Old Curiosity Shop from George Cattermole, an artist who specialized in drawing fussy Gothic architecture and cluttered interiors
and who had already provided illustrations for the novel's serial
publication. The pictures, one showing the Curiosity Shop and the
other Nell's Grandfather sitting inconsolably on her grave in the
country church, remained in the novelist's collection until his death
(the former is now at Dickens House; the latter in the Victoria and
Albert Museum). Dickens professed himself delighted by both pictures in which, he claimed, 'the whole feeling and thought and
expression of the little story is rendered to the gratification of my
inmost heart' (*Letters*, iii. 397–8: 20 Dec. 1842). Dickens also owned
two paintings of his characters by another of his friends, Frith, for
which he paid the artist £40: a *Dolly Varden, looking back at her
Lover* and a *Kate Nickleby at Madame Mantalini's* (1842; private
collections) both of which were later hung prominently in his dining
room at Gad's Hill Place. Frith was to corner a market in representations of Dolly Varden, a character from *Barnaby Rudge* whose distinctive eighteenth-century costume struck him as providing a
splendid contrast to 'the ugliness of modern dress' and whose flir-
tatiousness evidently appealed to the mid-Victorian imagination.[13]
Dolly's hooped-up chintz overskirt, lovingly depicted by Frith, even
served to inspire a peculiarly English fashion in the early 1870s.[14]
When the 'Dolly Varden' picture was sold after Dickens's death, the
sale catalogue described it as a 'masterpiece' and it fetched the not
inconsiderable sum of £1,050 (the *Kate Nickleby* went for a mere
£210).[15] Dickens did not possess any painting representing a character or a scene from any novel later than *Dombey and Son* but it is
worth noting that in 1852 he bought a pair of matched paintings by
the Scottish artist Robert Hannah from the walls of the Royal Academy's Summer Exhibition. The subject of one of these paintings was
The Play. Its companion piece, entitled *The Novel*, showed two
young women seated in an 'easy open calash' (an open carriage), one
of whom was reading a monthly part of *Bleak House* aloud to the

other.[16] The subject must have proved flattering to the novelist, but it may also be significant that he was content to purchase a picture showing two contented *readers* of his most recent fiction rather than a scene from the novel itself.

Subjects from Dickens's earlier, rather than his later, novels continued to appeal to Victorian artists. At least they seem to have appealed to the more staid amongst them rather than to those painters who shared the Pre-Raphaelite predilection for far earlier literature and for more fanciful costumes than were sported by their contemporaries. Perhaps the finest of all the pictures inspired by Dickens is Robert Braithwaite Martineau's delightful *Kit's Writing Lesson* (exhibited at the Royal Academy in 1852; Tate Gallery). This shows a scene from chapter 3 of *The Old Curiosity Shop* where Kit Nubbles 'tucked up his sleeves and squared his elbows and put his face close to the book and squinted at the lines' in order to be instructed by Nell in an attempt to improve his writing skills. Sir William Quiller Orchardson, best known for his slightly sentimental representations of Regency amours, painted two pictures of Nell early in his career, in 1855 and 1863, the latter of which shows *Little Nell and her Grandfather in the Wood* (Sheffield City Art Galleries). In 1888 William Maw Egley exhibited his *Florence Dombey in Captain Cuttle's Parlour* (Victoria and Albert Museum). This picture is somewhat surprising for its date, for it suggests more of a reverence for the painterly fashions of the 1840s than a penchant for the refinedly 'Aesthetic' aspirations of the 1880s. Indeed, apart from those who provided illustrations for new editions of his novels, such as the once highly rated Frederick Barnard,[17] relatively few artists since the 1880s have sought to draw direct inspiration from Dickens's novels. By the turn of the twentieth century, Dickensian subjects would almost certainly have been seen as too distinctly rooted in the previous century. Moreover, the whole manner of painting, sculpture, and even book illustration were rapidly and radically changing. The extent of the shift away from representation to abstraction, and the offence that shift often provoked in the eyes of older conservatives, was wittily suggested in a cartoon published in the satirical magazine *Punch* in April 1933. The cartoon shows a group of staid, middle-aged men and women recoiling in horror from a dwarfish, angular, and gesticulating figure sculpted in the manner of Jacob Epstein The inscription under the cartoon reads: 'The Dickensian Society refuses

Charles Dickens, 1839, by Daniel Maclise.

'Kit's Writing Lesson' by Robert Braithwaite Martineau, 1852.

the gift of a statuette of Little Nell by a Modern Sculptor'. It is in the essential incongruity of matching that particular, 'sentimental' Dickensian subject with the starkly provocative and innovatory mode of an Epstein that the real wit lies.

Dickens and Dickensians

The conventionally besuited and predominantly middle-aged 'Dickensian Society' shown in the *Punch* cartoon is a reference to the flourishing Dickens Fellowship. The Fellowship had been established in October 1902 under the presidency of novelist's youngest surviving son, Sir Henry Dickens. By 1905 it had 6,500 members, some twenty-five British branches, and seven overseas branches (in the United States, Canada, Australia, and even the Gold Coast). These early members coupled a real enthusiasm for Dickens's life and work with an often uncritical, even blinkered, zeal for the eternal memory of 'the Inimitable'. The most far-sighted early achievement of the Fellowship was the acquisition in 1925 of Dickens's house at 48 Doughty Street and the conversion of the late Georgian building, which had long served as a boarding-house, into a museum and memorial library. This is now the only surviving London home of the novelist and it contains a remarkable and expanding collection of paintings, manuscripts, and objects associated with the novelist and his works. Equally significantly, in January 1905, the Fellowship began publishing a journal, *The Dickensian*, as 'a Magazine for Dickens Lovers'. The illustrated journal has steadily developed as a much-respected vehicle for both scholarly investigation and critical debate. As the pages of the early issues of the *Dickensian* show, the Dickens Fellowship was dedicated not only to maintaining the earnestness of its founding enthusiasts, but also to enhancing the public perception of Dickens's life and art. It did so by showing an active interest in charitable causes, by continuing the novelist's own tradition of public readings from his novels, and by an active sponsorship of amateur dramatics. The first number of the *Dickensian* records, for example, December readings in London of both *A Christmas Carol* and *The Cricket on the Hearth*, an evening of 'sketching recitals' in Portsmouth, and readings interspersed with musical interludes at Southampton and in the 'Ladies' Parlour' at Brixton Independent church. A Dickens Fellowship Dramatic Club was

'The Dickensian Society refuses the gift of a statuette of Little Nell by a Modern Sculptor.' Cartoon, *Punch*, April 1933.

formed in September 1905, under the presidency of the actor Sir Herbert Beerbohm Tree, and the Club mounted a production in December of an adaptation of scenes from *Nicholas Nickleby* (somewhat perversely entitled *The Gentleman in the Next House*) and a version of the Bardell *v.* Pickwick trial. The one dramatic event that attracted most attention from the press was 'A Debate in the form of *A Trial of John Jasper* for the murder of Edwin Drood' which was held at the King's Hall, Covent Garden in January 1914. The judge was played by G. K. Chesterton, and counsel for the defence was Chesterton's brother, Cecil. The prosecution was led by B. W. Matz, the editor of the *Dickensian*, and the jurymen, under the foremanship of George Bernard Shaw, included the writers Hilaire Belloc, William Archer, William De Morgan, and W. W. Jacobs. The proceedings did not run as smoothly as anticipated and came to an abrupt conclusion when Shaw, as foreman, announced, apparently on his own authority, a verdict of manslaughter. Thus John Jasper escaped the more serious charges of murder and attempted murder for which there was, it must be admitted, only limited warrant in the plot of Dickens's unfinished novel.

The 'Drood' Problem and Adaptations of *Pickwick Papers*

The Dickens Fellowship's early attempts to pin a murder on a man whom Dickens never actually identifies as a murderer was one of a large number of attempts to solve *The Mystery of Edwin Drood*. The fascination with solutions has continued unabated ever since the novelist's untimely death. Three quite distinct continuations of the novel were published in the United States in the early 1870s, all of which assumed that Edwin Drood had survived an attempt on his life. Edwin is also alive in 'Gillan Vase's' [Elizabeth Newton's] *A Great Mystery Solved* of 1878 (Newton supposes that he has escaped from the murder attempt, thanks to the fortunate interposition of one of Jasper's fits; he then goes on to marry Rosa Budd). In Richard Proctor's *Watched by the Dead* of 1887 the enigmatic Datchery turns out to be Edwin in a clever disguise and a man determined to pursue and expose his attacker. It was only with John Cuming Walters's *Clues to the Mystery of Edwin Drood* of 1905 that the now-common assumption that a murder *must* have been committed was carefully formulated (Walters was to act as a member of the Dickens

Fellowship's jury in 1914). Most twentieth-century 'solutions' have come to resemble complex, if often controversial, detective stories centred on a murder. John Jasper has been recruited to a sect of murderous Thuggees (in Howard Duffield's *John Jasper—Strangler* of 1930) and cast alternatively as Edwin's deliverer from a vicious band of Egyptian assassins in Felix Aylmer's *The Drood Case* of 1965. More recent, and equally ingenious, continuations include those by Charles Forsyte (1980), John Thacker (1990), and Leon Garfield (1980).

The Mystery of Edwin Drood is far from unique in having a distinct and sometimes unexpected afterlife. The first was *Pickwick Papers* and it is worth exploring the strange reconfigurations of that early novel in some detail. A *Pickwick Comic Almanac . . . Containing Sam Weller's Diary of Fun and Pastime* appeared in 1838. In the same year there appeared the anonymous *The Posthumous Papers of the Wonderful Discovery Club, formerly of Camden Town* and 1839 saw *The Posthumous Notes of the Pickwickian Club* (edited by one 'Bos') and the yet more cheeky *Pickwick Abroad; or, A Tour in France* by the popular writer of *The Mysteries of London*, G. W. M. Reynolds.[18] Of Reynolds's novel the critic of the *Sun* wrote: 'If "Pickwick Abroad" were not a work built upon another man's foundations, we should say it was one of the cleverest and most original productions of the modern British Press. We rise from the first Number with only the regret that Charles Dickens himself had not written it.' Its impact was such that a writer in the *Age* noted that the novel was 'so well done by G. W. M. Reynolds, that we must warn Boz to look to his laurels'.[19] But *Pickwick* did not only attract the attentions of prose writers anxious to pluck laurels and to cash in on Dickens's success. The novelist was to suffer worse humiliations at the hands of hack playwrights. Several of the earlier *Sketches by Boz* had been turned into comic burlettas—a once popular kind of musical farce—for performance on the London stage in the early 1830s, but the stage history of *Pickwick Papers* is particularly remarkable for its precocity. Even before the novel had completed its serial run, a dramatized version by Edward Stirling was produced at the City of London Theatre on 27 March 1837. A week later a second theatrical version by William Leman Rede opened at the Adelphi and soon transferred to the Surrey Theatre. In June a burletta entitled *Sam Weller: or The Pickwickians* by William T. Moncrieff was produced at the Theatre

Royal in the Strand and ran successfully for some eighty performances. It was followed in August by T. P. Taylor's *The Pickwickians*
which proved to be a flop at Sadler's Wells. This was still three
months before Dickens had actually finished his serialization, a factor which failed to deter three further theatrical hacks who had their
adaptations performed in theatres at Belfast, Sheffield, and even New
York.[20] Dickens's reaction to these piracies varied from amused
contempt to downright vexation. He was grudgingly prepared to
admit to John Forster that if Moncrieff's version had 'put a few
shillings in the vermin-eaten pockets of so miserable a creature,
and has saved him from the workhouse or a jail, let him empty
our little pot and welcome (Letters, i. 304: 7 Sept. 1837). On 29
November 1838, however, he complained to his friend Frederick
Yates:

My general objection to the adaptation of any unfinished work of mine
simply is, that being badly done and worse acted it tends to vulgarize the
characters, to destroy or weaken in the minds of those who see them the
impressions I have endeavoured to create, and consequently to lessen the
after-interest in their progress. (*Letters*, i. 463)

One cannot help suspecting, however, that Dickens was secretly flattered by the attentions of these pirates. As he must have divined, all
publicity was good publicity and his rivals' efforts certainly did nothing effective to dent the appeal of the genuine article.

Since 1837 *Pickwick Papers* has continued to attract an extraordinary number of would-be adaptors for a whole variety of media, both
old and new. In his exhaustive study of dramatizations of Dickens H.
Philip Bolton lists some 212 separate versions of the novel variously
reshaped for the stage, both professional and amateur, for film stu-
dios, for radio and, latterly, for television.[21] Pickwick has had a particularly varied musical life. A version of the interpolated story of
Gabriel Grub, somewhat portentously described as a 'Cantata Seria
Buffa', appeared in 1881, while in Manchester in 1884 *The Great
Pickwick Case* was adapted as a 'Comic Operetta' with music
arranged by Thomas Rawson. The most celebrated musical version
is that by Wolf Mankowitz, with music by Cyril Ornadel, which
opened at the Savile Theatre in London in July 1963. The comedian
Harry Secombe took the title role and went on to make something of
a popular hit with the show's leading musical number, the breezily

Stereo cards showing scenes from *Pickwick Papers*, *c.*1880s/90s.

'Pickwick in the wrong room.'

'Pickwick's apology.'

optimistic 'If I ruled the World'. The first *Pickwick* film (now apparently lost) appears to be the four-minute silent version of *Christmas at Wardle's* produced in Britain in 1901. Certain of the interpolated stories from the novel were filmed with such seemingly uninviting titles as *Gabriel Grub: The Surly Sexton* (1904) and *A Knight for a Night* (1909). These were outclassed some eleven years later by Thomas Alva Edison's surviving one-reeler entitled *Mr Pickwick's Predicament* (a silent retelling of the story of Pickwick and Mrs Bardell acted out with much gesticulation). This was followed a year later by a second American silent version directed by Lawrence Trimble and by a three-reel British movie of 1913, starring the rotund American comedian John Bunny, and notable for its attempts to reproduce authentic settings.[22] A British talkie version, with the celebrated Dickensian actor Bransby Williams as Sergeant Buzfuz, was premièred in London in November 1921. A fourth film, directed by Noel Langley, and starring James Hayter, was released in 1952. The novel proved to be equally popular with the pioneers of broadcasting in Britain. Two scenes from *Pickwick Papers* were performed on BBC radio in February 1930, but a twelve-part serialization, which was broadcast on the 'Home Service' from October 1939 to March 1940, offered a more thorough dramatic reading of the novel. This was at a period when such easygoing, morale-raising distractions would probably have been regarded as a helpful contribution to the 'War Effort'. Interestingly enough, the first drama shown on the fledgling BBC television on 6 and 11 July 1938 was a further version of the trial scenes from the novel. It was rebroadcast, once the service had begun again after the end of the Second World War, in September 1946.

Dickens and the Stage

The varied afterlife of *Pickwick Papers* can to some degree be paralleled by that of other Dickens novels (and most notably by *Oliver Twist* and *A Christmas Carol*). Tracing the history of such adaptations is not truly the business of a study such as the present one, but it is worth pausing to consider certain of those plays, films, and television dramatizations which can be said to have had a lasting impact on the public perception of Dickens and his work. Dickens is a rare phenomenon amongst novelists in that his work flourishes in the imaginations of many who never get round to actually reading his books. The novelist, who once declared to his friend John Forster that he had often thought that he 'should certainly have been as successful on the boards as [he had] been between them', began this process by taking with such avidity to public readings from his work.[23] He was both a great self-publicist and a supremely talented projector of himself. Charles Kent, who appreciatively witnessed these performances, noted in 1872:

These Readings were throughout so conspicuously and so radiantly a success, that even in the recollection of them, now that they are things of the past, it may be said that they have already beneficially influenced, and are still perceptibly advancing, the wider and keener appreciation of the writings themselves. In its gyrations, the ball then rolling at the Reader's foot imparted a momentum to one far nobler and more lasting—that of the Novelist's reputation, one that in its movement gives no sign of slackening.[24]

Since Kent's time a string of actors have built careers either on imitating 'the Inimitable' as public readers or in establishing reputations in playing specific Dickens characters on stage. In the closing years of the twentieth century both Simon Callow (who starred in a one-man show scripted by Dickens's biographer, Peter Ackroyd) and Miriam Margolyes (who concentrated on Dickens's women) succeeded in opening up fresh and illuminating dramatic investigations of the way in which Dickens's characters bore on the life of their creator. When the Callow/Ackroyd performances were revived in 2002 as *The Mystery of Charles Dickens* they were floridly described by Callow himself in the advance publicity as offering audiences an opportunity 'to reacquaint themselves with some of the funniest and saddest characters ever created, expressed in language so exuberant and so naturally theatrical that it positively demanded to be spoken out loud on a stage'. Emlyn Williams, who had enjoyed a considerable success as a Dickens reader in the years following the Second World War, also believed that the novelist himself had left an opening in the market by means of which a new generation of his theatrical heirs could profit:

To me, Dickens the actor—and without having seen him, let us grant that he was as gifted as he may well have been—Dickens the actor did not do full justice to Dickens the author, in the material he chose to perform: I am emboldened to give that opinion after a long and arduous search through the entire Dickens canon, for my own stage material. To me, Dickens the actor chose to ignore the richest and most exciting vein in the whole treasure-cave: the descriptive writing. He neglected Dickens the man of literature.[25]

Dickens himself had therefore set a precedent, but he had equally declined to establish limits for reconfigurations of his work beyond which his successors could not presume to pass. Above all he seemed to allow for the fact that 'acting out' a page of Dickens was neither presumptuous nor sacrilegious. Despite the broken-backed attempts by his contemporaries to reinvent his fiction in the form of parodies, continuations, burlettas, and melodramas, the novels themselves appear to have always won the day. Indeed, as the passage of time has suggested, those novels have proved to have an innate integrity and resilience. It is this resilience that enables them to withstand the potential threats represented by translations into another medium, however brilliantly, or, conversely, vulgarly those translations might be executed. Verdi's *Rigoletto* may have almost totally eclipsed its theatrical original, Victor Hugo's *Le Roi s'amuse*, but, despite its success on both the stage and the screen, Lionel Bart's musical *Oliver!* (1960) has never diminished the distinctive quality of *Oliver Twist*. In a similar way, a reading of the singularly redoubtable *A Christmas Carol* is not damaged by an awareness that the part of Scrooge has been interpreted by actors as diverse as Sir Seymour Hicks (on stage in 1901 and in a film adaptation in 1935), Alastair Sim (in a fine British film of 1951), Basil Rathbone (in an American television broadcast of 1957), and Donald Duck (in Walt Disney's animated cartoon *Mickey's Christmas Carol* of 1983).[26] Dickens's first Christmas Book has also managed to survive its inventive trans-mogrification into *The Muppet Christmas Carol* in 1992. Time and again history has seemed to suggest that whereas rewritings, reinterpretations, and ideological readings of Dickens have been transitory, the texts themselves have retained their ability to open up often unexpected, but nonetheless suggestive, imaginative vistas. In the second act of Tom Stoppard's play *Travesties* (1975), Nadezhda Krupskaya refers to the fact that her husband, Lenin, had been so vexed by the 'saccharine sentimentality' of a dramatic version of *The Cricket on the Hearth* that he had walked out of the theatre. In his play Stoppard is calling Lenin's politically determined aesthetics into question rather than criticizing any real shortcoming on Dickens's part. The particular production of *The Cricket on the Hearth* to which Stoppard refers had in fact become a particular favourite with audiences at the still experimental Moscow Arts Theatre in the years immediately following the Russian Revolution. It might therefore be further posited that it was Lenin, and not his fellow Russians, who was reacting against a *Zeitgeist*, a particularly charged *Zeitgeist* at that, which may well have needed a serving of Dickensian 'sentimentality' as a relief from the obligatory diet of socialist realist gruel.[27]

Pre-twentieth-century audiences for Dickensian dramas certainly seem to have relished both sentimentality and a concomitant suspension of disbelief. Few people are now likely to recall the success of J. P. Burnett's tear-jerking stage version of *Bleak House*, a play baldly entitled *Jo*. The play is now remarkable for one thing only: the prominence it gave to a woman who is, to date, the longest-serving Dickensian actor, Burnett's wife Jennie Lee. Miss Lee gave her first performance in the title role in Liverpool in 1875. The play transferred to the Globe Theatre in London in 1876 (though here a censor in the Lord Chamberlain's office insisted on the omission of Jo's dying recitation of the Lord's Prayer). *Jo* brought Jennie Lee fame on both sides of the Atlantic and, much to Bernard Shaw's chagrin, she was still playing the role some twenty-one years later. In 1921, when the actress was in her seventies, she returned to the role for a charity benefit performance at the Lyric Theatre in London in aid of the 'Charles Dickens Children's Library'.[28] Thus, ironically, the illiterate boy Jo, played by a superannuated actress, raised money in order to encourage literacy amongst children. It is unlikely that *Jo* will be revived again, but the critical fortunes of *Bleak House* have suffered not a whit. The same is probably true of the once-celebrated version of *A Tale of Two Cities*, *The Only Way*, first performed at the Lyceum Theatre on 16 February 1899. This play has now been committed to much the same literary limbo as the drama which perhaps inspired the novel, Watts Phillips's *The Dead Heart* (1857), and Tom Taylor's elaborate stage version which opened at the Lyceum in January 1860. It was *The Only Way*, written by Lieutenant-Colonel the Reverend Freeman Wills and the Canon Frederick Langbridge, that probably helped render Sydney Carton's dying words so familiar to many who were otherwise unacquainted with the novel (they figured prominently in a final tableau and were printed in the programme). By the end of the year the play had run for 260 performances in London and had opened successfully in New York.[29] *The Only Way* starred John (later Sir John) Martin-Harvey, a protégé of Sir Henry Irving's, as Sydney Carton and it was Martin-Harvey and his company who kept the play alive in London and the provinces over the succeeding thirty-odd years (even appearing in a silent-film version in 1925 when its star was in his sixties).[30] Martin-Harvey had in fact managed to keep his status as a matinée idol well into his career as the impersonator of Carton, fostering it with a series of picture postcards in which he glowers soulfully or poses heroically on the steps to the scaffold. His starring role was also enhanced by a special souvenir programme, produced at the end of 1899 for the Lyceum, which published photographs of the leading actors and of the most dramatic scenes and also printed Hamilton Clarke's poignant musical theme associated with 'Mimi' (a new character, unthought of by Dickens, who has been rescued by Carton from the slums of Paris and who pines with unrequited love for him. She finally kills Defarge to save Lucie from arrest and goes to the guillotine with the hero).

The success of *The Only Way* depended on its histrionics, on its elaborate sets, and on its highly charged action (which cut down on Dickens's plot by eliminating Jerry Cruncher, Miss Pross, and Madame Defarge from the story). In terms of British theatrical history it represents the last great fling of the high-flown late Victorian tradition most readily associated with Sir Henry Irving. The later twentieth century's greatest Dickensian adaptation stands in stark contrast to it. This was the version of *Nicholas Nickleby* scripted by David Edgar for the Royal Shakespeare Company and produced at the Aldwych Theatre in London in June 1980. The play, which ran for eight and a half hours, was performed over two successive nights.[31] Despite the positively Wagnerian demands it made on its audiences, it proved to be one of the greatest triumphs brought off by the Royal Shakespeare Company in its prime. The production's genius lay in the originality and inventiveness of its staging. Edgar's script was evolved in association with the thirty-nine actors taking part and with the active participation of its directors, Trevor Nunn and John Caird. This new version kept far more of Dickens's text than any earlier stage version. Rather than eliminate much of the linking narrative, and many of the descriptive passages, it divided them up, sharing them between actors who were required to move in and out of character as much as they doubled up on minor parts. The directors determined that 'the whole company should be regarded as the story-teller of the whole tale'. Edgar was later to write of the guiding principles behind the planning of the production:

The collective voice would not be silenced even now: the rewriting and rehearsal processes would be influenced by the fact that the company as a whole was pursuing a collective purpose. This . . . was a familiar process to most of us; but none of us had even attempted it on anything like this scale. We began by sitting round in a large, 45-person circle, to talk about the novel, our reaction to it, our memory of other Dickens adaptations— we saw one or two of the movies—and so on. Then we began the exercise work, which was to last four or five weeks, before a single part was cast or a single word written.[32]

Edgar's key phrase is 'collective purpose'. Rarely before had such a long novel been allowed the integrity to express itself. Gone were the artificial and outmoded divisions into three or four acts with scene changes and elaborate tableaux. Instead there were broad lines of development, a delight in detail, a multiplicity of short scenes, a flexible use of the stage, and a sense that actors had actually *evolved* their characters prompted by a real understanding of how and why Dickens worked as a writer. The play was transported triumphantly to New York in 1981 and on its revival in Great Britain was broadcast on Channel 4 in November 1982. Such was its impact that it rendered the Royal Shakespeare Company the victim of an elaborate hoax, for letters were sent out to hundreds of supporters of the Company with the heading RDT ('Royal Dickens Theatre') offering them roles in forthcoming Dickens productions! The director John Barton was asked to complete *Edwin Drood* and posters advertising a spoof new production of *Little Dorrit* actually appeared outside the theatre itself.[33] Alas, so far, *Nicholas Nickleby* has proved to be a unique theatrical phenomenon.

Dickens and Film

A very select number of twentieth-century film adaptations of Dickens's novels have shared something of the boldness, the inventiveness, and the sheer verve of the Royal Shakespeare Company's

Nicholas Nickleby. Silent movies of *The Old Curiosity Shop* had been made in 1909, 1911, 1912 (all one-reelers), 1914, 1921, and 1922 (a lost Italian version) but in 1935 a British talkie, made in black and white and directed by Thomas Bentley, captured a fascinating range of vintage acting styles and of voices, orotund, plummy, and precise. The film is far from a masterpiece, but despite its creaks and stiff-nesses it has both period charm and genuine flair (it was photo-graphed by Claude Friese-Greene, the son of the great pioneer of cinema). Grandfather was played by Ben Webster (who, despite his advancing years, was to go on to a distinguished Hollywood career). His is a highly sentimentalized performance that Dickens's con-temporaries would probably have relished as much as did the rela-tively unsophisticated cinema audiences of the 1930s. That is not to say that it possesses an immediate rapport with latter-day viewers. In the last scene, for example, Webster milks the old man's incompre-hension of the import of Nell's demise for all its tear-jerking worth. The real star of the film is, however, Hay Petrie as a quirkily malefic and splendidly Gothic Quilp, a Quilp who leers, sneers, and cavorts very much as Dickens demanded. The sets, too, vividly recall the fussy architecture delineated so lovingly by George Cattermole in the original illustrations. Equally memorable, if largely for W. C. Fields's idiosyncratic and surprisingly warm interpretation of Wilkins Micawber, is George Cukor's Hollywood version of *David Copperfield* (1935). The movie was a huge popular success at a time when Dickens's reputation stood at a low ebb amongst many would-be highbrow readers and critics. The movie cut corners and condensed in terms of the plot and its characters (no Traddles, Creakle, Dr Strong, or Rosa Dartle), but it does manage to capture the essentials of the story with considerable vivacity. Alas, despite the fact that the screenplay was in part the work of the British novelist Hugh Walpole, Micawber's famous definition of the eco-nomic distinction between happiness and misery was simplified lest the mention of sixpences might disconcert transatlantic audiences. The celebrity cast also included Edna May Oliver as a particularly fine Betsey Trotwood and Basil Rathbone as a splendid Murdstone who shows off his aquiline profile to cruel effect. Cukor's *David Copperfield* is, however, more a vehicle for its actors than it is a cinematic triumph.

The accolade 'triumph' must be reserved for the two finest

black-and-white versions of Dickens novels, David Lean's *Great Expectations* (1946) and his *Oliver Twist* (1948). Both films were beautifully designed by John Bryan. Lean uses chiaroscuro to singular effect, notably in his haunted nightscapes and cloudscapes. This is especially true of the famous opening sequences of both films— the twilit marshes, the twin gibbets, and the aching trees in the windswept churchyard in *Great Expectations* and the agonies of Oliver's pregnant mother as she struggles through pelting rain to the workhouse in *Oliver Twist*. Throughout the latter film Lean seems to pay an animated tribute to the images of Dickens's characters so vividly established by his original illustrator, George Cruikshank (notably so in the nightmarish presentation of Fagin). Blacks, whites, shadows, glooms, and cobwebs are also used with formidable effect in the Satis House scenes in *Great Expectations*. Lean's Miss Havisham, Martita Hunt, is an unrivalled piece of casting, matched by two finely attuned Estellas from the young Jean Simmons and the adult Valerie Hobson. Notable too are the fine performances coaxed from John Mills as the adult Pip (who also acts as narrator), Finlay Currie as Magwitch, Bernard Miles as Joe, and Alec Guinness as a winsome Herbert Pocket. Although his film eliminates Orlick and conveniently disposes of Mrs Joe in order to introduce Biddy, Lean's only major deviation from Dickens's plot is his revision of the admittedly ambiguous ending. Here there is no ambiguity. Pip returns to the rundown but undemolished Satis House to find that Estella has established herself in Miss Havisham's rooms and has begun to adopt the solitary habits of her sometime guardian (she too has been jilted, Bentley Drummle having found out about her unfortunate parentage). Pip decides otherwise. 'I have come back, Miss Havisham,' he proclaims, 'I have come back. To let in the sunlight' and he proceeds to pull down the heavy, dust-infused curtains which have shrouded the room for so long. The film ends with Pip and Estella 'starting again', rushing out into the sunlight and closing the gates of Satis House behind them.

It was Alec Guinness, who had played a young, biddable, slightly foppish Herbert in *Great Expectations*, who persuaded a sceptical Lean that he had it in him to take on the part of Fagin. It proved to be one of the triumphs of a long and distinguished acting career. Guinness's Fagin is unsurpassed in its menace, its energy, and its ambiguity, at once the 'merry old gentleman' and the murderous

W. C. Fields as
Wilkins Micawber
in George Cukor's
film of *David
Copperfield*, 1935.

Martita Hunt as
Miss Havisham,
Jean Simmons as
Estella, and
Anthony Wager as
Pip from David
Lean's film of *Great
Expectations*, 1946.

father of lies (so effective was this performance that it occasioned charges of anti-Semitism in post-Holocaust Palestine and gave rise to a two-year ban in the United States, a ban which lasted until twelve 'offensive' minutes of the film's action were cut).[34] Again Lean assembled a fine supporting cast, notably Robert Newton as a brutish Sikes, a fly Anthony Newley as the Dodger, and John Howard Davies as an Oliver who manages to capture the essential vulnerability and the incongruous gentility that Dickens insists upon. If Lean's *Oliver Twist* lacks the subdued atmospheric intensity of his *Great Expectations*, it compensates by exploring visually much of what Graham Greene recognized in a roughly contemporary essay as Dickens's 'Manichaean' vision of a war between spiritual forces.[35]

Dickens has proved to be less fortunate in attracting talented film directors since the release of Lean's two great classics of the 1940s. Carol Reed's finely crafted film of Lionel Bart's musical *Oliver!* (1968) has none of the tension or inventiveness of Lean's *Oliver Twist* but it at least has the advantage of good choreography and a well-cast Fagin (Ron Moody). The same cannot be said of a 'politically correct', but singularly dull, version of the novel directed by Clive Donner (1982) with George C. Scott crudely attempting to render a victimized Fagin sympathetic (a virtually impossible task, though an equally politically correct Independent Television version of 1999 made Fagin into a non-Jewish magician from Prague!). Joseph Hardy's *Great Expectations* (1975) had a potentially interesting cast (including James Mason and Robert Morley) but it managed to be singularly unenthralling. Far more interesting is Alfonso Cuaron's updated, trans-Atlanticized version of the same novel (1998), starring Robert de Niro as Magwitch and with Anne Bancroft as 'Miss Dinsmoor' (formerly Havisham) with her wedding banquet laid out on a South Florida lawn. Pip (renamed 'Finn') has no pretensions to be a gentleman, and Mrs Joe has a lover, but Cuaron's updating generally makes for a persuasive reading, particularly in his acceptance of Dickens's revised ending with 'Finn' reunited with a surprisingly provocative Estella (played by Gwyneth Paltrow). Although his film wrenched the novel's story unnaturally, even brutally, into the American twentieth century, Cuaron recognized that there was sufficient resonance in Dickens's plot and characterization to license the recontextualization of the most powerful aspects of both. Far less persuasive and enterprising was Delbert Mann's brave attempt to use appropriate locations in his 1970 film of *David Copperfield*. The film was designed to coincide with the Dickens centenary of that year and in celebration an all-star British cast was assembled. Edith Evans played Betsey Trotwood, Emlyn Williams Mr Dick, Ralph Richardson Micawber, Michael Redgrave Mr Peggotty, and Ron Moody Uriah Heep. Nevertheless, the movie can now only be judged as uninspired and ultimately dispiriting.[36] The only post-war colour film to prove truly sympathetic to the real spirit of Dickens is Christine Edzard's quirkily brilliant *Little Dorrit* of 1987. Edzard, who wrote her own screenplay, styled her film 'A Story Told in Two Parts'. Abandoning Dickens's own division of his story into 'Poverty' and 'Riches', she determined to retell the substance of the story from the points of view of Arthur Clennam (176 minutes) and Amy Dorrit (181 minutes), allowing the two perspectives to overlap and to blend. The action is often slow but, unlike most other Dickens movies, this one is expansive rather than condensed. It has epic proportions but, like the original novel, few epic pretensions. Although the film was made in a London studio and not on location, it adeptly evokes untidy street scenes and jostling crowds. The interior scenes use colour tellingly and often with superb effect, variously suggesting the blistered chocolate of the wainscot of the Clennam house, the sense that wallpaper has seen many better days in the shabby Marshalsea, and the rinsed-out tones of the otherwise sumptuous reception rooms of the rich. As with her sense of crowds and subdued colours, Edzard's cast is outstanding. Derek Jacobi is a deeply wounded but singularly plausible Arthur Clennam (playing the part of one of Dickens's least engaging heroes) and the veteran Alec Guinness gives a beautifully nuanced performance as William Dorrit. Just as remarkable, in their various ways, are the actors taking smaller roles: Patricia Hayes (Affery); Miriam Margolyes (Flora Finching), and Eleanor Bron (Mrs Merdle), and even the vignette performances put in by Robert Morley (as Lord Decimus Barnacle) and Alan Bennett (as the Bishop). Throughout her film Edzard used orchestral music arranged, with great flair, from operas by Verdi, music which variously expresses repressed or unexpressed emotion, dramatic tension, or a brassy confidence with an ease which would probably have delighted Dickens.

Poster for David Lean's *Oliver Twist*, 1948, featuring Alec Guinness as Fagin and Robert Newton as Bill Sikes.

Borough High Street, in Christine Edzard's *Little Dorrit*, 1987.

Dickens and Television

As the great Russian director Sergei Eisenstein asserted in the late 1940s, Dickens was one of the unacknowledged 'fathers' of the cinema.[37] Although many ill-informed speculators suggest that Dickens is also the 'father' of the television serial, he should not be readily claimed as a soap-opera scriptwriter *manqué*. He has, however, been consistently well served by those who have adapted his novels for television, particularly so once it was generally recognized that, if sufficient time were allotted in the schedules, the narratives of the longer novels could be allowed to develop over five or six substantial episodes. As with adaptations of much shorter Jane Austen novels, BBC television dramatizations of Dickens were originally relegated to an early evening slot on Sundays. They thus took on something of the status of morally uplifting sabbath reading. *David Copperfield* appeared in this form in thirteen half-hour episodes in 1956 and again in 1966 (both scripted by Vincent Tilsley).[38] A new, over-condensed version, by Hugh Whitemore, was broadcast in only six episodes in 1975 and repeated in 1976.[39] Most of these early television dramatizations suggested that Dickens's fiction was little more than diversion and entertainment, and best suited to children. Although all of the major novels appeared in some form or another on the screen, surprising as it may now seem, *Little Dorrit* has never been adapted for British television. A real breakthrough occurred in the late 1970s, a breakthrough that coincided with the revisionist criticism of the novels which began to appear in the years following the centenary of the novelist's birth. The old taste for a benign or predominantly comic Dickens was steadily superseded by a new-found relish for a darker, more expansive, more demanding, and more cerebral novelist. In the spring of 1976 the BBC broadcast a memorable dramatization of the then still largely overlooked *Our Mutual Friend*. It was adapted by Julia Jones and Donald Churchill and serialized in seven weighty episodes. Each episode was introduced with images of a murky, eddying Thames, accompanied by a particularly evocative and appropriate sub-Brahmsian score by Carl Davis. It was also fortunate in the casting of Leo McKern as Boffin, of the comedian Alfie Bass as Silas Wegg, and of Warren Clarke as an especially unnerving and clumsily intense Bradley Headstone. It was filmed in consistently subdued colour. Colour was also used with

great effect in Arthur Hopcraft's subtle adaptation of the equally
neglected *Hard Times*, broadcast in four episodes by Granada TV (a
company appropriately based in Manchester). It had a strong cast, a
fine sense of period, and offered an impressive evocation of an
unlovely, polluted, industrial landscape. Although the BBC produced an adequate, if ultimately uninspired, *Pickwick Papers* in 1985,
there has since been a real shift in interest away from the sprawling,
predominantly comic, early novels to the later, moodier, more
intense ones. This switch has entailed a considerable investment of
time and money, and it has also demanded the careful choice of
actors who can move beyond 'character' parts into a more persuasive
'realism'. Three such serialized productions stand out, each of
which was later released on video: a six-and-a-half-hour *Bleak House*
of 1987; a five-and-a-half-hour *Martin Chuzzlewit* of 1995; and a
five-hour-fifty-minute *Our Mutual Friend* of 1998. The *Martin
Chuzzlewit* had the novelist David Lodge as its adaptor. 'Adaptation
is a form of criticism', Lodge claimed in a lecture he gave in 1994,
though he also admitted that he had been obliged to make substantial
cuts both in the dialogue that he had selected ('verbal redundancy')
and in the plot (the American scenes had, alas, been reduced to a
minimum to save both time and money).[40] He also diverged from
Dickens's ending. Lodge recognized, as all good writers for the
medium know, that television is mimetic: it shows, not tells, but unlike a feature film, it allows for expansiveness, for episodic transmis-
sion, and for an extensive use of the spoken word. *Martin Chuzzlewit*
had a fine cast, including Paul Scofield as old Martin Chuzzlewit,
the ageing John Mills as Chuffey, and Tom Wilkinson as a slightly
subdued Pecksniff. Sadly, though, the Mrs Gamp proved to be a
damp squib of a performance. Lodge's adaptation had real merits,
but it was in many senses a rereading and redrafting of Dickens's
original. It was outclassed on all levels by the *Bleak House* of
1987. Here the teleplay was the work of the excellent Arthur
Hopcraft (who had worked on the Granada *Hard Times*). Hopcraft
intelligently dispensed with the double narrative and the time shift
between Esther's sections and those told by the third-person narrator. He therefore made a complex story more straightforward by
seeming to tighten the lines of plot into a single progressive movement and by cleverly juxtaposing scenes and, occasionally, dexter-
ously redistributing dialogue. In the scene of Jo's death, for example,

it is Esther who recites the Lord's Prayer and John Jarndyce who splenetically explodes with the third-person narrator's rage ('Dead, your Majesty. Dead, my lords and gentlemen. Dead, men and women, born with Heavenly compassion in your hearts. And dying thus around us every day'). Neither Esther nor Jarndyce is in fact present at the death-bed in the novel. The serial, which was subtly directed by Ross Devenish, ultimately lost very little of Dickens's story in terms of character or plot. What Devenish and his designers added, however, was a fine evocation of a heterogeneous London shrouded in fog and of a landscape beyond London mired in mud. It was filmed in a grainy colour which somehow managed to suggest an interrelationship between fog and sunlight, haze and lamplight, cloud and candle. The subdued lighting of the interior scenes certainly helped to enhance the middle-aged beauty of Diana Rigg's beautifully poised Lady Dedlock. Rigg was not the only impressive member of the cast (the veteran comedian Charlie Drake was inspiredly cast as Grandfather Smallweed), but the general impression left by this highly distinguished production is of a homogeneous group of actors working superbly both with and against one another. Many individual scenes fix themselves in the memory, but perhaps the most haunting is the image of Richard Carstone walking out into the fog from Lincoln's Inn Hall, arm in arm with the frail Miss Flite. They disappear into the murk but, as we sense, they are taking the fog of Chancery with them into a larger, pervasive fog.

Late twentieth-century television has enhanced the long tradition of refiguring Dickens very considerably. Having successfully kept the novels alive to popular audiences in the 1950s and 1960s, television, and the BBC in particular, began to discover the dramatic potential of the variety, the subtlety, the spiritual depths, and the extraordinary fertility of Dickens's narratives. The Dickens adaptations of the 1980s and 1990s were major cultural achievements which may well prove to be unrivalled, given the prejudices against 'costume drama' which seem to prevail in the penny-pinching, anti-élitist opening years of the twenty-first century. Television demonstrated that it could explore narrative territory beyond what the resources of the stage and the cinema could offer. Above all, it returned to the tensions and the suspense of serialization, but not as Dickens himself would have understood tension and suspense or the serial form in which he presented them. In their original green

wrappers Dickens's monthly parts offered readers both entertainment and stimulus, both solace and release, both companionship and
provocation, a sense both of the profound sadness of the world and
of the intensity of its joy. Dickens's serials also demanded patience
and concentration. Given that these monthly parts included illustrations which were integral to the text and that the novelist himself
recognized the ready transmutability of his completed stories into
public readings, no one nowadays should be disturbed by their
attractiveness to those who adapt them for television, the medium
that so easily links words with images and then projects them, like
the original monthly parts, into private rather than public spaces. It
is idle to speculate as to whether or not Dickens would have relished
the 'art' of television and as to whether or not he would, had he been
born in the twentieth century, have recognized it as the medium in
which he would have chosen to work. He is in every sense a product
of the nineteenth century and he worked in a long literary tradition
of which he was intensely proud to be an heir. In terms of what and
how he wrote he is emphatically *not* our contemporary. In terms of
the ramifications of what he wrote, his work is, as W. H. Auden said
of that of the dead W. B. Yeats, 'modified in the guts of the living'.
Dickens is intensely alive both in the immediate legacy of his fiction
and in the 'modifications' that his heirs develop from that fiction.
The fact that he has been so readily and easily recontextualized, both
within and beyond his lifetime, is perhaps best seen as a tribute to
the very resilience of his genius.

NOTES

Place of publication is London unless otherwise stated.

CHAPTER 1. Dickens's Life

1. The notice appeared in both the *Hampshire Telegraph and Sussex Chronicle* and in the *Hampshire Chronicle*. See Michael Allen, *Charles Dickens' Childhood* (1988), 18 and 126 n. 23.

2. George Dolby, *Charles Dickens as I Knew Him: The Story of the Reading Tours* (1885), 37–8.

3. Robert Langton, *The Childhood and Youth of Dickens* (1891), 224. Michael Slater disputes Langton's claim that Mary was the nurse in question in his *Dickens and Women* (1983), 4, 382–3.

4. Allen, *Charles Dickens' Childhood*, 101–3.

5. See Michael Slater (ed.), *'Gone Astray' and Other Papers from Household Words 1851–1859* (1998), 35–42. For Dickens's education see also Philip Collins, *Dickens and Education* (1963), 12–13.

6. Allen, *Dickens' Childhood*, 106–12.

7. For Dickens as a legal clerk see William S. Holdsworth, *Charles Dickens as a Legal Historian* (New Haven, 1928) and Peter Ackroyd, *Dickens* (1990), pp. 115–19.

8. For the background to the stories collected as the *Sketches by Boz* see Michael Slater (ed.), *Sketches by Boz and Other Early Papers 1833–1839* (1994), pp. xi–xxii.

9. See also Ackroyd, *Dickens*, 128.

10. Abraham Hayward, *Quarterly Review*, 59 (Oct. 1837), 484–518; repr. in Philip Collins (ed.), *Dickens: The Critical Heritage* (1971), 56–62. For a discussion of this review see Andrew Sanders, *Dickens and the Spirit of the Age* (1999), 21–2.

11. These diaries are reprinted in *Letters*, vols. i and ii.

12. Philip Collins (ed.), *Charles Dickens: The Public Readings* (Oxford, 1975), 1–4.

13. He found Browne's sketch 'frightfully and wildly wide of the mark' (*Letters*, iv. 671: Nov.–Dec. 1846).

14. For a detailed discussion of the dating of the autobiography see pp. xvii–xxii of Nina Burgis's Clarendon edition of *David Copperfield* (Oxford, 1981).

15. For the journalism published in *Household Words* see Michael Slater (ed.), *'The Amusements of the People' and Other Papers: Reports, Essays and Reviews 1834–1851* (1996) and *'Gone Astray' and Other Papers from Household Words*.

16. For these working titles see Harry Stone (ed.), *Dickens' Working Notes for his Novels* (Chicago, 1987), 186–205.

17. For these reviews see Collins (ed.), *Dickens: The Critical Heritage*, 300–14.

18. For a commentary on 'On Strike' and the other *Household Words* essay of this period see Slater (ed.), *'Gone Astray' and Other Papers from Household Words*, 196–210.

19. For the breakup of Dickens's marriage and its professional ramifications see Slater, *Dickens and Women*, ch. 7 'Catherine: The End of the Marriage' pp. 135–62.

20. For the best introduction to these essays see Michael Slater and John Drew (eds.), *'The Uncommercial Traveller' and Other Papers 1859–1870* (2000), pp. xi–xxiii.

21. Dolby, *Charles Dickens as I Knew Him*, 11.

22. Charles Kent, *Charles Dickens as a Reader* (1872), 87.

23. For these 'Farewell' readings see Collins, *Dickens: The Public Readings*. See esp. the introduction to 'Sikes and Nancy', 465–70.

CHAPTER 2. 'These Times of Ours': Dickens, Politics, and Society

1. Queen Victoria's diary for 15 Oct. 1851. Quoted in Paul Greenhalgh, 'The Art and Industry of Mammon: International Exhibitions 1851–1901', in John M. Mackenzie (ed.), *The Victorian Vision: Inventing New Britain* (2001), 265.

2. Quoted by Patrick Beaver in *The Crystal Palace* (1970), 42.

3. For the Central Working Class Committee see *Letters*, vi. 57 n. 3.

4. Jeffrey A. Auerbach, *The Great Exhibition of 1851* (New Haven and London, 1999), 3, 130.

5. 'The Great Exhibition and the Little One', *Household Words* (5 July 1851). This article, written in collaboration with R. H. Horne, is reprinted in Harry Stone (ed.), *The Uncollected Writings of Charles Dickens: Household Words 1850–1859*, 2 vols. (1969), i. 319–20, 329.

6. *Letters*, vi. 796–7 and n. (4 Nov. 1852); 801 (11 Nov. 1852); 805 (19 Nov. 1852).

7. For Dickens's response to funerals see Andrew Sanders, *Charles Dickens: Resurrectionist* (1982), 39–46.

8. 'Trading in death', *Household Words* (27 Nov. 1852); repr. in Michael Slater (ed.), *'Gone Astray' and Other Papers from Household Words 1851–1859* (1998), 95–105.

9. G. M. Young, 'Portrait of an Age', in *Early Victorian England 1830–1865*, 2 vols. (1934; 2nd impression 1951), ii. 455.

10. Ibid. 438.

11. Notes to *Caesar and Cleopatra* (1898), quoted by Dan H. Lawrence and Martin Quinn in their *Shaw on Dickens* (New York, 1985), pp. xxix–xxx.

12. Foreword to *Great Expectations* (1937); repr. in Lawrence and Quinn (eds.), *Shaw on Dickens*, 51.

13. James Fitzjames Stephen, 'Mr. Dickens as a Politician', *Saturday Review*, 3 (3 Jan. 1857), 8–9; repr. in Philip Collins (ed.), *Dickens: The Critical Heritage* (1971), 344–5.

14. Walter Bagehot, 'Charles Dickens', *National Review*, 7 (Oct. 1858), 458–86; repr. in Collins (ed.), *Dickens*, 397–8.

15. John Ruskin in a letter to Charles Eliot Norton (19 June 1870); repr. in Stephen Wall (ed.), *Charles Dickens* (Penguin Critical Anthology, Harmondsworth, 1970), 191.

16. 'Old Lamps for New Ones', *Household Words* (15 June 1850); repr. in Michael Slater (ed.), *'The Amusements of the People' and Other Papers: Reports, Essays and Reviews 1834–1851* (1996), 242–8.

17. Ibid. 247.

18. Ibid. 244.

19. For the debates over Catholic Emancipation see Owen Chadwick, *The Victorian Church*, pt. 1 (1966), 7–24.

20. 'Snoring for the Million', *Examiner* (24 Dec. 1842), repr. in Slater (ed.), *'Amusements of the People'*, 51–5.

21. 'Gone Astray'; repr. in Slater (ed.), *'Gone Astray' and Other Papers*, 161.

22. 'The Noble Savage', *Household Words* (11 June 1853); repr. in Slater (ed.), *'Gone Astray' and Other Papers*, 141–8.

23. For two contrasting but complementary studies of Dickens's attitudes towards women see Michael Slater, *Dickens and Women* (1983) and Patricia Ingham, *Dickens, Women and Language* (Hemel Hempstead, 1992).

24. For Miss Peecher see Philip Collins, *Dickens and Education* (1963), 128–9.

25. *Letters*, v. 416–17 and nn. 1 and 3. The article, 'A Bundle of Emigrants' Letters', is repr. in Stone (ed.), *Uncollected Writings: Household Words 1850–1859*, i. 85–96.

26. 'Sucking Pigs', *Household Words* (8 Nov. 1851); repr. in Michael Slater (ed.), *'Gone Astray' and Other Papers*, 42–9.

27. Slater, *Dickens and Women*, 269.

28. K. J. Fielding (ed.), *The Speeches of Charles Dickens* (Oxford, 1960), 407.

29. Ibid. 410–11.

CHAPTER 3. The Literary Context

1. G. H. Lewes, *Dickens in Relation to Criticism* (Feb. 1872); repr. in Rosemary Ashton (ed.), *Versatile Victorian: Selected Critical Writings of George Henry Lewes* (1992), 77.

2. The May 1844 inventory of Dickens's books at Devonshire Terrace is included as app. C in *Letters*, iv. 711–25.

3. R. H. Horne, *A New Spirit of the Age*, 2 vols. (1844), i. 307.

4. Ibid. 48–9.

5. Ibid. 57, 70.

6. J. H. Stonehouse (ed.), *Catalogue of the Library of Charles Dickens from Gadshill etc.* (1935), 5–120.

7. John Stuart Mill, *Autobiography* (1873), ch. 5, pp. 146–8.

8. Hallam Tennyson, *Alfred Lord Tennyson: A Memoir*, 2 vols. (1897), i. 118.

9. Stonehouse (ed.), *Catalogues*, 109.

10. Arthur Hallam, review of *Poems, Chiefly Lyrical, Englishman's Magazine*

(Aug. 1831); repr. in John D. Jump (ed.), *Tennyson: The Critical Heritage* (1967), 41.

11. Horne, *New Spirit*, ii. 256–7.

12. Thomas Carlyle, *Chartism* (1840), ch. 10; repr. in *English and Other Critical Essays* (Everyman edn., 1967), 226–7.

13. Ibid. 227–8.

14. Thomas Carlyle, *Past and Present* (1843), 340–1.

15. Carlyle, *On Heroes, Hero-Worship and the Heroic in History* (1840), lecture v; repr. in *Sartor Resartus: On Heroes and Hero Worship* (Everyman edn., 1956), 383.

16. Gordon N. Ray, *Thackeray: The Uses of Adversity 1811–1846* (1955), 427.

17. Ray, *Thackeray: The Age of Wisdom 1847–1863* (1958), 138.

18. '*In Memoriam*. W. M. Thackeray', repr. in Michael Slater and John Drew (eds.), *'The Uncommercial Traveller' and Other Papers 1859–1870* (2000), 328, 329.

19. For Trollope and Dickens see Andrew Sanders, *Anthony Trollope* (Writers and their Work series, Plymouth, 1998), 24–6.

20. *The Letters of Anthony Trollope*, ed. N. John Hall, 2 vols. (Stanford, Calif., 1983), ii. 557–8.

21. Anthony Trollope, *An Autobiography*, 2 vols. (1883), ed. David Skilton (Penguin Classics edn., Harmondsworth, 1988), 159.

22. 'The Natural History of German Life', *Westminster Review* (July 1856); repr. in *Essays and Leaves from a Notebook* (Edinburgh, 1884), 236.

23. For Gaskell's relationship with Dickens see Hilary Schor, *Scheherazade in the Marketplace* (1994). See also Andrew Sanders, 'Serializing Gaskell: From *Household Words* to *The Cornhill*', *Gaskell Society Journal*, 14 (2000), 45–58.

24. Quoted by Catherine Peters in her *The King of Inventors: A Life of Wilkie Collins* (1991), 352.

25. For Dickens's use of serial publication see John Butt and Kathleen Tillotson, *Dickens at Work* (1957) and John Sutherland, *Victorian Novelists and Publishers* (1976).

26. For Dickens's illustrators see Frederick G. Kitton, *Dickens and his Illustrators* (1899). For a more recent study see also Jane R. Cohen, *Charles Dickens and his Original Illustrators* (Columbus, Oh., 1980).

27. For this see 'English Influences on Vincent Van Gogh', *Vincent* (Bulletin of the Rijksmuseum, Amsterdam), 4/1 (1975), 18–22.

CHAPTER 4. Urban Society: London and Class

1. Hippolyte Taine, *Notes on England* (1860–70), trans. and introd. Edward Hyams (1957), 13.

2. Anon., *The Pictorial Handbook of London Comprising Its Antiquities, Architecture, Arts, Manufacture, Trade, Social, Literary and Scientific Institutions, Exhibitions, and Galleries of Art* (1854), 1.

3. For a varied view of the phenomenon of London in the first half of the

nineteenth century see Celina Fox (ed.), *London: World City 1800–1840* (New Haven and London, 1992).

4. Friedrich Engels, *The Condition of the Working Class in England* (1845), ed. Victor Kiernan (Harmondsworth, 1987), 68.

5. Ibid. 68–9.

6. For these statistics see K. Theodore Hoppen, *The Mid-Victorian Generation 1840–1886* (Oxford, 1998), 56, 58–9.

7. Ibid. 46.

8. George Brimley in his review of *Bleak House* published in the *Spectator* (24 Sept. 1853); repr. in Brimley's *Essays* (1860), 291.

9. For this issue see Andrew Sanders, *Dickens and the Spirit of the Age* (Oxford, 1999), 23–6.

10. Hoppen, *Mid-Victorian Generation*, 46.

11. For Dickens's concern for the employment of his sons in worthy professions see Sanders, *Dickens and the Spirit of the Age*, 147–9.

12. For Bradley Headstone, Charley, and the teaching profession see Philip Collins, *Dickens and Education* (1963), 92–3, 149–50, 159–71.

13. Henry Mayhew, *London Labour and the London Poor; a Cyclopaedia of the Condition and Earnings of Those That Will Work, Those That Cannot Work, and Those That Will Not Work*, 4 vols. (1861), i. 272.

14. Ibid. iv. 366–71.

15. Edward Baines Jun. quoted by David Cannadine in his *Class in Britain* (1998), 78.

16. Matthew Arnold, 'The Incompatibles', *Nineteenth Century*, 9 (June 1881), 1034–42; repr. in Philip Collins (ed.), *Dickens: The Critical Heritage* (1971), 267–9.

17. George Bernard Shaw, 'Foreword to *Great Expectations*' (1937, 1947); repr. in Dan H. Laurence and Martin Quinn (eds.), *Shaw on Dickens* (New York, 1985), 45–6.

18. Ibid. 58.

CHAPTER 5. Utilitarianism, Religion, and History

1. William Hazlitt, *The Spirit of the Age* (1825; World's Classics edn., 1935), 4.

2. Ibid. 4.

3. John Stuart Mill, 'Bentham', *Westminster Review* (Aug. 1838); repr. in *Early Essays* (1897), 330.

4. John Stuart Mill and Jeremy Bentham, *'Utilitarianism' and Other Essays*, ed. A. Ryan (Harmondsworth, 1987), 65.

5. Ibid.

6. Mill, 'Bentham', in *Early Essays*, 354.

7. This was argued by E. P. Whipple in his 'On the Economic Fallacies of *Hard Times*', *Atlantic Monthly* (1877); partially repr. in *Hard Times*, ed. George Ford and Sylvère Monod (Norton Critical Edn., 1966), 323–7.

8. For this see Andrew Sanders, 'Dickens and the Millennium', in Juliet John and Alice Jenkins (eds.), *Rethinking Victorian Culture* (2000), 81–91.

9. For Dickens and Unitarianism see *Letters*, iii. 455 n. 5.
10. 'Report of the Commissioners Appointed to Inquire into the Condition of the Persons Variously Engaged in the University of Oxford', *Examiner* (3 June 1843); repr. in Michael Slater (ed.), *'The Amusements of the People' and Other Papers: Reports, Essays and Reviews 1834–1851* (1996), 62.
11. Humphry House, *The Dickens World* (1941; 1960 edn.), 34.
12. Ibid. The book titles are listed in full in the short pamphlet by D. J. Carlisle, *Imitation Books in Charles Dickens's Study, Gad's Hill Place* (Gad's Hill School, Higham-by-Rochester, 1998).

CHAPTER 6. Science and Technology

1. John Ruskin to Charles Eliot Norton, 19 June 1870; repr. in Philip Collins (ed.), *Dickens: The Critical Heritage* (1971), 443–4.
2. These two articles are reproduced in Michael Slater (ed.), *Sketches by Boz and Other Early Papers 1833–1839* (1994), 513–50. See also G. A. Chaudhry, 'The Mudfog Papers', *Dickensian*, 70 (1974), 104–12.
3. 'The Poetry of Science' (Dec. 1848); repr. in Michael Slater (ed.), *'The Amusements of the People' and Other Papers: Reports, Essays and Reviews 1834–1851* (1996), 129–34.
4. For these contentions see K. J. Fielding and Shu-Fang Lai, 'Dickens, Science and *The Poetry of Science*', *Dickensian*, 93 (1997), 5–10. See also Philip Collins's riposte that this is 'going beyond the evidence' (ibid. 136). For an extended account of Dickens's interest in science and for a survey of the articles published by him in his journals see Shu-Fang Lai: 'Dickens and Science: Summaries of Contributions Related to Science in *Household Words* and *All the Year Round* with an Introduction' (Ph.D. thesis, University of Glasgow, 1999).
5. 'Poetry of Science', 131.
6. Fielding and Shu-Fang Lai, 'Dickens, Science', 6.
7. These articles appeared on 2 June 1860, 7 July 1860, and 9 Mar. 1861.
8. See e.g. K. J. Fielding and Shu-Fang Lai, 'Dickens, Science, Evolution and "The Death of the Sun"', in Anny Sadrin (ed.), *Dickens, Europe and the New Worlds* (1998), 200–11. George Levine's contention that there are Darwinian elements in Dickens is contained in his *'Little Dorrit* and Three Kinds of Science', in Joanne Shattock (ed.), *Dickens and Other Victorians: Essays in Honour of Philip Collins* (1988).
9. See e.g. 'Comets and their Tails of Prophets', *Household Words* (23 May 1857); 'A Sweep through the Stars', *Household Words* (22 May 1858); 'Five Comets', *Household Words* (20 Nov. 1858); 'A Lady on the Peak of Tenerife', *All the Year Round* (16 Feb. 1865); 'Respecting the Sun', *All the Year Round* (22 Apr. 1865).
10. 'Proposals for Amusing Posterity', *Household Words* (12 Feb. 1853); repr. in Michael Slater (ed.), *'Gone Astray' and Other Papers from Household Words 1851–1859* (1998), 122–6.
11. 'A Flight', *Household Words* (30 Aug. 1851); repr. in Slater (ed.), *'Gone Astray' and Other Papers*, 26–35.

12. 'Railway Dreaming', *Household Words* (10 May 1856); repr. ibid. 369–76.
13. Figures from Benjamin Vincent, *Haydn's Dictionary of Dates and Universal Information, Relating to all Ages and Nations* (17th edn., 1881), 656–8.
14. W. M. Thackeray, 'De Juventute', *Roundabout Papers* (10 Oct. 1860); repr. in George Saintsbury (ed.), *The Oxford Thackeray: The Wolves and the Lamb, Lovel the Widower, Denis Duval, Roundabout Papers* (1980), 424.
15. For this address see K. J. Fielding (ed.), *The Speeches of Charles Dickens* (Oxford, 1960), 397–408.
16. Ibid. 404.

CHAPTER 7. Recontextualizing Dickens

1. The banknote was designed by Roger Withington, the Bank of England's 'artist-designer'. An exhibition to mark the appearance of the note was held at the Bank of England Museum, Apr.–Sept. 1992.
2. Quoted by Madeline House and Graham Storey in *Letters*, vol. i, p. ix, pref.
3. Ibid. pp. ix–x.
4. Although separate collections of letters to individual correspondents appeared during the later years of the nineteenth century and in the first quarter of the twentieth century, the next 'collected' edition had to wait for the three-volume limited Nonesuch edition of 1938. This was in turn replaced by the superb, twelve-volume Pilgrim edition which began publication in 1965.
5. Robert Langton, *The Childhood and Youth of Charles Dickens: With Retrospective Notes, and Elucidations from his Books and Letters* (1891), Preface to the Enlarged and Revised Edition, p. ix.
6. Mary Dickens, *Charles Dickens: By his Eldest Daughter* (1885; repr. 1911).
7. Gladys Storey, *Dickens and Daughter* (1939), 133–4.
8. Claire Tomalin, *The Invisible Woman: The Story of Nelly Ternan and Charles Dickens* (1990). In an appendix to the subsequent paperback edition of her biography Tomalin considers the possibility that Dickens died not at Gad's Hill but at Ellen's house in Peckham. There seems to be little foundation for this story.
9. For these busts see Paul Atterbury (ed.), *The Parian Phenomenon: A Survey of Victorian Parian Porcelain Statuary and Busts* (Shepton Beauchamp, Somerset, 1989), 233, 241, 248.
10. There is a collection of such figurines at the Dickens House Museum in London.
11. For Dickens and art see the two pioneer articles by Leonée Ormond, 'Dickens and Painting: The Old Masters' and 'Dickens and Painting: Contemporary Art', *Dickensian*, 79 (1983), and 80 (1984) respectively.
12. Hunt was not pleased with the picture in later life, complaining to William Michael Rossetti in 1907 that he had 'used salad oil for the sky which, never drying got very dirty and messed in the course of years'. See Mary Bennett, *William Holman Hunt* (catalogue for an exhibition arranged by

the Walker Art Gallery and shown in Liverpool and London in 1969), 19–20, no. 5.

13. See Vanda Foster, 'The Dolly Varden', *Dickensian*, 73 (1977), 19–24.

14. For Frith's painting see the Catalogue to the 1970 Charles Dickens Exhibition at the Victoria and Albert Museum, F18 and pl. 43. For the 'Dolly Varden' style see Foster, 'Dolly Varden', and C. Willett-Cunnington and Phillis Cunnington, *Handbook of English Costume in the Nineteenth Century* (1959; 3rd edn. 1970), 493–4, 510. The costume is described as 'a form of Polonaise, its essential feature being its material, chintz or cretonne, the underskirt being bright silk or cotton'. The 'Dolly Varden Hat' had a crown surrounded by ribbon trimming, sometimes with what were described as 'follow-me-lads' streamers.

15. J. H. Stonehouse (ed.), *Catalogue of the Library of Charles Dickens from Gadshill etc.* (1935), 127.

16. For these paintings see Ormond, 'Dickens and Painting', 7.

17. For Barnard see Frederick G. Kitton, *Dickens and his Illustrators* (1899), 228–9. Barnard published three series of 'extra-illustrations' in 1879, 1884, and 1885. These eighteen photogravures were reprinted in Thomas Archer's expensively produced *Charles Dickens: A Gossip about his Life, Work and Characters* (n.d. [1886?]).

18. For these and other reconfigurations of *Pickwick Papers* see Percy Fitzgerald's *The History of Pickwick* (1891), app.

19. These press reviews are quoted in the Preface added to the 1864 reissue of the novel.

20. For these performances see the exemplary list of Dickensian dramatizations in H. Philip Bolton, *Dickens Dramatized* (1987), 75–103.

21. See ibid.

22. For these versions see Graham Petrie, 'Silent Film Adaptations of Dickens: Part II—1912–1919', *Dickensian*, 97 (Summer 2001), 110–11.

23. Quoted by Philip Collins in *Charles Dickens: The Public Readings* (Oxford, 1975), p. xvii.

24. Charles Kent, *Charles Dickens as a Reader* (1872), 21.

25. Emlyn Williams, 'Dickens and the Theatre', in E. W. F. Tomlin (ed.), *Charles Dickens 1812–1870: A Centenary Volume* (1970), 192.

26. For these see Bolton, *Dickens Dramatized*, 241, 246, 250, 266.

27. Tom Stoppard, *Travesties* (1975), 89. See also Bolton, *Dickens Dramatized*, 292. The Moscow Arts Theatre's popular production of *The Cricket on the Hearth* was seen in 1921–2. It finally ran foul of ideological objections from senior Bolsheviks. A Russian film of the story was, however, made in 1931 (Bolton, *Dickens Dramatized*, 293).

28. Ibid. 349, 353–4, 363.

29. Ibid. 395 ff.

30. For the film version of *The Only Way* see Graham Petrie, 'Silent Film Adaptations of Dickens: Part III—1920–1927', *Dickensian*, 97 (Winter 2001), 210–12.

31. See the review of the production in the *Dickensian*, 76 (1980), 174–5.

32. David Edgar, 'Adapting Nickleby', *Dickensian*, 79 (1983), 22.

33. *The Times*, 31 July 1980.
34. For this see Joss March, 'Dickens and Film', in John O. Jordan (ed.), *The Cambridge Companion to Charles Dickens* (Cambridge, 2001), 218–19.
35. Graham Greene, 'The Young Dickens', in *The Lost Childhood and Other Essays* (1951).
36. A commemorative paperback book by George Curry, *Copperfield '70: The Story of the Making of the Omnibus 20th Century-Fox Film of Charles Dickens' David Copperfield* (1970), describes the shooting of the film and reprints some of its lame screenplay (by Jack Pulman and Frederick Brogger).
37. Sergei Eisenstein, 'Dickens, Griffith and the Film Today', in *Film Form: Essays in Film Theory*, ed. and trans. Jay Leyda (New York, 1949), 232.
38. Bolton, *Dickens Dramatized*, 345.
39. See ibid. 347 and the review in *Dickensian*, 71 (1975), 104.
40. Reported in *Dickensian*, 91 (1995), 66–7.

FURTHER READING

BIOGRAPHICAL MATERIAL

Ackroyd, Peter, *Dickens* (London: Sinclair Stevenson, 1990).

Adrian, Arthur A., *Georgina Hogarth and the Dickens Circle* (London: Oxford University Press, 1957).

Allen, Michael, *Charles Dickens' Childhood* (London: Macmillan Press, 1988).

Collins, Philip (ed.), *Dickens: Interviews and Recollections*, 2 vols. (London: Macmillan, 1981).

Dickens, Mary, *Charles Dickens: By his Eldest Daughter* (1885; repr., Cassell & Co., 1911).

Dolby, George, *Charles Dickens as I Knew Him: The Story of the Reading Tours* (London: T. Fisher Unwin, 1885).

Forster, John, *The Life of Charles Dickens* (3 vols. 1872–4), ed. J. W. T. Ley (London: Cecil Palmer, 1928).

Kent, Charles, *Charles Dickens as a Reader* (London: Chapman & Hall, 1872).

Langton, Robert, *The Childhood and Youth of Dickens* (London: Hutchinson & Co., 1891).

Storey, Gladys, *Dickens and Daughter* (London: Frederick Muller Ltd., 1939).

Tomalin, Claire, *The Invisible Woman: The Story of Nelly Ternan and Charles Dickens* (London: Viking, 1990).

DICKENS'S LETTERS, SPEECHES, READINGS, AND JOURNALISM

Collins, Philip (ed.), *Charles Dickens: The Public Readings* (Oxford: Clarendon Press, 1975).

Fielding, K. J. (ed.), *The Speeches of Charles Dickens* (Oxford: Clarendon Press, 1960).

House, Madeline, Storey, Graham, Tillotson, Kathleen, *et al.* (eds.), *The Letters of Charles Dickens*, 12 vols. (The Pilgrim Edition, Oxford: Clarendon Press, 1965–2002).

Lehmann, R. C., *Charles Dickens as Editor* (London: Smith, Elder & Co., 1912).

Lohrli, Anne, *'Household Words': A Weekly Journal 1850–1859, Conducted by Charles Dickens* (Toronto: University of Toronto Press, 1973).

Oppenlander, Ella Ann, *Dickens' 'All the Year Round': Descriptive Index and Contributor List* (Troy, NY: Whitston Publishing Co., 1984).

Slater, Michael (ed.), *Sketches by Boz and Other Early Papers 1833–1839*

(Dent Uniform Edition of Dickens' Journalism, vol. i; London: J. M. Dent, 1994).

—— (ed.), *'The Amusements of the People' and Other Papers: Reports, Essays and Reviews 1834–1851* (Dent Uniform Edition of Dickens' Journalism, vol. ii; London: J. M. Dent, 1996).

—— (ed.), *'Gone Astray' and Other Papers from Household Words 1851– 1859* (Dent Uniform Edition of Dickens' Journalism, vol. iii; London: J. M. Dent, 1998).

—— and Drew, John (eds.), *'The Uncommercial Traveller' and Other Papers 1859–1870* (Dent Uniform Edition of Dickens' Journalism, vol. iv; London: J. M. Dent, 2000).

Stone, Harry (ed.), *The Uncollected Writings of Charles Dickens: Household Words 1850–1859*, 2 vols. (London: Allen Lane, The Penguin Press, 1969).

DICKENS'S LIBRARY, MEMORANDA, WORKING METHODS, AND PUBLISHERS

Butt, John, and Tillotson, Kathleen, *Dickens at Work* (London: Methuen & Co., 1957).

Kaplan, Fred (ed.), *Charles Dickens' Book of Memoranda* (New York: New York Public Library, 1981).

Patten, Robert L., *Charles Dickens and his Publishers* (Oxford: Clarendon Press, 1978).

Stone, Harry (ed.), *Dickens' Working Notes for his Novels* (Chicago: University of Chicago Press, 1987).

Stonehouse, J. H. (ed.), *Catalogue of the Library of Charles Dickens from Gadshill etc.* (London: Piccadilly Fountain Press, 1935).

Sutherland, John, *Victorian Novelists and Publishers* (London: Athlone Press, 1976).

PERIODICALS

Dickens Studies (Boston: Emerson College, 1965–9), continued as *Dickens Studies Annual: Essays on Victorian Fiction* (New York: AMS Press, 1970–).

Dickens Studies Newsletter (Louisville, Ky.: Dickens Society of America, 1970–83), continued as *Dickens Quarterly* (Amherst, Mass.: Dickens Society of America, 1984–).

The Dickensian (London: The Dickens Fellowship, 1905–).

COMPANIONS AND DICTIONARIES

Bentley, Nicholas, Slater, Michael, and Burgis, Nina, *The Dickens Index* (Oxford: Oxford University Press, 1988).

Cotsell, Michael, *The Companion to Our Mutual Friend* (London: Allen & Unwin, 1986).

Davis, Paul, *The Penguin Dickens Companion* (London: Penguin, 1999).

Hawes, Donald, *Who's Who in Dickens* (London: Routledge, 1998).

Jacobson, Wendy, *The Companion to The Mystery of Edwin Drood* (London: Allen & Unwin, 1986).

Newlin, George, *Everyone in Dickens*, 3 vols. (Westport, Conn.: Greenwood Press, 1995).

—— *Every Thing in Dickens* (Westport, Conn.: Greenwood Press, 1996).

Paroissien, David, *The Companion to Oliver Twist* (Robertsbridge: Helm, 1992).

—— *The Companion to Great Expectations* (Robertsbridge: Helm, 2000).

Sanders, Andrew, *The Companion to A Tale of Two Cities* (London: Unwin Hyman, 1988).

Schlicke, Paul (ed.), *Oxford Readers' Companion to Dickens* (Oxford: Oxford University Press, 1999).

Shatto, Susan, *The Companion to Bleak House* (London: Allen & Unwin, 1988).

Simpson, Margaret, *The Companion to Hard Times* (Robertsbridge: Helm, 1997).

DICKENS AND HIS ILLUSTRATORS

Browne, Edgar, *Phiz and Dickens* (London: James Nisbett & Co., 1913).

Cohen, Jane R., *Charles Dickens and his Original Illustrators* (Columbus, Oh.: Ohio University Press, 1980).

Kitton, Frederick G., *Phiz (Hablot K. Browne): A Memoir* (London: W. Satchell & Co., 1882).

—— *Dickens and his Illustrators* (London: George Redway, 1899).

Steig, Michael, *Dickens and Phiz* (Bloomington, Ind.: Indiana University Press, 1978).

DICKENS'S LONDON

Anon., *The Pictorial Handbook of London Comprising Its Antiquities, Architecture, Arts, Manufacture, Trade, Social, Literary and Scientific Institutions, Exhibitions, and Galleries of Art* (London: Henry G. Bohn, 1854).

Chancellor, E. Beresford, *The London of Charles Dickens* (London: Grant Richards, 1924).

Cunningham, Peter, *Hand-Book of London: Past and Present* (London: John Murray, 1850).

Dexter, Walter, *The London of Dickens* (London: Cecil Palmer, 1923).

Mayhew, Henry, *London Labour and the London Poor*, 4 vols. (London: Griffin, Bohn & Co., 1851–61).

Schwarzbach, F. S., *Dickens and the City* (London: The Athlone Press, 1979).

Sekon, G. A., *Locomotion in Victorian London* (London: Oxford University Press, 1938).

Stedman Jones, Gareth, *Outcast London: A Study in the Relationship between Classes in Victorian Society* (Oxford: Oxford University Press, 1971).

Weinreb, Ben, and Hibbert, Christopher (eds.), *The London Encyclopaedia* (London: Macmillan, 1983).

Welsh, Alexander, *The City of Dickens* (Oxford: Clarendon Press, 1971).

DICKENS: STAGE, FILM, AND TELEVISION ADAPTATIONS

Bolton, H. Philip, *Dickens Dramatized* (London: Mansell Publishing Ltd., 1987).

Fitzgerald, Percy, *The History of Pickwick* (London: Chapman & Hall, 1891).

Petrie, Graham, 'Silent Film Adaptations of Dickens: Part I—Beginnings to 1911', *Dickensian*, 97 (Spring 2001).

—— 'Silent Film Adaptations of Dickens: Part II—1912–1919', *Dickensian*, 97 (Summer 2001).

—— 'Silent Film Adaptations of Dickens: Part III—1920–1927', *Dickensian*, 97 (Winter 2001).

Pointer, Michael, *Charles Dickens on the Screen: The Film, Television and Video Adaptations* (Lanham, Md.: Scarecrow Press, 1996).

DICKENS: EUROPE, AMERICA, AND THE EMPIRE

Collins, Philip, 'Dickens and French Wickedness', in Sylvère Monod (ed.), *Dickens et la France* (Lille: Presses Universitaires de Lille, 1978).

Lazarus, Mary, *A Tale of Two Brothers: Charles Dickens's Sons in Australia* (Sydney and London: Angus & Robertson, 1973).

Moss, Sidney P., *Charles Dickens' Quarrel with America* (Troy, NY: Whitston Publishing Co., 1984).

Sanders, Andrew, 'The Dickens World', in Michael Cotsell (ed.), *Creditable Warriors: English Literature and the Wider World 1830–1876* (London and Atlantic Highlands, NJ: The Ashfield Press, 1990), 131–42.

Slater, Michael (ed.), *Dickens on America and the Americans* (Austin and London: University of Texas Press, 1978).

VICTORIAN AND EARLY TWENTIETH-CENTURY CRITICISM

Ashton, Rosemary (ed.), *Versatile Victorian: Selected Critical Writings of George Henry Lewes* (London: Bristol Classical Press, 1992).

Chesterton, G. K., *Charles Dickens* (London: Methuen & Co., 1906).

Collins, Philip (ed.), *Dickens: The Critical Heritage* (London: Routledge & Kegan Paul, 1971).

Coustillas, Pierre, 'Gissing's Writings on Dickens: A Bio-Bibliographical Survey', *Dickensian*, 61 (1965).

Eliot, George, *Essays and Leaves from a Notebook* (Edinburgh: William Blackwood & Sons, 1884).

Gissing, George, *Charles Dickens: A Critical Study* (London: Blackie & Son, 1898).

Horne, R. H., *A New Spirit of the Age*, 2 vols. (London: Smith, Elder & Co., 1844).

Laurence, Dan H., and Quinn, Martin (eds.), *Shaw on Dickens* (New York: Frederick Ungar Publishing, 1985).

TWENTIETH-CENTURY COLLECTIONS OF CRITICISM

Connor, Steven (ed.), *Charles Dickens* (Longman Critical Readers; London: Longman, 1996).

Gross, John, and Pearson, Gabriel (eds.), *Dickens and the Twentieth Century* (London: Routledge & Kegan Paul, 1962).

Giddings, Robert (ed.), *The Changing World of Charles Dickens* (London: Vision Press, 1983).

Hollington, Michael (ed.), *Charles Dickens: Critical Assessments*, 4 vols. (Robertsbridge: Helm, 1995).

Jordan, John O. (ed.), *The Cambridge Companion to Charles Dickens* (Cambridge: Cambridge University Press, 2001).

MacKay, Carol Hanbery (ed.), *Dramatic Dickens* (London: Macmillan, 1989).

Nisbet, Ada, and Nevius, Blake (eds.), *Dickens Centennial Essays* (Berkeley & Los Angeles: University of California Press, 1971).

Sadrin, Anny (ed.), *Dickens, Europe and the New Worlds* (London: Macmillan, 1999).

Schad, John (ed.), *Dickens Refigured: Bodies, Desires and other Histories* (Manchester: Manchester University Press, 1996).

Shattock, Joanne (ed.), *Dickens and other Victorians: Essays in Honour of Philip Collins* (London: Macmillan Press, 1988).

Tomlin, E. W. F. (ed.), *Charles Dickens 1812–1870: A Centenary Volume* (London: Weidenfeld & Nicolson, 1970).

Wall, Stephen (ed.), *Charles Dickens* (Penguin Critical Anthology; Harmondsworth: Penguin Books, 1970).

SELECT CRITICAL STUDIES

Andrews, Malcolm, *Dickens and the Grown-Up Child* (Iowa City: University of Iowa Press, 1994).

Bowen, John, *Other Dickens: Pickwick to Chuzzlewit* (Oxford: Oxford University Press, 2000).

Carey, John, *The Violent Effigy: A Study of Dickens's Imagination* (London, Faber & Faber, 1973; 2nd edn., 1991).

Chittick, Kathryn, *Dickens and the 1830s* (Cambridge: Cambridge University Press, 1990).

Collins, Philip, *Dickens and Crime* (London: Macmillan & Co., 1962).

—— *Dickens and Education* (London: Macmillan & Co., 1963).

Connor, Steven, *Charles Dickens* (Oxford: Blackwell, 1985).

Fielding, K. J., *Charles Dickens* (London: Longmans, 1958).

Flint, Kate, *Dickens* (Brighton: Harvester, 1986).

Gilmour, Robin, *The Idea of the Gentleman in the Victorian Novel* (London: Allen & Unwin, 1981).

Hardy, Barbara, *The Moral Art of Dickens* (London: Athlone Press, 1970).

House, Humphry, *The Dickens World* (London: Oxford University Press, 1941).

Ingham, Patricia, *Dickens, Women and Language* (Hemel Hempstead: Harvester Wheatsheaf, 1992).

Lucas, John, *The Melancholy Man: A Study of Dickens's Novels* (London: Methuen & Co., 1970).

Marcus, Steven, *Dickens from Pickwick to Dombey* (London: Chatto & Windus, 1965).

Meckier, Jerome, *Hidden Rivalries in Victorian Fiction: Dickens, Realism, and Revaluation* (Lexington, Ky.: University of Kentucky Press, 1987).

Miller, J. Hillis, *Charles Dickens: The World of his Novels* (Cambridge, Mass.: Harvard University Press, 1958).

Sadrin, Anny, *Parentage and Inheritance in the Novels of Charles Dickens* (Cambridge: Cambridge University Press, 1994).

Sanders, Andrew, *Charles Dickens: Resurrectionist* (London: Macmillan Press, 1982).

—— *Dickens and the Spirit of the Age* (Oxford: Clarendon Press, 1999).

Schlicke, Paul, *Dickens and Popular Entertainment* (London: Allen & Unwin, 1985).

Schor, Hilary, *Dickens and the Daughter of the House* (Cambridge: Cambridge University Press, 1999).

Slater, Michael, *Dickens and Women* (London: J. M. Dent & Sons, 1983).

—— *An Intelligent Person's Guide to Dickens* (London: Duckworth, 1999).

Welsh, Alexander, *From Copyright to Copperfield: The Identity of Dickens* (Cambridge, Mass.: Harvard University Press, 1987).

Wilson, Angus, *The World of Charles Dickens* (London: Secker & Warburg, 1970).

222 *Further Reading*

HISTORICAL AND SOCIAL BACKGROUND

Briggs, Asa, *Victorian Cities* (London: Odhams Press, 1963).

Cannadine, David, *Class in Britain* (New Haven and London: Yale University Press, 1998).

Hoppen, K. Theodore, *The Mid-Victorian Generation 1846–1886* (Oxford: Clarendon Press, 1998).

Thompson, F. M. L., *The Rise of Respectable Society: A Social History of Victorian Britain 1830–1900* (London: Fontana Press, 1988).

Waller, P. J., *Town, City and Nation: England 1850–1914* (Oxford: Oxford University Press, 1983).

Wiener, Martin J., *English Culture and the Decline of the Industrial Spirit 1850–1980* (Cambridge: Cambridge University Press, 1981).

WEBSITES

http://humwww.ucsc.edu/dickens/index.html   The Dickens Project at the
University of California
http://lang.nagoya-u.ac.jp/~matsuoka/Dickens.html   Mitsuharu Matsuoka's
Dickens Page
http://www.fidnet.com/~dap1955/dickens/   The Dickens Page
(All the above sites have extensive lists of links to other, more specialized
websites)
http://www.dickens.fellowship.btinternet.co.uk/   The Dickens Fellowship
http://www.dickensmuseum.com/   The Dickens House Museum

FILM AND TELEVISION ADAPTATIONS
OF DICKENS'S NOVELS

Since 1903 there have been at least 180 films or TV adaptations of Dickens's fiction. Many of the TV versions have been in multiple episodes, raising the total to about 400 separate films. The novel most frequently adapted has been *Oliver Twist*. All the novels, including *Edwin Drood*, have been filmed at least once.

Bleak House (GB; BBC, 1959)
Bleak House (GB; director Ross Devenish, 1985)

Mickey's Christmas Carol (US; director Burney Mattinson, 1983)
Scrooged (US; director Richard Donner, 1988)
The Muppet Christmas Carol (US; director Brian Henson, 1992)
Christmas Carol, the Movie (GB; director Jimmy Teru Murakami, 2002)

David Copperfield (US; director George Cukor, 1935)
David Copperfield (GB; director Stuart Burge, 1956)
David Copperfield (GB; director Joan Craft, 1966)

Dombey and Son (GB; director Joan Craft, 1969)
Dombey and Son (GB; director Rodney Bennett, 1983)

Great Expectations (GB; director David Lean, 1946)
Great Expectations (GB; BBC, 1959)
Great Expectations (GB; director Alan Bridges, 1967)
Great Expectations (GB; director Julian Amyes, 1981)
Great Expectations (GB; director Julian Jerrold, 1998)

Hard Times (GB; Granada Television, director John Irvin, 1977)
Hard Times (GB; BBC, director Peter Barnes, 1994)

Little Dorrit (GB; BBC, director Christine Edzard, 1987)

Martin Chuzzlewit (GB; director Joan Craft, 1964)
Martin Chuzzlewit (GB; director Pedr James, 1994)

Nicholas Nickleby (GB; director Alberto Cavalcanti, 1947)
Nicholas Nickleby (GB; director Eric Tyler, 1957)

Nicholas Nickleby (GB; director Joan Craft, 1968)
Nicholas Nickleby (GB; director Christopher Barry, 1977)

The Old Curiosity Shop (GB; director Thomas Bentley, 1934)
The Old Curiosity Shop (GB; director Joan Craft, 1962)

Oliver Twist (GB; director David Lean, 1948)
Oliver Twist (GB; BBC, 1962)
Oliver! (GB; based on the Lionel Bart musical, 1968)
Oliver Twist (GB; director Gareth Davies, 1985)

Our Mutual Friend (GB; director Eric Tyler, 1958)
Our Mutual Friend (GB; BBC, director Peter Hammond, 1976)
Our Mutual Friend (GB; BBC, director Julian Farino, 1998)

The Pickwick Papers (GB; producer Douglas Allen, 1952)
Pickwick (GB; director Terry Hughes, 1969)
The Pickwick Papers (GB; director Brian Lighthill, 1985)

A Tale of Two Cities (GB; director Ralph Thomas, 1958)
A Tale of Two Cities (GB; director Joan Craft, 1965)

INDEX